Modern Judgements

RACINE

MODERN JUDGEMENTS

General Editor: P. N. FURBANK

Dickens   A. E. Dyson
Henry James   Tony Tanner
Milton   Alan Rudrum
Sean O'Casey   Ronald Ayling
Pasternak   Donald Davie and Angela Livingstone
Walter Scott   D. D. Devlin
Racine   R. C. Knight
Shelley   R. B. Woodings
Swift   A. Norman Jeffares

IN PREPARATION

Matthew Arnold   P. A. W. Collins
Ford Madox Ford   Richard A. Cassell
Freud   F. Cioffi
Marvell   M. Wilding
Pope   Graham Martin

Racine

MODERN JUDGEMENTS

edited by

R. C. KNIGHT

MACMILLAN

Selection and editorial matter © R. C. Knight 1969

First published 1969 by
MACMILLAN AND CO LTD
Little Essex Street London WC2
and also at Bombay Calcutta and Madras
Macmillan South Africa (Publishers) Pty Ltd Johannesburg
The Macmillan Company of Australia Pty Ltd Melbourne
The Macmillan Company of Canada Ltd Toronto

Printed in Great Britain by
WESTERN PRINTING SERVICES LTD
Bristol

Contents

6 CONTENTS

Acknowledgements

C. M. Bowra, 'The Simplicity of Racine', the Zaharoff Lecture for 1956 (The Clarendon Press); Professor T. Spoerri, 'Trieb und Geist bei Racine', from *Archiv für das Studium der neueren Sprachen*, CLXIII; Professor J. C. Lapp, 'Racine's Symbolism', from *Aspects of Racinian Tragedy* (University of Toronto Press); Professor Georges Poulet, 'Notes sur le temps racinien', from *Études sur le temps humain*, vol. 1, translated as *Studies in Human Time* by Elliott Coleman (Librairie Plon and Edinburgh University Press) (the Editor is much indebted to Mr Elliott Coleman for permission to adapt his translation); Jean Starobinski, 'Racine et la poétique du regard', from *L'œil vivant* (Éditions Gallimard); Professor L. Goldmann, 'Structure de la tragédie racinienne', from *Le Théâtre tragique* (Centre National de la Recherche Scientifique); Professor L. Spitzer, 'Die classische Dämpfung in Racines Stil', from *Romanische Stil- und Literaturstudien*, vol. 1 (Professor Anna C. Hatcher, literary executrix of Professor Spitzer, and Universitäts- und Verlagsbuchhandlung N. G. Elwert); R. A. Sayce, 'Racine's Style: Periphrasis and Direct Statement', from *The French Mind: studies in honour of Gustave Rudler*, ed. W. Moore, R. Sutherland and E. Starkie (The Clarendon Press); Professor E. Vinaver, 'L'Action poétique dans le théâtre de Racine', the Zaharoff Lecture for 1960 (The Clarendon Press); Professor Jules Brody, 'Racine's *Thébaïde*: an analysis', from *French Studies*, XIII (1959); Professor J. Pommier, 'Tradition littéraire et modèles vivants dans L'*Andromaque de Racine*', Presidential Address to the Modern Humanities Research Association 1962 (Modern Humanities Research Association); Professor P. F. Butler, 'La Tragédie de *Bérénice*', from *French Studies*, III (1949); Jean Dubu, 'Quelques raisons esthétiques pour le silence de Racine après *Phèdre*', from *XVIIe Siècle*, XX (1953) (the Editor would also like to thank M. Dubu for his collaboration in revising and translating his text for this volume).

General Editor's Preface

LITERARY criticism has only recently come of age as an academic discipline, and the intellectual activity that, a hundred years ago, went into theological discussion, now finds its most natural outlet in the critical essay. Amid a good deal that is dull or silly or pretentious, every year now produces a crop of critical essays which are brilliant and profound not only as contributions to the understanding of a particular author but as statements of an original way of looking at literature and the world. Hence, it often seems that the most useful undertaking for an academic publisher might be, not so much to commission new books of literary criticism or scholarship, as to make the best of what exists easily available. This at least is the purpose of the present series of anthologies, each of which is devoted to a single major writer.

The guiding principle of selection is to assemble the best *modern* criticism – broadly speaking, that of the last twenty or thirty years – and to include historic and classic essays, however famous, only when they are still influential and represent the best statements of their particular point of view. It will, however, be one of the functions of the editor's Introduction to sketch in the earlier history of criticism in regard to the author concerned.

Each volume will attempt to strike a balance between general essays and ones on specialised aspects, or particular works, of the writer in question. And though in many instances the bulk of the articles will come from British and American sources, certain of the volumes will draw heavily on material in other European languages – most of it being translated for the first time.

P. N. FURBANK

Introduction

RACINE is now probably, of all French writers of his time, the most widely discussed, and perhaps the most variously interpreted. This promotion is recent, and goes back no further than a few decades; a hundred years ago, in an English series such as 'Modern Judgements', he would have had no place at all.

The fault, as far as the English-speaking world is concerned, lies with the incompetence and incomprehension of the so-called translators who put versions of six of Racine's tragedies on the London stage between 1674 and 1723. As Katherine E. Wheatley[1] has shown, what passed there for tragedy – and for imitation of the latest French models and theories – was highly coloured style, heroics, horror, suspense and 'poetic justice'. None of Racine's peculiar merits remained in the English versions. What little the London public was allowed to see of his realism in the treatment of human passions, it thoroughly disliked. So, in fact, behind the sins of the English translators there lie the shortcomings of English taste.

In his own country Racine was an establishment figure before he died, and quickly became a figurehead – for opponents of the Shakespearian vogue in the eighteenth century, as later for opponents of romanticism and realism in their turn. This can have done nothing to dissuade those outside the Latin tradition from regarding him as the very type of what was insular, artificial and off-putting in French taste. He early became looked on as the exemplar of classicism – meaning here traditional correctness, formal perfection according to accepted canons. It was to him, according to the *Oxford English Dictionary*, that the English epithet 'classic' was first applied in its literary sense:

> And classic judgement gain'd to sweet Racine
> The temperate strength of Maro's chaster line.
>
> (Collins, 1744)

[1] Important works referred to will be found in the Bibliography, unless the subject of a special footnote.

Romantics everywhere felt obliged to decry him because they were fighting his admirers and imitators; the German A. W. Schlegel,[1] who allowed him many merits, nevertheless wrote that his plays had the atmosphere of a palace antechamber, in which 'les spectateurs et l'auteur lui-même se pénétraient de l'idée que la politesse est un des éléments primitifs de la nature humaine'.

A change set in as the nineteenth-century *classiques* disappeared, and by the 1880s Brunetière[2] was demonstrating that Racine possessed the same virtues as the naturalist novel. Most of his tragedies remained on the repertory of the Comédie Française, though there the results of a hybrid and run-down tradition were producing strange and depressing results up to a generation ago. But at the turn of the century Sarah Bernhardt was using *Phèdre* as one of the favourite vehicles (with *la Dame aux Camélias* and *l'Aiglon*!) of an emotional art that moved multitudes wherever her world tours took her.

The first significant blow struck for Racine in England – Lytton Strachey's essay, which appeared in 1908 – seems to have been in advance even of French opinion. The study brought out in the same year by the dramatist and critic Jules Lemaître[3] was still crying up the tragedies for the romantic virtues of emotion and picturesqueness, and the realistic violence and boldness of the characterization. Strachey starts – as an Englishman perhaps must – from another of the old themes, the parallel with Shakespeare, but he can see and analyse the merits of both kinds of art. He accepts Racine's unities and stage conventions, but as factors making, in his hands, for concentration. Before the day of scientific linguistics, he showed as well as anyone ever has how a style can be abstract, general and low-pitched and still carry as much poetry as Shakespeare's (cf below, p. 41 ff); and as much music – thereby demonstrating that no part of the mystery is necessarily inaccessible to alien ears and minds. In fact that part of Racine that depends on economy and understatement can be particularly attractive to the modern Englishman; more so, one may suspect, than to a Frenchman of the Midi.

By about 1930, after another heavy crop of original studies in France (with Vossler in Germany and Lugli in Italy), most of the

---

[1] *Cours de littérature dramatique*, trans. Madame Necker de Saussure (Paris and Geneva, 1832) II 146.

[2] Cf his *Histoire de la littérature française classique* (1905, and reissues) II ch. viii.

[3] *Jean Racine* (1908).

positions had been taken up which, between them, held the field until the experimental approaches of the sixties. Classicism had been redefined as voluntary submission to a discipline, implying 'un romantisme antérieur' (Valéry), 'romantisme dompté' (Gide).

In 1930 that subtle and sensitive critic Henri Bremond tried to interpret Racine in the light of another notion due to Valéry – that of 'la poésie pure' – 'une volonté remarquable', to quote the latter, 'd'isoler définitivement la Poésie, de toute autre essence qu'elle-même', conceived almost a century before by Edgar Allan Poe and envisaged as an (admittedly unattainable) goal by the greatest French poets, so Valéry thought, since Baudelaire. In the same year a wilfully paradoxical essay of Giraudoux denied all connexion between Racine's poetical world and the real world of his very ordinary life. Thierry Maulnier, in 1935, saw the plays as an absolute, not of poetry, but of tragic drama.

But Giraudoux's *boutade* was a reaction against a new, romantic, attitude to the poet. If, as it seemed, a drama of volcanic passions had been produced by a sedulous professional author who turned into an adroit and successful courtier, romantic conceptions of the relation between life and art could only be satisfied by rewriting the life. Masson-Forestier,[1] in an unbalanced and unscholarly book of 1910, forced all the evidence he could lay hands on to suggest that the supposedly 'tendre Racine' (but *tendre*, when that phrase was coined, meant 'susceptible') was an almost poetically ferocious egoist, a sort of monster. François Mauriac's *Racine* (1928) was a Mauriac character, who loved life and art and therefore sin, a lost sheep finally gathered back into the Jansenist fold.

The romantic tendency has never ceased since then; for one thing it is so much easier to write about a poet's loves or his religion than about his art; for another, the fallacy will never die that art is good in proportion as the emotion behind it is stormy and 'sincere'. It has lately been represented in a particularly long, erudite and aggressive work by R. Jasinski, according to whom life and works, art and character, must infallibly correspond, and who consequently goes through the plays picking out, not one, but several independent cycles of allusions – allusions to public events, allusions to Racine's strict education by Jansenist teachers and subsequent revolt (cf below, p. 170), to rivalry with Corneille, and to a love-life of which we know nothing except from a little contemporary tittle-tattle – all which, he tells us, we must

---

[1] *Autour d'un Racine ignoré* (1910).

grasp before we can receive the Racinian message. Jasinski too is in a sense a reaction – against the most solidly documented study yet devoted to the poet's career (rather than his life), by R. Picard, who had deliberately played down all motives and factors other than the material and materialistic ones which could be established by objective methods, producing what looked like the portrait of a self-seeking careerist which some found so unsympathetic as to be incredible.

But in this introduction we ought to limit ourselves to the progress that has been made in appreciating Racine's literary legacy. All links between life and art are in his case purely conjectural; too many letters have been destroyed, too much evidence of his motives and sentiments obliterated, for the most important phases of the life ever to be established with any certainty. Far too much attention has been lavished on the author to the detriment of the works; and biography is only really relevant to our present subject if we believe, with Jasinski, that without the one we cannot have a true view of the other. We therefore record this conviction and pass on.

Probably it was this extreme that has pushed many critics in the same direction as Giraudoux, making them look at the dramatic works as a kind of absolute, isolated from any historical context – or, if Racine's times, their civilisation and artistic ideals, are mentioned at all, to see him as so miraculous a climax of all that was good in them that still he stands alone. The tendency is very pronounced in Thierry Maulnier's book (already mentioned), which employs so many super-latives, so many hyperboles, to laud the tension, the violence, the 'purity', the 'nudity', the hardness of the tragedies that the reader who thought he knew them rubs his eyes.

Very much more scholarly, and more nuancé despite its deliberate one-sidedness, is the view supported by the great authority of E. Vinaver, depicting a Racine distinguished from his whole century by being the only man to understand and – consciously, he thinks – to strive towards the genuine tragic emotion; despising, though he had to use them, the elements which for all his rivals were paramount, or at least primordial, the 'dramatic' elements of suspense or surprise aroused by manipulation of the plot.

Hardly had 'classicism' been put in its historical place, when in the 1940s a new abstract concept was swept into fashion – the baroque. This term had been applied first to architecture, then to the fine arts, and lastly by followers of the art-historian Wölfflin to literature. It defines – in terms which are fairly unclear – an art of tension, dwelling on phenomena of transience or unreality; it is open to the immediate objection that in Italy and elsewhere it describes an art following an era considered classical, whereas in France room can only be found for it *before* the age of Louis XIV, which has always borne the latter title. The baroque concept has done some service by revealing beauties in certain underrated or quite unknown poets, while creating considerable confusion and waste of effort by the utter disunanimity among its historians as to its limiting dates and the figures and art-forms considered characteristic of it. For instance the typically baroque drama is for R. Lebègue[1] the irregular horror tragedy of 1575–1610, for the Danish V. Vedel[2] and many others it inspires the atmosphere of tragi-comedy from A. Hardy onwards, and Corneille's love of the extraordinary situation arousing admiration rather than pity; but for P. Butler, in his excellent study of conventional and original trends in Racine, the baroque is also the *romanesque* or *galant* taste exemplified by Thomas Corneille or Quinault in the years preceding and surrounding the appearance of *Andromaque*. A notion that has been made to include Bach and Scarron, Rubens and Bosch, D'Aubigné and Saint-Amant, Montaigne, Pascal and Racine's *Alexandre*, has surely been strained beyond all usefulness.

At least no French critic will admit that the essential Racine is baroque, though others have; and Butler shows the tide lapping all round him and flooding the lower levels.

Most of the other tendencies represented by the most recent Racine criticism are gathered into a quite illusory suggestion of unity by the term 'la nouvelle critique', which has been applied to them and adopted by them.[3] Only a few principles unite them: rejection of the ideal of impartial and objective appraisal, and of the belief that what an author meant to say in his work is something that can be established, and constitutes the only legitimate meaning; together with an inductive method which begins by deciding intuitively what elements ('themes') in his work are of significance, however foreign to his expressed intentions, and works back from them to a principle – a

---

[1] *Le Théâtre baroque en France* (1942).

[2] *Deux Classiques français vus par un critique étranger*, trans. E. Cornet (1935).

[3] See R. Barthes, *Sur Racine* (1963); R. Picard, *Nouvelle Critique ou nouvelle imposture?* (1965); S. Doubrowski, *Pourquoi la Nouvelle Critique: critique et objectivité* (1966); J.-P. Weber, *Néo-critique et paléo-critique* (1966); J. Pommier, 'La Querelle', in *Revue d'histoire littéraire* LXVII (1967) 82 ff.

single principle usually – which, *ex hypothesi*, can be made to explain the whole.

Many of the *néo-critiques* are inspired by one or another of the *sciences humaines*: L. Goldmann is a Marxist, explaining Racine by the Jansenist Weltanschauung (as he sees it) and the Jansenists by the frustration of the *noblesse de robe* in seventeenth-century France. G. Poulet and J. Starobinski (if they really belong here in any strict sense) are phenomenologist philosophers. R. Barthes is a Freudian, and, as may be imagined, not the first Freudian to fish in these waters. Most of them appeal to the principle (developed by sociologists out of F. de Saussure's linguistic concepts) of structuralism; that is to say, that languages or cultures, social groups or aesthetic movements, the total production of any artist, or for some even an individual work, are all 'structures' – systems bound together by an inner consistency in which every ingredient depends on the whole and can only be fully understood by reference to it.

In such an approach all depends, manifestly, on the correctness and exhaustiveness of the analysis: the account given can at most be shown to be consistent and self-supporting – *valable*, as the expression goes, but not objectively true. The theories at present in the field offer us a choice of determining factors, from childhood memories or traumata, conscious or unconscious, to a Weltanschauung, several philosophical concepts, a religious conflict determined by an economic and political set-up, and a selection of archetypal symbols; so it is impossible to point to any universally acceptable results after all the efforts that have been made so far.

The interesting part of the discussion has been about the methods of criticism itself. One side has had to look again at the notion of the 'significance' of a work of literature, the other has, laudably, tried to explore new approaches, and has, at its best, contributed stimulating insights. Several of these find a place in this collection, less for their representative value, nearly always, than because they seemed to the editor to enrich experience of the tragedies. The attentive reader, especially if versed in conventional methods of scholarship, may note here and there a mutilated quotation or an untenable interpretation of a text – but these accidents are not confined to our contemporaries. (The present writer would not endorse Spitzer's reference to Andromaque's 'pride', p. 120.)

What we have called a discussion has in fact been a quarrel, a twentieth-century *Querelle des Anciens et des Modernes* which has been the joy and scandal of cultured French readers for over two years. It was provoked by the scholarly and conservative Sorbonne professor R. Picard, who immediately found himself lumped with all other scholars – though in fact university teachers are quite numerous on the other side – as *la critique universitaire*, allegedly tied by a hidebound historical approach to fallacious views on the nature of literary originality and poetic composition.

Of course, scholarship has occupied itself with Racine in its own ways, ever since it has taken modern literature into its province, and it is time to say something of the contribution of professional scholars to our understanding of his work. To the present writer – for reasons which will be readily appreciated – it appears by no means uniformly deserving of such a condemnation.

The first monument of pure Racinian erudition goes back well before the day of serious university studies – to 1865 in fact, when Paul Mesnard began to bring out his great eight-volume edition of the *Œuvres* in Hachette's 'Grands Écrivains' series. New knowledge since then has changed our views on literary influences and on contested points of biography, changes of taste have dated some of Mesnard's judgements on both the life and works; but his standards of probity and accuracy in establishing the texts of published works and unpublished papers, historical records and testimonies, are those we still try to apply, and every student of Racine since then is deeply in this great scholar's debt.

The big battalions of university researchers appeared, in France, Great Britain, the U.S.A., the dominions, Germany and Italy, mainly after the last war. Modern literary studies were still quite near their beginnings in the 1920s and 1930s. But from 1929 to 1942, at Johns Hopkins University, H. Carrington Lancaster brought out his *History of French Dramatic Literature in the Seventeenth Century*, a vast repository of all the known facts concerning theatres, actors, playwrights and every play performed or merely printed of which record remains.

Even earlier, R. Bray had begun the serious history and analysis of the theories and rules constituting 'classicism' (*La Doctrine classique*, 1926), complemented only much later by J. Scherer's *Dramaturgie classique* (1950), which examines what the playwrights of the century actually did.

The thirties and forties saw the publication of D. Mornet's contribution – an *Histoire de la littérature française classique* (1947), an edition of Racine, a students' manual – drawing attention to the borrowings, the similarities, the affinities of taste linking Racine with the (not altogether undeservedly) forgotten dramatists of his day or just before. He overdid this aspect, no doubt; for originality is not simply what is left when all the borrowings have been accounted for, and the notion of literary 'influences' is not a simple one. But Mornet was a disciple of Gustave Lanson (who ruled over French studies in Paris from 1900, and set their course at a crucial moment, not only for France but for French departments abroad); and Lanson was under the spell of scientific method. He saw which was the science that could confer respectability on his subject – he turned it into a branch of history, *l'histoire littéraire*: an autonomous branch, but bound by the same laws, outlook and techniques. Lanson never denied the primary importance of what is inside books; but researchers of the Lanson school more easily got the feeling that they were dealing with facts when they inquired into the play of influences that could be considered as having determined literary creation, or simply prospected for 'sources'. This misplaced emphasis, and the misconceptions it encouraged, are what *la critique universitaire* is expiating today at the hands of its adversaries.

Nevertheless the Lansonian approach brought solid gains: it taught respect for facts and high standards in the handling of facts (if not always caution in their interpretation); and among the facts were many which forced us to correct, and no doubt enrich, our views of Racine's originality and his relation to his own age and the classical past, his taste, and – if not his methods of composition, since the modern critics tell us it is presumptuous to think we can ever know that – at least the elements with which his creative powers had to work. As a result we realise that, while he was unique in the width of his literary background and the boldness yet selectiveness of his taste, yet it was a taste that underwent a development and always included limitations (cf below, pp. 161 ff).

One humble but valuable contribution has been to the particular credit of this country – scholarly texts of single plays presented with a care, competence and taste that make them helpful to the relative beginner and attractive to the expert. Our Bibliography devotes a special section to these English editions, from which only *Andromaque* and *Iphigénie*, of the great tragedies, are now missing.

A different outlet for the historical or scientific spirit is found in linguistics. Racine's style, which has long been the subject of fascinated attention (cf pp. 41 ff), has often been analysed, and with increasing precision, for instance by Spitzer (pp. 117 ff), who returned to the subject later, and by Sayce (pp. 132 ff). Cahen has studied the vocabulary of the tragedies and its limits. Concordances of several plays are now available to guide further investigation. Combining modern linguistic approaches with historical study of the rhetorical doctrines and concepts of Racine's day, P. France has given a comprehensive account of *Racine's Rhetoric*.

This effort, to replace the poet in his context and at the same time to see what sets him apart, is timely and necessary. Much stylistic study has neglected the problem (cf p. 118). This is the one reservation made by Professor Vinaver in a review[1] of Sir M. Bowra's essay (which we reprint) – the 'confusion between Racine's handling of his medium and the medium itself. There is nothing surprising in the fact that Racine's flowers "are never described more closely than as 'fleurs'." Many French poets share this and other apparent limitations, not because French poetry is "unlyrical", but because, as an English philosopher has recently remarked, "different languages offer different temptations"...'

The opposite pitfall awaits the academic literary historian, and it is again Professor Vinaver who has described it most pungently – 'the temptation to plunge the writer into his milieu until he vanishes in it.'[2] Only too true of not a few of us; and yet whoever attempts to pin down and name the thing that, for him, differentiates Racine and makes him valuable as his contemporaries were not, leaves the door always open on the doubt: was it truly towards this that Racine was struggling – consciously? unconsciously? – or is the modern critic reading his own tastes and values into the work that (sometimes) satisfies them?

The virtual impossibility, here, of fully objective criticism explains why Racine has been served up to nearly every known sauce. He has been successively *tendre*, correct (as a term of praise), formal (as the contrary), the realistic connoisseur of passion, the pure artist, cruel perhaps but detached, the fugitive from God, the psycho analytical casebook, the only Frenchman to attain the tragic.

There is no agreed picture. Only a nonentity can be seen objectively. To make evaluation harder, the art form he used is now a museum

[1] *French Studies* xx (1956) 275. [2] *Racine and Poetic Tragedy*, p. 7.

piece. It did not really survive him (his worst enemies were the *epigoni* who 'pullulated' on his corpse, as Hugo put it, openly and shamelessly pillaging every turn of style which in Racine had been original and bold; timidly experimenting only in occasional changes of subject matter or details of production) – and in a sense he killed it, by giving it a model impossible to equal and impossible to ignore.

The present editor has no illusion of being exempt from the preconceptions of his generation (which is not precisely that of the *néo-critiques*). But as a balanced statement it is difficult to quarrel with the threefold formula offered in 1950 by R. Picard to an American public:

> An accomplished drama whether we approach it from the point of view of plot, of tragedy, or of poetic genius. And in this threefold excellence lies one of the explanations for our poet's present fortune. ... Critics and lovers of Racine there are, who value his plays first and foremost for the compactness and the violence of their action; next, there are those who admire him mainly as the originator of a new conception of tragedy, more adapted than anything the Greeks devised, to the philosophy of our modern world; while others, finally, are sensitive to his poetic quality alone.[1]

The study of his magical use of the dramatic form seems at the moment to interest only academic critics (J. Lapp, whose book still holds the field, B. Weinberg, O. de Mourgues), but it is rewarding and revealing. A rather silly notion of stage illusion, substituted for verisimilitude in the true Aristotelian sense, had robbed tragedy, while Racine was still a boy, of all visual, physical movement and appeal, and Corneille's great successes had maintained this austere model in the face of the great scenic advances which rival genres (the machine-play and then the opera) exploited to the full. But Racine brought in the outside world as much as he wished to, imaginatively, as seen or remembered in his characters's minds. He used his constraints as stimuli. Thus, to take a different example, it was a 'rule' (as it is obviously common sense) that no entrance or exit should take place without a plausible motive existing and being stated: hence rather frequent invitations to go and sacrifice to the gods when the stage had to be cleared at the end of an act; but hence also Andromaque's unforgettable first appearance:

Pyrrhus.   Me cherchiez-vous, Madame?
   Un espoir si charmant me serait-il permis?
Andromaque. Je passais jusqu'aux lieux où l'on garde mon fils.
   Puisqu'une fois le jour vous souffrez que je voie ... (I iv 258–61)

[1] 'Racine among us', in *Yale French Studies*, v (1950) 47–8.

Pyrrhus's obsequious eagerness, Andromaque's complete – and yet modest and touching – ignoring of it, both arise out of a technical necessity.

This mastery is one of the bases of Racine's art; the other, technical also, is his mastery of poetic language: another case of poverty turned into riches. A search for clarity had pruned the French language of all the exuberance some poets love; figurative speech had become un-fashionable; concrete terms were considered 'low'. The Alexandrine metre, in the process of avoiding the slipshod, had developed habits which only computerized research[1] has revealed in all their hidebound uniformity. (We realize now the explosive emotion indicated in the last line of *Bérénice*:

Bérénice. Pour la dernière fois, adieu, Seigneur.
Antiochus.   Hélas!

though we can never feel it as we should; because no-one now would shrink, as every poet did then, from placing an *adieu* or an *hélas* in the second hemistich.) Valéry gives the impression of writing like Racine, but only a pasticheur or a parodist could submit to all the restrictions Racine accepted.

This poetry has fascinated many, sometimes for the wrong reasons, as in the days of 'la poésie pure' – for its wonderful melody alone, as if this could in any poetry be divorced from the sense of its words. More lately, its deliberate avoidance of images and all other obvious poetic devices has acted like a challenge to the ingenuity of seekers after hidden systems of key-words and symbols.

More important, to some critics today (E. Vinaver, P. Butler), is something far deeper than this – the spirit of tragedy, captured of old in Athens, at times by Shakespeare, and by no-one else in the modern world but Racine. The question is delicate; for if Racine rediscovered tragedy he rediscovered it for himself – it was not easy for seventeenth-century writers to grasp what the Greeks had meant by the word. They never spoke of *le tragique* in this sense:[2] when they spoke of *a* tragedy, it is clear that they thought only of a work cast in a dramatic form characterised by great dignity of characters and style, and a plot never

---

[1] P. J. Wexler, 'On the grammetrics of the classical alexandrine', in *Cahiers de lexicologie* IV (1964) pp. 61 ff.

[2] As H. T. Barnwell has pointed out (*The Tragic in French Tragedy*, Inaugural lecture, the Queen's University, Belfast, 1966).

entirely fictitious in which death, or a fate as dreadful, descended at the dénouement, or had been clearly threatened if it did not actually descend. A loose formula admitted a great variety of tones and effects. There can be no doubt that Racine attained something purer and loftier than this suggests; but it may be doubted how clearly he could define it to himself, although he had personally wrestled with the Greek texts of Aristotle, Sophocles and Euripides; it may be doubted too if he ever aimed exclusively at attaining it, since it is admitted that he did not always succeed. To credit him with too precise a conception of this elusive quality – and whenever this is done, it is always with reference to one or another quite modern definition of it – is inevitably to force him into a modern mould. Perhaps this is inevitable: but we should know when we are doing it, and sacrifice none of the truth that we can see.

Racine has nothing like the span of Shakespeare, but he is not restricted to a single note. He has scenes which shocked contemporaries, and please at least some today, by recalling the quiet psychological comedy of Terence. He has created only four of the jealous tigresses whom some see as dominating his entire drama. He is not wholly pessimistic, though he has characters which can be taken as warnings of the danger of human passions, embodiments of the ethics of the Jansenist Nicole or the analysis of La Rochefoucauld, whose desires become their fate and turn them into monsters of unconscious egoism and cruelty. But not all end in despair and defeat: some uphold the standards by which the rest claim to act, and by which all must be judged; some of them suffer with magnanimity and inner peace, and what may quiet us in a death so noble; some are spared death. These rarely seem as vital as the others in our eyes – but this may be the effect of the responsiveness of our age to accents of despair. The almost passive Andromaque was Marquise du Parc's part, not Hermione: la Champmeslé played Atalide, not Roxane. Our age has seen much tragedy in its world, and created strangely little in its art; it is not wrong for it to dwell on the tragic aspects of Racine.

What may yet emerge as a more balanced picture, however, is a conception of a wonderfully complete *poetry*, transcending its limitations and forging into a single whole the indigence and the music of its language, its cruel or courtly irony and the human truth and imaginativeness of its study of men's passions and sufferings; to form, not the richest, but one of the purest and intensest forms of art devised by man.

The choice of passages to represent Racine criticism of the last few decades was of course not easy to make, and few or none will approve of it *in toto*. We cannot hope that it will provide a clear and coherent picture of its subject. The aim was to hold the balance even between several different considerations – to exhibit the principal trends (while exercising the editorial privilege of deciding what was too aberrant for inclusion); to make available papers that were (or chapters taken from books that had become) inaccessible, but usually not to reprint what was readily available in a complete book devoted to our author; and at the same time to collect the contributions of as many countries as possible, including of course that of the English-speaking world, habitually ignored in France. Not however by Professor Pommier, who opened his essay, in its original form as a lecture read in Oxford, with a graceful tribute to 'the pleiad of excellent *racinistes*' of which this country can boast. 'They may recognise contributions of their own in my remarks. If I say no more, it is not for lack of gratitude, but of time.'

Our contributors have all consented to dispense with the apparatus of footnotes which is less appropriate in the framework of the present collection. Any reader, therefore, who requires chapter and verse for some statement which here appears unsupported, is warned to consult the original version, where he will find the exigencies of scholarship more fully complied with. Every alteration has been authorised, and sometimes requested, by the writer (or, in one case, his literary executrix). For this, and many other examples of forbearance and consideration which have eased his task, the editor wishes to express all his gratitude.

R. C. KNIGHT

Chronology

1639   (Dec) Born at La Ferté-Milon (modern Département de l'Aisne), only son of a tax official.

1641   (Jan) Birth of his only sister and death of his mother.

1643   Death, after remarriage, of his father, leaving nothing to his family.

1649   Death of his maternal grandfather, with whom he had lived. The widow joined her sister and a daughter in the convent of Port-Royal-des-Champs near Paris (under strong Jansenist influence), almost certainly taking with her Racine, to be admitted *gratis* to the famous 'Petites Écoles' conducted by Jansenist recluses living round the convent.

1653–5   Interval at the college of the town of Beauvais.

1656   'Petites Écoles' closed by royal command. He remained in the vicinity.

1658–9   A year at the Collège d'Harcourt in Paris.

1659   Introduced by his cousin Vitart into the Duc de Luynes's household.

1660   A lost play, *Amasie*, rejected by the Théâtre du Marais. First publication – an ode on the king's marriage.

1661–2 (or –3) Visit to Uzès in Languedoc where an uncle was vicaire-général of the bishop. Hopes of an ecclesiastical living were realized only six years later.

1664   First play, *La Thébaïde ou les frères ennemis*, produced by Molière.
First royal gratification, of 600 *livres*, soon raised to 800 then 1200 per annum.

1665   *Alexandre le Grand* produced by Molière, and a fortnight later, without warning to the latter, by the Hôtel de Bourgogne. Molière was justly offended.

1666   A *Lettre à l'auteur des Hérésies imaginaires*, replying to a slighting remark about playwrights in a pamphlet by the Jansenist Nicole, confirmed Racine's estrangement from Port-Royal.

1667   (Nov) *Andromaque*, produced at the Hôtel de Bourgogne, as his other plays will be, up to *Phèdre*; a brilliant success.

1668   (Autumn) *Les Plaideurs*, his one comedy.

        (Dec) Death of Marquise du Parc, the actress who had created the role of Andromaque. Racine appeared 'half-dead' with grief at her funeral. She is said to have borne him a daughter who lived eight years.

1669   (Dec) *Britannicus*.

1670   (Nov) *Bérénice*.

        Rival production of Corneille's *Tite et Bérénice* produced by Molière.

1672   (Jan) *Bajazet*.

        (Dec) Elected to the Académie Française (despite considerable opposition).

1673   (Feb) *Mithridate*.

1674   (Aug) *Iphigénie* produced at a royal fête at Versailles. It became his greatest popular success.

1675   (May) Rival tragedy of *Iphigénie* by Leclerc and Coras.

1676   First edition of *Œuvres complètes*, with new prefaces. (Revised editions 1687, 1697.)

1677   (Jan) *Phèdre et Hippolyte* (title changed to *Phèdre*, 1687). Rival tragedy of *Phèdre et Hippolyte* by Pradon.

        (June) Marriage.

        (Sept) Ordered to write the history of the reign, with Boileau.

        (Thereafter, ceased to write for the stage, was reconciled with Port-Royal, attended court, obtained appointments conferring nobility, and brought up a family of six.)

1689   *Esther*, commissioned by Madame de Maintenon, performed before the court at Saint-Cyr by girls of the school she had founded.

1691   *Athalie*, composed for the same purpose, has 'rehearsals' attended by the king, but no public performance (until 1702).

1694   Four *cantiques spirituels* published with music.

1699   (21 Apr) Died. Buried in the churchyard of Port-Royal.

SIR MAURICE BOWRA

The Simplicity
of Racine (1956)

VERY few poets have fashioned a world which is at once so rich and
so strictly circumscribed as that of Racine. To us, who inevitably judge
most poetry by Shakespeare, he seems to come from another order of
being. Instead of bursting luxuriance, we find trimness and formality;
instead of experiment and innovation, the intensive exploitation of a
selected range of effects. Each poet had some fifty years of dramatic art
behind him, and each followed the main lines marked out by his
predecessors, but whereas Shakespeare continued to the end extending
the capacities of drama by exploring new territory, Racine narrowed
them and confined himself to what he believed to be its essential task.
In his wish to surpass Corneille he eliminated much to which Corneille
owed his chief renown – his heroic and chivalrous elements, his resonant
maxims, his majestic irrelevances, his moral disquisitions, his stage
effects. Racine asked himself what tragedy ought to be, and came to a
firm answer, which he followed from *Andromaque* to *Phèdre*. With
unrelaxed determination he admitted nothing which did not agree with
it. In the desire to conform, which lay so deep in his nature, he obeyed
the main precepts of Aristotle with a piety beyond the emulation of his
contemporaries or the precedent of the Attic tragedians.

Though Racine owed his profound knowledge of human nature to
his observation of his contemporaries and especially of those whom he
saw at the court of Louis XIV, where a high style and irreproachable
manners were often a mask for formidable passions and unscrupulous
ambitions, he did not copy them directly but used them as material for
his own realm of the imagination, in which the fundamental workings
of human nature could be displayed with a special clarity and emphasis.
The classic idea of tragedy, as it was understood in his time, provided
him with a ritual whose ceremonial demands he observed with affec-

tionate fidelity. The very strictness of the form appealed to his love of order and satisfied his desire to make every detail play an indispensable part in the main design, while the obligation to transpose his experience into distant spheres enabled him to maintain a majestic tone beyond the indignity of contemporary fashions and controversies. With the powerful convention behind him, he could create characters and situations which were at once particular and universal, and, by stirring many familiar chords in his audiences, force them to look on fundamental matters with a refreshed and sharpened vision. Just as the Greeks found the material for tragedy in a dateless, heroic past and were able through this to give a peculiarly vivid form to the problems which beset them, so Racine used the limitations of his art to isolate his subjects and make them more cogent and more impressive than if he had dramatized his own familiar world or made concessions to mere modernity. In selecting what he thought to be most dramatic in humanity Racine was able to do full justice to it by fitting it into a strict frame which allowed nothing but the most essential issues to be presented on the stage.

In this spirit Racine not only accepted the unities of time, place, and action but applied them rigorously to his tragedies and made them serve his central purpose. All his scenes are set indoors, in palaces which may be in Greece or Rome or Constantinople, but are equally indefinite and uncharacterized, differentiated by almost no suggestion of local colour or specific decoration. They hardly need any scenery on the stage, and too much of it spoils their authentic effect. Racine places his action at some distance from ordinary life on the principle that it adds reverence to the view (*Bajazet*, Préface). If he usually secures this by choosing themes from remote ages like heroic Greece and imperial Rome, in *Bajazet* he makes a comparatively modern subject no less remote by setting it in the alien world of the seraglio at Constantinople. He does not need to vary the scenes of a play, since they are of no importance in comparison with what is said in them. What matters is that the dramatic action should be as concentrated as possible, and with this any change of scene would interfere. It means that most of Racine's catastrophes take place off the stage and are reported by witnesses. When Atalide kills herself before our eyes, it is but another tribute to the precarious and brutal conditions of Turkish life. It is more characteristic of Racine that he does not follow Euripides in bringing the dying Hippolyte back on the stage and that Phèdre has already taken poison before she returns to speak her last words. He uses the unity of place to enforce his conviction that the first task of tragedy lies in its words, that these are more important even than its actions, since they reveal what happens in the hearts of his characters and should be hampered as little as possible.

The conditions of dramatic performance also forced Racine to observe the unity of time. Because he was compelled to confine a whole drama to less than two hours, he could not afford to waste precious moments on preliminaries and diversions. Everything must be relevant to a single end, and that means that he begins a tragedy with the sustained crisis which is its subject. In his opening words he always strikes a note of tension or alarm or anxiety, which shows his characters in the grip of their fatal obsessions, whether it is Agrippine fuming at her son's neglect of her, or Antiochus steeled at last to break with Bérénice, or Xipharès confessing his long-concealed love for Monime, or Agamemnon tortured by the oracle which tells him to sacrifice his daughter. Racine increases the emotional pressure as he proceeds, but it is already in strong blast when he begins. His plots are not unfolded with a Shakespearian elaboration but consist almost entirely of a single complex of events which sweeps all to the fatal end. The convention that the plot must be confined to one day suits this art, which deals only with the last stage of a process, when all the different stresses and conflicts come together in a crash of passion and doom. None of Racine's plots would gain from being spread beyond the conventional day, and indeed the shortness of time implied by his intervals is neces- sary to the breathless movement of his action, in which events crowd on each other in the relentless hurry of a crisis reeling to catastrophe.

The unities of time and place are demanded by the unity of action, and to no aspect of his art does Racine devote more vigilant care. In all his tragedies he makes every word and every situation relevant to a central theme, and this is always the relations between the members of a small group of human beings, who, by changing their positions with regard to one another, break the precarious balance on which they live, and precipitate disaster. The pattern of these relations is different in each play, from the complex movements of the quartet in *Andromaque*, each of whom is in love with someone who loves someone else, to the predominance in *Phèdre* of a single woman who drags everyone with her in her own ruin. Behind the leading figures are the confidants, whose main task is to draw out their patrons and to complete their interior monologues by apt suggestions, questions, and criticisms, and who act as mirrors to reveal what forces lie in wait to inflame and destroy. Only exceptionally do they have, like Narcisse and Œnone, an active part, and even then they are extensions of the chief characters, reflections of their desperate desires and instruments of their unconscious purposes. Racine conforms with exemplary fidelity to Aristotle's definition of the unity of action as

a complete whole, with the parts of its action so closely connected that the transposal or removal of any one of them will alter and dislocate the whole.

Racine secures this unity not only by making each situation rise with relentless necessity from what precedes it, but by basing the whole development of his plots on the personalities of those who take part in them. The march of events, which has so predestined an air, is determined entirely by the behaviour of human beings, who, in obeying the commands of their imperious natures, come into conflict with one another and create havoc and disaster. Racine never allows any irrelevance, however alluring, to turn his eyes away from the plot.

This consummate art embodies Racine's highly individual vision of existence, his selection from experience and his transformation of it into a coherent and impressive form. In his own critical comments no word appears more often than 'simplicité', and though, by misinterpreting it, we can convict him of failure in something which he did not attempt, it stands for what is most characteristic and distinctive in his work. The simplicity which he seeks and attains is certainly not artless or unsophisticated or merely instinctive. Everything is carefully weighed and calculated; nothing is left to chance. Racine's simplicity is a form of simplification, in which he omits much that might seem relevant to us but does not seem relevant to him. He concentrates on what he considers to be the most forceful and most assertive element in humanity – the passions. These provide him with the driving power of all his plots and are set to work in the most dramatic and most economical way. If he simplifies, it is because he sees that the passions are responsible for all that is most exciting in human existence and form an incomparable basis for a convincing, lifelike art, for that 'vraisemblance' which he values almost as much as 'simplicité'. Few other dramatists see tragedy quite in this way or work with so firm and undeviating idea of what it ought to be.

In his desire for this kind of simplicity Racine avoids much that we might expect to find in the presentation of societies far from his own. He was blamed for not making *Bajazet* sufficiently Turkish, and he certainly had no love for the picturesque accessories which delighted Corneille. But he was not totally blind to some relevant aspects of historical or geographical atmosphere and gives alike to his Greeks, his Romans, and his Turks characteristics which are undeniably their own and almost peculiar to them. But he does this because it is indispensable to his plot. The sacrifice of Iphigénie, the reasons of state which impel Titus to reject Bérénice, the 'grande tuerie' which startled Madame de Sévigné in *Bajazet* arise inevitably from the worlds to which they belong. But Racine knew that any generous indulgence in local colour would spoil his most important effects. Having set his events in a separate sphere of the imagination, he could not break their isolation by adding details which would detract from its austere distinction. He had to keep the distance between his characters and the common scene, because otherwise he would not be able to display them in their authentic, unconcealed humanity. To make too much of their Greek or Roman background would be in some sense to dress them up, to give them delusive disguises, when what mattered was to show them in their all too human selves. Just as he avoided French subjects because they would inevitably suggest contemporary references which would interfere with his selective and concentrated art, so in his treatment of ancient or alien societies he eliminated any details, however attractive in themselves, which were likely to spoil the fundamental simplicity of his tragic vision.

 Racine enhances this sense of distance by choosing his characters from kings and queens, their companions and their attendants. In this he not only followed the precedent of Attic tragedy but conformed to social distinctions as they were observed at the court of Louis XIV. But he had better reasons than these. If it is a main duty of tragedy to display how men fall from prosperity to disaster, their fall is the more appalling when they start with all that the world most honours. Such men and women have a detachment which makes them respond with unusual candour to the malice of events. In the closed circles in which they move there is ample room for them to be unrestrainedly themselves, to know one another with a remorseless intimacy, to speak with an unquestioning consciousness of their own superiority, and not to be afraid of unlocking their innermost thoughts. Yet in the midst of their pomp they are isolated with the dangerous loneliness of those who are forbidden to mingle with the multitude. They stand exposed and unprotected in the grandeur of their heredity and their station. Because power offers opportunities of indulgence denied to ordinary men, they follow their ambitions and desires with an alarming eagerness and self-confidence. In their uncurbed individuality corruption finds a ready prey, and feeds remorselessly on it. Racine's characters are so little broken to discipline that they plunge into the most desperate courses with no care for the consequences and are prevented by self-will, pride, and the voracity of their appetites from abandoning anything that they have begun. Tragedy justifiably deals with these privileged and uninhibited people, because they are free to pursue their own desires and through their exalted position present in sharp outline much that would be blurred in the pressure of common life.

The key to Racine's art is that character is destiny; that, by being what they are, men and women forge their own fates; and for him character means in the first place the passions. It is they which compel decision and action, which smash through the restraints imposed by society, and drive human nature to assert itself in primitive violence. Racine's persons have an extraordinary degree of reality, which is in no sense realistic or even familiar, since this is not the manner in which people ordinarily speak and act, but is none the less impressively real because it embodies something which everybody knows, and which is all the more striking because it has been simplified by discriminating insight and reduced to its indispensable essence. By eliminating all ornament or irrelevance or even idiosyncrasy from his characters Racine gives them an extraordinary degree of life, of convincing personality; for it is through their salient, ruling proclivities that we form our notions of people and think that we know them. This not only makes Racine's characters more 'heroic' in the sense that their motives are less confused and less hesitant than those of ordinary men and women, but also more real, since they having nothing but the authentic self, the irreducible element which remains when everything transitory or local has been removed. Despite all their capacities and their proud air of independence they cannot escape from the central laws of their being. They remain always and ineluctably themselves, and this is their glory, their pathos, and their doom.

Racine knows human nature too well to shape a character to suit a single passion, and prefers to show how one passion, however strong, may so foster others and be so infused by them that a new complex unity arises. Though he presents a whole galaxy of women in love, from the innocent Junie and the less innocent Atalide to the furious and tormented Hermione, Roxane, and Phèdre, in none of them is love the only thing that counts. Junie has her tendency to fear the worst and to compromise with circumstances; Atalide is not above jealousy and not always happy about the sacrifices which she is prepared to make for her beloved; Hermione is so deeply absorbed in herself that she loses her sense of reality in criminal irresponsibility; Roxane hardly distinguishes between her love of Bajazet and her love of power; Phèdre is racked by a conviction of defeat and guilt. Though Racine's men are notable for pride and ambition, these are countered in Acomat by worldly opportunism, in Mithridate by crafty suspicion, in Agamemnon by a father's affection. In Néron a cold-blooded egoism and a thirst for violent sensation are the more formidable because he conceals them in an accomplished talent for histrionic deceit. Racine disagrees with those moralists of his time who find the mainspring of behaviour in self-interest or self-regard; he knows that human nature is not so easily explained. His assumption is that, though a single passion may seem to be in command, it summons others to its service and reveals the complex unity which is the self.

Racine formed his characters on the psychological insight which his generation learned alike from the court and the confessional and which found such uncompromising exponents as La Rochefoucauld and Pascal. This taught that virtues and vices are more intimately allied than common decency is ready to admit and that nothing in human nature should really surprise us. This means that Racine not only is far more subtle than the Attic tragedians in his analysis of motives and vagaries of character but sometimes admits to tragedy psychological conditions which, but for his art in assimilating them, might seem to be below its dignity. He was fully awake to the paradoxes of behaviour and did not shrink from making them responsible for some of his most dramatic shocks. When Hermione hears from Oreste that, in obedience to her wishes, he has killed Pyrrhus, her immediate and obliterating reaction is contempt and hatred for him:

> Tais-toi, perfide,
> Et n'impute qu'à toi ton lâche parricide.
> Va faire chez tes Grecs admirer ta fureur.
> Va, je la désavoue, et tu me fais horreur.

> Barbare, qu'as tu fait? Avec quelle furie
> As-tu tranché le cours d'une si belle vie?
>
> *(Andromaque,* V iii 1533–8)

When Roxane, who has offered marriage and powers to Bajazet, hears him falter in his acceptance, her whole temper changes to freezing hatred:

> Non, je ne veux plus rien.
> Ne m'importune plus de tes raisons forcées.
> Je vois combien tes vœux sont loin de mes pensées.
> Je ne te presse plus, ingrat, d'y consentir.
> Rentre dans le néant dont je t'ai fait sortir.
>
> *(Bajazet,* II i 520–4)

When Bérénice, who has denounced Titus for his heartless treatment of her and regarded him as a cowardly and dissembling traitor, sees that after all he acts from motives of the highest honour, she changes her whole outlook and speaks with the tenderest understanding:

> Mon cœur vous est connu, Seigneur, et je puis dire
> Qu'on ne l'a jamais vu soupirer pour l'empire.
> La grandeur des Romains, la pourpre des Césars
> N'a point, vous le savez, attiré mes regards.
> J'aimais, Seigneur, j'aimais, je voulais être aimée.
> Ce jour, je l'avoûrai, je me suis alarmée;
> J'ai cru que votre amour allait finir son cours.
> Je connais mon erreur, et vous m'aimez toujours.
>
> *(Bérénice,* V vii 1475–82)

There is no need to show how these changes of heart and purpose take place; it is enough to display them in their full dramatic impact when they come, and then there is no doubt of their truth.

The quality of Racine's insight can be seen in his characterization of Néron. The plot of *Britannicus* turns on the crisis when the young emperor, who is thought to show promise of being a model ruler, suddenly reveals himself as a murderous monster. Agrippine is at the start aware of the danger, but others, notably Burrhus, are deceived by him. Racine takes a hint from Tacitus, who says that Néron hid his hatreds under deceitful flattery, and shows how a man who is all too ready to deceive others deceives also himself. When Néron first appears, gloating over the abduction of Junie, he says, with apparent fervour, that he is passionately in love with her:

> Depuis un moment, mais pour toute ma vie.
> J'aime (que dis-je aimer?), j'idolâtre Junie.
>
> (*Britannicus*, ii ii 383–4)

But we soon see from his horrible glee in making her suffer that he is moved not by love but by lust for some new and violent sensation. The man, who so lies to himself, lies with practised skill to others. When his mother has made her long appeal to him, he says that he will do all that she asks and speaks in words of affectionate reconciliation:

> Oui, Madame, je veux que ma reconnaissance
> Désormais dans les cœurs grave votre puissance;
> Et je bénis déjà cette heureuse froideur,
> Qui de notre amitié va rallumer l'ardeur.
>
> (Ibid. iv ii 1295–8)

Racine leaves us to guess whether Néron has already decided to defy his mother and is lying to her or for the moment means what he says; and this is just the doubt which we feel with a man who is so corrupted by falsehood that he himself does not always know whether he means what he says or not.

It might be argued that, though Racine is invariably successful with his more violent characters, he is less successful with their victims, whose very innocence entails a certain lack of personality in comparison with the exorbitant passions and merciless claims of their persecutors. If this were true, it would illustrate W. B. Yeats's words that 'passive suffering is not a theme for poetry'; and indeed if Racine's victims went unresisting and uncomplaining to their doom, it would be too painful to endure. But he avoids this by giving to them a power of initiative which brings them to life and invests them with a tragic dignity. Andromaque has buried her heart with Hector, but he still lives for her in her son, and, when the boy's life is in peril, she shrinks from no stratagem or sacrifice to save him. Britannicus is only a boy, but, when Néron bullies and threatens him, he answers with a proud, defiant courage. Monime is in an impossible position, when both Mithridate and his two sons are in love with her, and at first she yields to his dominating insistence, but in the end she rejects him, though she knows that it may mean her death. Aricie is almost an unconsidered sacrifice in a general devastation, but she too has her moments of grandeur,

when she stands by Hippolyte in his humiliation or defends his innocence to his frenzied father. In building his action on the passions a
lesser poet might have found it difficult to arouse interest in these sane
and unselfish characters, but Racine relies on more than the pathos of
their lot or the contrast between them and their persecutors. By giving
them their own pride and distinction he makes them live in their own
right and brings them closer to us.

Racine's dramatization of the passions gains a new dimension from
the clarity with which his characters speak. It is part of their grand manner, their distance from common men, their refusal to shirk issues or to
be anything but themselves. Their lucidity implies a high intelligence
and rises from their understanding of themselves and their circumstances. Racine makes great use of this and secures unique results from
it. His characters display a searching insight into one another, and this
is sharpened by the force of their passions. It is Agrippine's desire to
keep her hold on Néron which reveals to her his innate savagery;
Roxane's love for Bajazet which tells her that, despite his protestations,
he does not love her; Mithridate's self-centred arrogance which betrays
to him the love of Xipharès and Monime. The passions provoke the
discovery of truth because they sharpen the intelligence on many
matters which concern them. In opposition to La Rochefoucauld's
maxim that 'l'esprit est toujours la dupe du cœur', Racine shows how
the heart, no matter how agonized or how rotten, sets the intelligence
to work with an increased lucidity and penetration.

This formidable insight is also applied by the characters to themselves. Even Racine's gentler and less assertive heroines, when they are
called to make some supreme sacrifice, know exactly what it is and why
they make it. When Andromaque sees that the only way to save her
child is for her to marry Pyrrhus, she feels that this is none the less an
act of treachery to her dead husband, and that, once she has done it,
she must atone by killing herself. Faced by a situation which might call
for a dexterous display of casuistry, she follows the dictates of her
nature so scrupulously that she solves all her problems by a single
stroke:

> Mais aussitôt ma main, à moi seule funeste,
> D'une infidèle vie abrégera le reste,
> Et, sauvant ma vertu, rendra ce que je doi
> A Pyrrhus, à mon fils, à mon époux, à moi.
>
> (*Andromaque*, IV i 1093–6)

So Junie, terrified of the doom which Néron plots for Britannicus, thinks not of her own safety, but of what she might have done to save him. She has tried to warn him by signs, but knows that her efforts have been fruitless. With courageous candour she blames herself for not having dissimulated with more confidence and more success. Though her own fate is sealed with that of Britannicus, she thinks only of him and of what she might have done to help him. She makes no mistakes about herself and does not shrink from condemning her own failure:

> Quel tourment de se taire en voyant ce qu'on aime,
> De l'entendre gémir, de l'affliger soi-même,
> Lorsque par un regard on peut le consoler!
> Mais quels pleurs ce regard aurait-il fait couler!
> Ah! dans ce souvenir, inquiète, troublée,
> Je ne me sentais pas assez dissimulée. (*Britannicus*, III vii 1003–8)

In Andromaque and Junie affection, so powerful that it deserves the name of passion, enables them to see exactly what they are doing, without any obstruction either from forbidding self-control or from deluding self-pity.

A similar insight is displayed by those who are the prey of more violent and more destructive passions. They have at least no illusions about the nature and the demands of their desires. Agrippine deceives herself neither about the crimes which she has committed to make her son emperor nor about her own lust for glory and power; Agamemnon knows that in the last resort he prefers his own success in war to his love for his daughter; Phèdre sees both how strong and how wrong is her passion for Hippolyte. But this knowledge in no way impedes the course of passion. Racine's characters watch their own progress to destruction with an objectivity which never deserts them and yet can do nothing to save them; which stands apart from their tyrannous obsessions and yet is their helpless captive. We cannot but feel deeply for these men and women who are prevented by their own natures from helping themselves. Their dooms are the more appalling because they are dragged to them in full knowledge of what their actions mean and with a rational sense of responsibility for them. Living in an age which knew what self-examination is, Racine was able to turn it into a new force for tragedy by making his heroes and heroines spectators as well as agents in their own catastrophes.

Yet, though Racine endows his characters with this merciless insight and shows how it rises from the very force of their passions, he also shows how at a certain point it fails them and becomes an instrument in their fall. Though they remain almost clairvoyant in their knowledge of themselves, yet they make errors of judgement which hasten their ruin. They miscalculate the possibility of achieving their desires, and this is due to the violence of their passions, whether it is Oreste, who thinks that Hermione will yield herself to him if he does all that she demands, or Agrippine, that she can bring back Néron to her control by appealing to his affection and gratitude; or Antiochus, that Bérénice will accept his love if Titus rejects her; or Phèdre, that somehow she can seduce Hippolyte. The pathetic paradox of Racine's characters is that, though they know themselves and each other conspicuously well, they misjudge their ends. The very passions which enable them to see so much with an unsparing clarity blind them in the one thing which matters most to them; and this brings their ruin. They are so sure of themselves that they do not question their decisions until it is too late and there is no escape from disaster. Their doom is the more poignant because the intellectual penetration which gives them a singular distinction deserts them in their fatal crisis, and it is the cruellest of ironies when they fall through its treachery.

In this we may see Racine's bold and adroit adaptation of Aristotle's doctrine that the fall of tragic heroes should be due to some ἁμαρτία or error. In this Aristotle seems to combine, or confuse, an error of judgement with a fault of character, and this is natural enough in one who thought that right knowledge is an essential element in moral conduct. But he does not make his point very clearly and leaves the impression that a wrong judgement is in itself enough to create a tragic situation. Racine is not content to acquiesce in this uncertainty but consistently makes the fatal miscalculations of his characters rise directly from their passions, and thus builds his catastrophes on a satisfying and convincing scheme, which takes him far indeed from the practice of the Attic tragedians. With them the tragic action turns on the ignorance and the delusions of men, which grow and multiply until at last in the crash of disaster the victims learn that they can know nothing except their utter insignificance before the gods. Racine's characters are fully conscious of what they are doing, and their error is confined to one fatal blindness, but even then they dissect their feelings with unfaltering precision. Racine derives his catastrophes from the whole of a man's being and makes the intelligence almost as important as the passions, whether they sharpen it to see things with a peculiar clarity or delude it to work his ruin.

The notion that character is destiny excludes the play of chance. There are indeed moments when Racine allows coincidence to speed his action, but he does so only within strict limits. We cannot complain that Thésée arrives when he is rumoured to be dead, for it is in full accord with his unpredictable character; nor that Bajazet's love-letter to Atalide is found on her by Roxane's attendants after she has fainted, for it only hastens the revelation of what Roxane already suspects and is bound to know soon. In Racine chance plays an almost negligible part; for otherwise it would undermine his assumption that men act as they do because they are what they are. Though he naturally does not trouble himself with speculations about the freedom of the will, his characters are free in the sense which we usually give to the word: they make their own choices and in so doing act both from their emotions and their intelligence. They are not victims of some celestial savagery like the curse of bloodshed which ravages the House of Atreus or the doom to which the gods condemn Oedipus before he is born. Their faults are not in their stars but in themselves, and this makes it easier for us to participate in their aspirations and their anguish.

In his seven tragedies from *Andromaque* to *Phèdre* Racine chooses his matter from societies which are in no respect Christian. Later, when he broke his twelve years' silence with *Esther* and *Athalie*, he forsook his former practice for a kind of drama which reflected a change of outlook both in his patrons and in himself. But *Esther* is in no strict sense a tragedy, and though Athalie herself is a worthy sister and successor of Agrippine and Roxane, the magnificent poem to which she gives her name is in effect a morality which demonstrates the triumph of God and His servants. If in his creative heyday Racine avoided any specifically Christian colouring, it may well have been due to the contemporary taste for classical and heroic subjects, but, whatever the reason for it was, it had an incalculable influence on his art and brought special advantages to it. It meant that, despite his Jansenist education and the correct Catholicism of his patrons, he confined himself to a profane, pagan world, in which the lusts of the flesh and of the spirit determine and dominate the action, and, deeply though the fates of his characters may move us, they do so at a purely human level which rejects such consolations as religion might offer for their wounds. This suits something fundamental in the tragic vision of life, and Racine must surely have seen that the most authentic tragedy is based on a sense of irredeemable waste, of unresolved discords, of chaos at the heart of things, and that to advance some explanation or apology for these is to diminish their truly tragic character. For this reason perhaps he avoided not only any assumption that in the end all must be well but even any hint, such as we sometimes find in Shakespeare, that the ugliest catastrophes may be redeemed by love. Though Racine sometimes evokes pity, it is by no means his only or his chief effect, and with his more formidable characters he does not evoke it at all. In its place he offers sympathy in the sense that we enter into their souls and share their frenzies as if they were our own. What count with him are the intensity of passion and the emotional responses which it awakes. In this he resembles not Sophocles, who suggests that the most horrifying events must be accepted because the gods send them, but Euripides, who lets his catastrophes appeal to us in themselves without offering any solution or comfort, and is for this very reason 'the most tragic of the poets'.

It is true that in his Greek plays Racine gives some part to the gods, because he is compelled by his myths to do so. But not even in *Iphigénie* is this more than a dramatic device for developing the action. In *Phèdre* it is different, and Racine gives a new depth to his drama when Phèdre, torn between the claims of life and of death, shrinks alike from both:

> J'ai pour aïeul le père et le maître des dieux.
> Le ciel, tout l'univers est plein de mes aïeux.
> Où me cacher? Fuyons dans la nuit infernale.
> Mais que dis-je? Mon père y tient l'urne fatale.
> Le sort, dit-on, l'a mise en ses sévères mains.
> Minos juge aux enfers tous les pâles humains.

(IV vi 1275–80)

In this there is no need to see a transformation of Christian ideas into Greek. Phèdre has good reason to fear the punishments which await her after death, but these can be found in Tartarus as much as in any Christian Hell. None the less we must surely feel that here Racine does more than merely conform to ancient myth, that he tries to give a new substance to it, that his images of the Sun and Minos, of the light and the dark, are his way of stressing the implacable dilemma in which Phèdre finds herself. She cannot live, because in her guilt she shuns the light of day; she cannot die, because she dares not face what happens after death. Her position is tragically <u>human and familiar</u>, and in dramatizing it so closely to Greek ideas Racine displays his mastery of them and his <u>ability to give them a universal relevance.</u>

In this scene Racine deals with issues of good and evil as Phèdre sees them, and makes them perfectly consistent with her character and her situation. If their treatment is more searching and more revealing than we might expect, that is because he adds a new domain to his objective art. It is therefore surprising that in his Preface to *Phèdre* he speaks not as an artist but as a moralist:

> What I can guarantee is that I have done nothing in which virtue is set more in the light than in this play. In it the smallest faults are severely punished. The mere thought of crime is regarded in it with as much horror as crime itself. In it the weaknesses of love pass for true weaknesses. In it the passions are presented to the eye only to show the disorder of which they are the cause; and in it vice is painted throughout with the colours which make us know and hate its ugliness.

Racine is of course defending himself against the charge of stimulating to vice, and he states his case strongly. Something of what he says is true. Phèdre herself indeed shows the disorder which the passions create. But the more we look at these words, the less do they seem to be true of the play as a whole. Can Racine really mean that the love of Hippolyte and Aricie is a true weakness rightly punished? And what of Thésée, with the ruin of whose happiness the play closes? Does Racine even hint that this is a fit requital for his past loves and his passion for Phèdre? And even with Phèdre herself, is it true that we are so impressed by the justice of her end that we see in her a lesson and a warning? Even if Racine is more concerned with moral issues than hitherto, he does not present them as a moralist, still less on some facile theory, worthy of Miss Prism, that 'The good ended happily, and the bad unhappily. That is what fiction means.' If he does, we cannot even answer with Cecily: 'I suppose so. But it seems very unfair.'

In fact Racine's tragedies, including *Phèdre*, do not attempt to prove any such lesson. The <u>sufferings of the characters are by no means in proportion to their deserts.</u> Néron survives, not perhaps happily but at least defiantly, his first excursion into murder, and the innocent, whether Britannicus and Junie, or Bajazet and Atalide, or Hippolyte and Aricie, are as often ruined as the wicked. If they are punished for

anything, it is for their virtues – Britannicus for his outspoken resistance
to Néron, Atalide for her self-denying attempt to save Bajazet by
yielding him to Roxane, Hippolyte for his refusal to tell his father of
Phèdre's attempt to seduce him. And what are we to think of *Bérénice*,
in which all three of the chief characters are moved by the noblest
motives and rewarded by broken hearts? Some may perhaps take comfort from Mr T. S. Eliot's judgement:

> To my mind, Racine's *Bérénice* represents about the summit of civilisa-
> tion in tragedy; and it is, in a way, a Christian tragedy, with devotion to
> the state substituted for devotion to divine law.

That *Bérénice* is highly civilized nobody will deny, but even if we
admit that in it the state takes the place of divine law – and this is both
difficult in itself and unsupported by any evidence from Racine – are
we to believe that a tragedy is necessarily Christian because in it the
good suffer? Of course we might argue that in making their several
sacrifices Titus, Antiochus, and Bérénice have the consolation of knowing that virtue is its own reward, but, if that is so, it is strange that
Racine should close on a note of undisguised lament when he makes
Bérénice say:

> Adieu, servons tous trois d'exemple à l'univers
> De l'amour la plus tendre et la plus malheureuse
> Dont il puisse garder l'histoire douloureuse. (v vii 1502–4)

Whatever Racine may have felt about his characters, he did not distribute rewards and punishments among them according to their worth.
Racine indeed is too good a psychologist to divide his characters into
two classes on any moralistic plan. He knows that good and evil are to
be found inextricably compounded in the same person. Even his more
obviously virtuous characters have serious faults. Burrhus may be a
plain, blunt soldier, who prides himself on his hatred for any untruth,
but he is unduly complacent about his training of Néron. Bajazet is
undeniably ardent, courageous, and eager for renown, but there is an
element of corruption in the facility with which, after his first failure,
he succeeds in persuading Roxane that he returns her love. Moral
judgements on Mithridate are perhaps out of place, since he moves in
a sphere where what counts is not morality but honour, but on him
also our feelings are divided; for while he is savagely jealous, suspicious,
and cunning, we cannot but admire his superb self-confidence and his

unquenchable spirit. Even Agrippine, who is on her own admission an accomplished criminal and shrinks from nothing to win and keep power, redeems her arrogance by her unsparing confession of her iniquities to her son and her terrible denunciation of him after the murder of Britannicus. If Racine had really wished his plots to demonstrate the triumph of virtue and the discomfiture of vice, he would have discriminated more decisively between them.

Racine's refusal to allow the design of his tragedies to be dictated by obvious considerations of morality is deeper than this. Even when he depicts characters who are by the standards of almost any age lost souls, devoured by ugly passions and reckless self-gratification, he somehow sees them from inside and makes us enter into their inner selves, when they might otherwise horrify and appal us. This is true above all of Phèdre, and no doubt accounts for Racine's own attempt to disown the obvious truth about her. However much we may condemn her in absence or in abstract, yet, when she is present on the stage or in the imagination, we are swept away by the force of her passion and her misery and do not stop to judge her. We do not even feel it necessary to excuse her on the ground that she is the victim of forces beyond her control; for we are too close to her, too tightly caught in her feelings, to think of making excuses or to respond to anything but the overwhelming anguish of her human state. In the end it may perhaps be a comfort that she makes amends by confession and death, but in the long crisis of her passion we do not anticipate or desire this. The same is true of Racine's other *femmes damnées*, of Roxane and Hermione. They may indeed frighten and horrify us, but there is none the less a fierce fascination in their unbridled temperaments, and we cannot but respond to their pride of life and their truth to their own natures. However violent and vicious these women may be, in the uncontrollable attraction and excitement of their imperious presences we do not pass moral judgements on them. So too even Néron, who turns the blood cold by his murderous selfishness, is still undeniably human in his desire to escape from the bonds in which his mother holds him and in his inability to defy her when he is alone with her. We rightly shrink in horror from him, but he is not ultimately alien to something that we know and understand.

If what Racine says in his apology for *Phèdre* is true neither of his other plays nor of *Phèdre* itself, we must try to find what he thought the essential function of tragedy to be, by what means he hoped to solve its disturbing discords and to explain our need for it. He gives a hint in the Preface to *Bérénice*:

> It is sufficient that the action should be great, that the actors should be heroic, that the passions should be aroused, and that everything should be imbued with that majestic sadness in which the whole pleasure of tragedy lies.

In the last words, in which Racine speaks not as a moralist but as an artist who has his own task to perform, he comes near to uncovering his secret. We may supplement them with a story reported by the Abbé de la Porte in his *Anecdotes dramatiques*:

> I have heard Madame de la Fayette relate, said the Abbé de Saint-Pierre, that in a conversation Racine maintained that a good poet could get the greatest crimes excused and even inspire compassion for the criminals. He added that it only requires a fertile, delicate, and discriminating mind to reduce to such an extent the horror of the crimes of Medea or Phaedra as to make them acceptable to the spectators, and even to inspire pity for the criminals.

It is difficult not to believe that there is truth in this, since it amplifies and elucidates what Racine himself says about *Bérénice*; and surely the most important words are 'a good poet'. Racine's contention is that, if the poetry is only good enough, even the most criminal characters can be made sympathetic; and, if it is true, as the Abbé goes on to tell, that Racine wrote *Phèdre* to prove his point, we can judge his preaching by his practice. In other words, Racine trusted above all to his poetry to do what he thought right for tragedy. In the first and the last resort it is the poetry which counts and must be considered in its extraordinary and, for us, unaccustomed quality.

Racine's style has the same kind of simplicity as his dramatic structure and economy of action. It is formed by a resolute discrimination, a merciless rejection of anything which he considers below the proper majesty of his task. His vocabulary consists of no more than two thousand words, which is a tenth of the number in Shakespeare's, and he does not shrink from using the same phrase more than once if it meets a need. His is the antithesis of modern poetry which seeks at all costs to be individual and unusual and delights in unexpected images and unexploited observations. Though Racine admired Homer's gift for introducing the most humble details into poetry, he believed that this was impossible in French:

> 'Calypso lui donne encore un vilebrequin et des clous, tant Homère est exact à décrire les moindres particularités: ce qui a bonne grâce dans le

grec, au lieu que le latin est beaucoup plus réservé, et ne s'amuse pas à de si petites choses. La langue sans doute est plus stérile, et n'a pas des mots qui expriment si heureusement les choses que la langue grecque; car on dirait qu'il n'y a rien de bas dans le grec, et les plus viles choses y sont noblement exprimées. Il en va de même de notre langue que de la latine; car elle fuit extrêmement de s'abaisser aux particularités, parce que les oreilles sont délicates et ne peuvent souffrir qu'on nomme des choses basses dans un discours sérieux, comme une coignée, une scie, et un vilebrequin.'
(*Remarques sur l'Odyssée*)

He drew a firm line between what is 'sérieux' and what is 'bas', and excluded much that we assume to be at home in poetry of any kind. He has very few metaphors, and some of these are commonplace and conventional. He abounds in abstract words, especially when he deals with personal and even private emotions. He makes little appeal to the visual sense and is shy of mentioning colours. Even his flowers are never described more closely than as 'fleurs'. This exacting self-denial is dictated by his desire to keep his poetry serious; to make it conform to his notion that, if a drama is to have the universal character which is its right, it must be set at some distance from common life; to emphasize the difference of his characters, in the irresistible onslaught of their passions, from the common run of men; to maintain the majestic isolation in which they have their being. Racine's language conforms to his ideal of simplicity in doing exactly what his dramatic purpose demands.

The strength and the limitations of Racine's style lie in his unshakeable refusal to be lyrical. The spirit of song, which dances through Shakespeare and sheds a magic light on even the most obviously mechanical actions, would not only be distasteful to spectators who sharpened their thoughts on prose and expected poetry to share its virtues, but seem to Racine improper in tragedy. For him what matters is that the words should dominate the action, say exactly what it needs, and say no more, since even the smallest exaggeration or irrelevance must distract attention from the central, all-important task. In this he is far more ruthless than his Greek masters, whose words often take wing from the special situation to a larger and freer world which invites to vaster mysteries. Racine has an uncompromising notion of what dramatic speech ought to be, and lives rigorously up to it. Every line that he wrote cries to be spoken aloud and needs, if its full force is to be felt, to be spoken with care for every sound and intonation in it. So far from being monotonous, the flow of his couplets is in its own way as various as that of Virgil's hexameters; so skilfully does he shift his stresses and adjust his sounds. Even when a character speaks more than a hundred lines on end, like Mithridate in forecasting his plans to invade Italy, or Théramène in telling of the death of Hippolyte, the temper changes continually and many different sources of poetry are struck. The glory of this style lies partly in its texture, into which every theme is woven with a consummate feeling for its tone and temper, and partly in its continuity, which sustains the varied sequence of themes in unflagging and unfailing music.

There are moments when Shakespeare, towards the close of a tragic disaster, abandons imagery and makes his characters speak in the plainest of plain words, because any ornament would be untrue to their feelings and plain words alone fit the broken soul in its last agonies. So the dying Antony says to Cleopatra:

> Of many thousand kisses the poor last
> I lay upon thy lips.

So Racine, who begins a tragedy almost at the point at which Shakespeare begins a fourth act, not only shrinks from decoration but maintains his own kind of plainness through the whole length of a play. Though he is a master at varying his tone and making it suit all kinds of occasion, this is, in his view, always the right language for the passions, which are in themselves so personal and compelling that they do not need to be made more particular or to have their quality enriched by imagery. The words must fly straight to the target and hit the central point of emotion. Such an ideal would be unattainable if Racine did not build his plays on the contrast and conflict of many different passions, each of which demands its own kind of poetry. Nor would it be successful if he were not able to find their own appropriate poetry for the whole range of situations which make his plots. In his practised and immediate understanding of humanity nothing eludes him or defeats his capacity to present it in its full appeal. He has a dramatic, passionate poetry not only for all levels of love from the most selfish to the most self-sacrificing, but for almost every other emotion which troubles, inflames, or perverts the hearts of men. Clarified and toughened in his creative genius they come out in their primeval violence and compel our fascinated attention.

It is not enough to say that Racine's style is plain or simple. This it certainly is in its restricted vocabulary and its unfailing lucidity. But it is also supremely calculated in that its simplicity is shaped to a deliberate formality. This is necessary not only to give the right air of distance and majesty but to keep the passions in their place. Without it they would sweep all before them, and the whole discipline of the poetry would be ruined. But this formality takes a special form. It concentrates an extraordinary charge of emotion in a narrow space and makes this the more effective through its firm hold on it. Racine learned from the Greeks that, if the passions are to be displayed successfully, they must not be allowed to rant and rave. But he left his masters behind in imposing a far more rigorous formality, which indeed reflects something central to his being. Because he was himself at once extremely sensitive to the appeal of the passions and determined to master them by understanding them, he needed this stylistic discipline in his poetry to help him to fuse passions and understanding into an indivisible unity, in which each strengthens, completes, and absorbs the other. It is just because the passions with which he deals are so powerful that he curbs them with a highly precise, controlled, and formal language. Unlike Pushkin, who writes with a comparable clarity and simplicity, he does not venture far away from the passions; unlike Virgil, who is no less deeply concerned with them, he insists that everything must be clarified and understood beyond doubt or question. The fusion of the passions and the understanding means that Racine's style is often pointed and always concise and exact. His taut, powerfully charged lines rise from his unified outlook, from turning his whole compassionate attention to the engrossing spectacle of human behaviour.

This poetry is applied not to vague, general situations but to men and women, who are indeed compounded of familiar elements but are unmistakably individuals in their firmly articulated personalities. Racine treats of human nature in its conflicts and confusions, but seizes on the unity of impression which these produce and which has an intimate, personal appeal. His characters speak from their innermost, inalienable selves with an unfailing truth to the heart. They are as independent and self-sufficient as the characters of Homer or Shakespeare, and in none can we see an image of Racine himself or even a projection of his ideas and predilections. They live of their own right in their own passion-stricken world, and the strong light of poetry beats on them as they uncover the springs of their being. So in her reproof of Burrhus Agrippine reveals all that her pride of birth and station means to her:

> Certes, plus je médite, et moins je me figure
> Que vous m'osiez compter pour votre créature;
> Vous, dont j'ai pu laisser vieillir l'ambition
> Dans les honneurs obscurs de quelque légion,
> Et moi, qui sur le trône ai suivi mes ancêtres,
> Moi, fille, femme, sœur et mère des vos maîtres.
>
> (*Britannicus*, I ii 151–6)

So Ériphile describes how, after her first terror and horror of Achille, she sees him in quite a different light:

> Je le vis; son aspect n avait rien de farouche;
> Je sentis le reproche expirer dans ma bouche.
> Je sentis contre moi mon cœur se déclarer;
> J'oubliai ma colère, et ne sus que pleurer.
>
> (*Iphigénie*, II i 497–500)

So Phèdre, tormented by jealousy for the love of Hippolyte and Aricie, sees it in all its innocent happiness, when she throws the torment of her solitude and her guilt into her imagination of them:

> Les a-t-on vu souvent se parler, se chercher?
> Dans le fond des forêts allaient-ils se cacher?
> Hélas! Ils se voyaient avec pleine licence.
> Le ciel de leurs soupirs approuvait l'innocence.
> Ils suivaient sans remords leur penchant amoureux.
> Tous les jours se levaient clairs et sereins pour eux.
>
> (*Phèdre*, IV vi 1235–40)

Such passages record states of mind which are fundamentally not uncommon, but in Racine's passionate simplicity they are exalted to a peculiar power and given an extraordinary degree of life.

More remarkably, Racine provides a no less powerful poetry for characters who are swayed by passions so black and ugly that we might think them to be beyond the sway of so harmonious an art. But he rises without apparent effort to these criminal occasions and gives to wickedness its own revealing voice. When Iago discloses his hideous depths, he usually speaks in prose, but when Néron decides to break

his promise to Agrippine and kill Britannicus, his words of calculated,
cold-blooded savagery have their own terrible force:

> Elle se hâte trop, Burrhus, de triompher.
> J'embrasse mon rival, mais c'est pour l'étouffer.
>
> (*Britannicus*, IV iii 1313–14)

When Hermione rejects Andromaque's appeal for help in trying to
escape with her son to some remote refuge, her vanity and her jealousy
conspire to mask her hatred with a freezing disdain:

> Je conçois vos douleurs. Mais un devoir austère,
> Quand mon père a parlé, m'ordonne de me taire.
> C'est lui qui de Pyrrhus fait agir le courroux.
> S'il faut fléchir Pyrrhus, qui le peut mieux que vous?
> Vos yeux assez longtemps ont régné sur son âme.
> Faites-le prononcer; j'y souscrirai, Madame.
>
> (*Andromaque*, III iv 881–6)

When Roxane refuses Atalide's offer to surrender Bajazet to her, the
flood of her black fury is held in the bounds of an ironical, murderous
ambiguity:

> Je ne mérite pas un si grand sacrifice:
> Je me connais, Madame, et je me fais justice.
> Loin de vous séparer, je prétends aujourd'hui
> Par des nœuds éternels vous unir avec lui. (*Bajazet*, V vi 1621–4)

Racine's poetry rises directly from his understanding of human beings
in all their range and complexity and derives its strength from the
insoluble paradoxes of their nature.

This art is so fitted to human passions and so closely interwoven with
them that it lacks the sudden flights into the empyrean which we find
in Shakespeare. But if we wish to judge poetry by its impressive single
lines and to treat these as touchstones or talismans, many such can be
found in Racine. No one knows better how to clinch an occasion with
a line of astonishing force and concentration, and such lines may
legitimately be isolated and enjoyed for their own sake. But his true
strength lies in making them obey a commanding pattern and be
indispensable to it. They are not thrown in haphazard by an inspired
whim or merely as decorative additions; they contain the essence of an
occasion which has already been introduced with a wealth of powerful,
if less breathtaking, poetry. For instance the famous line

> Dans l'Orient désert quel devint mon ennui! (*Bérénice*, I iv 234)

is all the more impressive when it comes in Antiochus' speech to
Bérénice, because he has already declared his love for her and now tells
of his misery when he was left without her in Palestine. When Andromaque shrinks from the attentions of Pyrrhus, she begs him to go back
to Hermione in words which reflect all her helpless desire to be left
alone with her sorrows:

> Retournez, retournez à la fille d'Hélène. (*Andromaque*, 1 iv 342)

But this is only the crown of an appeal in which she has uncovered the
pathos of her unprotected widowhood. So an even more famous line,
which used to be quoted by advocates of 'la poésie pure', because it had,
as they claimed, little or no meaning, is actually the climax of Hippolyte's conviction that something fatal and accursed has broken into his
happy existence:

> Cet heureux temps n'est plus. Tout a changé de face
> Depuis que sur ces bords les dieux ont envoyé
> La fille de Minos et de Pasiphaé. (*Phèdre*, 1 i 34–6)

Though these lines caress the ear, they fascinate and hold us because
they are charged with dismay and horror. Racine's poetry yields its
full reward only when we respond alike to its intellectual strength and
its emotional intensity.

Racine is singularly free of double or ulterior meanings, vague
echoes, symbolical intentions, and indeed most means which seek to
extend the domain of poetry beyond its immediately intelligible subject. He aims at making every thought and emotion clear, at showing
their union in its provocative, indissoluble strength. He insists that this
must be itself in all its richness, with all its own attraction, and he sheds
on it the life-giving splendour of his style. So far from encouraging
our thoughts to range in vast speculations about the nature of things,
he pins them down to the special case, and demonstrates how absorbing
it is. No matter how complex it may be, he presents it in a transparently
simple form, which leaves no room for doubt and grips our whole
conscious and emotional attention. This poetry is indeed not always
maintained at the same point of intensity. Not only does it vary with
the moods of the characters, but there are some moments when the
need to explain a situation invites no more than merely machining
lines, and other moments when the passions have not yet burst into full
flame and must be treated with a quiet decorum. But this variety of

tone is essential to the whole effect. It prepares the way for the tremendous occasions when the poetry soars effortlessly to the most difficult
tasks and with its radiant lucidity presents a crisis in its full imaginative
appeal. For example, when Hippolyte defends his innocence to his
father, he breaks into a line which is as limpid as the day which it
invokes:

Le jour n'est pas plus pur que le fond de mon cœur. (*Phèdre*, IV ii 1112)

In this, which Paul Valéry calls 'le plus beau des vers', intellectual
meaning and poetical enchantment are inextricably fused, and each
strengthens and completes the other. If we wish to know what pure
poetry is, we need not waste effort in trying to distil some magical or
metaphysical essence; it is enough to respond to lines like this, which
do all that poetry can and embody all the qualities which we ask from
it.

Racine knew and interpreted in his own way the famous saying of
Aristotle that the function of tragedy is to arouse pity and fear and in
so doing to purge us of such emotions. But it is not always very
relevant and certainly not central to his art. The formula is too narrow
for his achievement, in which almost every emotion is aroused and the
purgation which follows is not a mere negative riddance but a transformation into something positive and enthralling. He does not attempt
to show that the disasters which he dramatizes are resolved by some
ultimate harmony, or that they can be explained and justified by
religion or philosophy, but through his imaginative insight into his
characters, who are so fatal to themselves, the emotions aroused by
their destinies are mastered and transcended in what he calls 'majestic
sadness'. This is his solution for the problems raised by tragedy, and for
it he relies on the power of his poetry. Without its transfiguring
influence his events would often be unbearably painful, but through it
their horror is absorbed in an excited and exalted understanding. Its
special, its overwhelming claim is that it is a poetry of humanity in its
complexity and its contradictions, in its errors and its crimes, often
ruined by its own violence, often corrupt and unredeemed, but for that
very reason close to much that we know in ourselves and cannot,
without betraying our human ties and loyalties, reject or deny.

SOURCE: The Zaharoff Lecture for 1956.

THEOPHIL SPOERRI

Racine: Impulse and Mind (1933)

(A Contribution to the Understanding of Classical Form)

> To live poetically cannot mean remaining in the dark about oneself or
> sweating it out in repulsive sultriness; it must mean becoming clear and
> lucid about oneself. KIERKEGAARD

> Mais il ne s'agit plus de vivre, il faut régner. RACINE

IT is strange what different impressions Racine makes on either side of
the Rhine. Whereas the predominant mood in French audiences, from
the start, is surprised shock at the untamed wildness of his heroes,
German audiences see the same poetic figures as the embodiment of
reserve, self-control and cool social restraint. Vossler's masterly little
book (*Racine*, Munich, 1926) sums up the entirety of Racine's form in
a single gesture of renunciation. Spitzer's sensitive and lavishly documented study indicates its main theme in the title: 'The Muting Effect
of Classical Style in Racine' (see p. 117). 'In Racine's work passion is
vital and irrepressible,' says on the other hand a new French interpreter
of Racine, Jean Giraudoux. 'Racine has discovered the ideal altitude
for tragedy . . . black souls flying at full speed, at full height.'

Instead of continuing along one of these parallel tracks, let us take
precisely this disparity between interpretations as the guide-line to our
investigation. It might perhaps be that the secret of Racine's greatness
lies in the fact that the parallel lines of his work meet, if at all, at
infinity.

If we look in the first place at the element of unrestraint and daemonic
terror in Racine's work, we cannot escape the fact that his language and
the attitude of his characters seldom go beyond a certain cool and
elegant reserve. Racine is never permitted to sound a loud, savage note
like Shakespeare. And yet he achieves the same effect by his masterly
use of the spatial and temporal elements in the dramatic action. He sees

to it that the quiet voice is amplified by the sinister acoustics of the
chosen setting. The actor may not let himself go in vehement gestures.
But the poet creates around the actor an atmosphere of such tension
that the slightest movement can precipitate the most monstrous catastrophe.

Bajazet is Racine's most ferocious play. The characters are subject to
the pressure of the sultry air of the seraglio, which reeks of blood and
is pregnant with deathly fear. The first lines already indicate the
sinister nature of the place. One may note how frequently and with
what emphasis the expression 'ce lieu', 'ces lieux', is repeated.

The effect of the setting is strengthened by the power of the moment.
All Racine's plays press on to the final decision. The characters all
move on the brink of a precipice. The ground at their feet is already
giving way. It is always, in the most ominous sense, 'high time'. In
Bajazet this element again is distorted in a sensational manner. Everything depends upon the fall of Babylon. The Sultan's messenger may
arrive at any moment. It will then be too late for Roxane's plans.
Roxane's first words present the decisive alternative:

> Enfin, belle Atalide,
> Il faut de nos destins que Bajazet décide.
> *Pour la dernière fois* je le vais consulter.
> Je vais savoir s'il m'aime. (I iii 257-60)

'Pour la dernière fois . . .' Notice how often this fateful phrase is
heard in Racine's work, each time with another meaning, now like a
whiplash, driving on to the final deed, now like the terrified shriek of a
man who is tortured to death. It repeatedly reminds us that it is
'ultimum tempus'. Both forces – setting and time – are embodied in a
ghostly way in the figure of Orcan. The name by itself throws a
terrifying shadow when first we hear it from the lips of the slave-girl
Zatime, who dares to disturb the Sultana with her news in the midst
of a soliloquy (III viii).

Roxane herself is mortally terrified at this dark incarnation of fate.
'Le temps presse,' she calls. And Atalide too now knows that the last
hour has struck:

> Ah! sais-tu mes frayeurs? sais-tu que dans ces lieux
> J'ai vu du fier Orcan le visage odieux?
> En ce moment fatal, que je crains sa venue! . . . (IV i 1123 ff)

The tearing pace of the action is from the beginning terrifyingly intensified – to the inescapable pressure of outside forces is added the equal inescapability of the inner action. Racine's characters may give us no doubt the impression of cool restraint. They do not utter their feelings. But precisely because the instincts are not dispersed in lyrical fireworks, they retain their sinister explosive quality. One only hears from time to time the sound of a gun being cocked, or one sees how a cannon is being shifted. But when the moment has come, the explosion takes place with tremendous violence. For the most part the situation is such that on the one side there are the frantic figures in whom passion is intensified to an unbearable degree, and on the other side good, harmless people who carry on their way without troubling about all the dark, menacing situations around them. It is precisely because of their innocent clumsiness that they bring down disaster upon themselves. Passion, spurred on to a daemonic savagery, pours itself out in a few fearful convulsions. In the end the innocent and the guilty all lie strewn on the ground, dismembered and bleeding. For the most part there is no thought of a morally satisfying conclusion. The beasts of prey, it is true, lacerate themselves in their fury. But the chief blow has fallen upon the innocent sacrifice. Seen from this preliminary point of view the solution is a purely dynamic one: the terrible tension has been discharged in a destructive explosion.

Whoever observes the outer vulnerability and the inner lack of control of these figures will no longer allow himself to be deceived by their outward pose, by the choiceness of their phrases, or by the parsimony of their gestures. He will acquire a keen ear for the slightest vacillations of tone that may reveal the advent of disaster. He will know that the concentrated emotions, which at the beginning of the play still inhibit one another while the action is not yet clarified, will break forth all the more terrifying in the explosion of the contrasting forces.

It needs a masterly creative artist like Racine to produce effects of such violence and such long-reverberating resonance, without outward apparatus, by means of purely linguistic suggestion in the narrowly confined ambit of the classical stage and of court convention. One is repeatedly astonished at the simplicity and force of his means. Let us observe, in just one example, how he lays his mines. Already in the course of the first meeting of Roxane and Bajazet (II i) all the decisive motifs are to be heard. At once Roxane makes her partner feel the pressing nature of the place and the time.

Here all the forward-moving factors have a positive sign. They lead to the *nœud* on which everything depends as far as Roxane is concerned: marriage with Bajazet after first removing the Sultan. Yet Bajazet hesitates. He conceals the true reason by recalling his constrained outer situation. Roxane, irritated that he is only thinking of himself, now shows him the menacing aspect of her power:

> Songez-vous que je tiens *les portes du Palais,*
> Que je puis vous l'ouvrir ou *fermer pour jamais,*
> Que j'ai sur votre vie un empire suprême,
> *Que vous ne respirez qu'autant que je vous aime?* ...
>
> (II i 507 ff)

Now as Bajazet once more hesitates, she bursts out into a first paroxysm of rage. Suddenly she addresses him as 'tu'. And then she pulls herself together again with effort, but one notices that the threat is now all the more conscious, and all the more dangerous:

> Bajazet, écoutez: *je sens que je vous aime.*
> Vous vous perdez. *Gardez de me laisser sortir.*
> *Le chemin est encore ouvert au repentir.*
> *Ne désespérez point une amante en furie.*
> *S'il m'échappait un mot, c'est fait de votre vie.* (II i 538–42)

Once more Bajazet side-steps. Now this is too much for Roxane:

> Ah, c'en est trop enfin: tu seras satisfait.
> *Holà! gardes, qu'on vienne.* (II i 567–8)

After all the fluctuation of the intrigue of love and power, now that Roxane has palpable proof that Bajazet is in love not with her but with Atalide, the most terrible of all machines of destruction is prepared. Roxane rages:

> Ah! je respire enfin; et ma joie est extrême
> Que le traître une fois se soit trahi lui-même.
> Libre des soins cruels où j'allais m'engager,
> Ma tranquille fureur n'a plus qu'à se venger.
> Qu'il meure. Vengeons-nous. Courez. Qu'on le saisisse,
> Que la main des muets s'arme pour son supplice.
> Qu'ils viennent préparer ces nœuds infortunés
> Par qui de ses pareils les jours sont terminés. (IV v 1273–80)

Strachey comments in this context:

> To have called a bowstring a bowstring was out of the question; and
> Racine, with triumphant art, has managed to introduce the periphrasis in
> such a way that it exactly expresses the state of mind of the Sultana. She
> begins with revenge and rage, until she reaches the extremity of virulent
> resolution; and then her mind begins to waver, and she finally orders the
> execution of the man she loves, in a contorted agony of speech.

And now Bajazet is given a final chance. But Roxane's preparations
reveal how cruel the situation of this final decision is:

> Oui, *tout est prêt*, Zatime:
> *Orcan* et *les muets* attendent *leur victime.*
> Je suis pourtant toujours maîtresse de *son sort.*
> Je puis le retenir. Mais s'il *sort, il est mort.* (v iii 1453–6)

The dark accord in the last half-line gives us indelibly the impression
that for Bajazet the exit is identical with being killed. Once more the
question is put to him:

> *Pour la dernière fois*, veux-tu vivre et régner? (v iv 1540)

'Vivre et régner!' – epitome of the fullness of life! Bajazet in his
helplessness tries to evade the issue once more. He believes he can
persuade the Sultana to change her mind by appeals to affection:

> Ajoutez cette grâce à tant d'autres bontés,
> Madame; et si jamais je vous fus cher . . .

Here the line breaks off – a device which Racine only employs at vital
points. The explosion follows in a single word, the meaning of which
is, however, terrifying clear to us:

> Sortez. (v iv 1563–4)

[Here the critic discusses *Andromaque*, *Britannicus* and *Bérénice*.]
Bérénice in particular makes it clear that the power of poetry does not
depend on the brutality of the methods used. What is of importance
is solely the form. It is precisely the evenness of tone, which is the
norm for the classical poet, that permits the creation of a neutral
background making even the slightest addition of colour effective.This
is valid for every aspect of artistic form. In prosody it is precisely the
strict obedience to law and the regularity of the alexandrine (the
twelve syllables, the ban on *enjambement*, the strong medial caesura,

for example) that allow a special effect to be achieved by means of the uneven distribution of stresses (inhibition of movement by accumulation, acceleration by reduction of stresses, obstruction by double stresses), by syntactical tensions spanning the caesura, and by interruptions of the line. In the use of language it is precisely the almost abstract, elegant manner that enables the occasional incursions into the colloquial and concrete, and also the rare outcries of yearning rising from the depths of the soul, to make their appearance with such force. In the outward stance of the heroes it is once more the persistent reserve which gives force and resonance to the slightest overstepping of the bounds. And thus generally in the shaping of a work of art: it is the economy of means and the restraint in the use of effects that give indeed full efficacy to the devices so cautiously handled (especially the use of proper names, the alternation of 'tu' and 'vous', the calculated perspective of the characters, the visionary style of the *récits*, the unexpected turn of conversation, the repetition of fundamental concepts in the way of leitmotif or refrain – to call to mind only a few of Racine's means of expression that have been illustrated). In addition to these comes the inner and outward tension of the action which gives an infinite reverberation to the faintest notes. (See the author's 'Le rythme tragique', in *Trivium*, 1945, and 'Das Problem des Tragischen', ibid. 1947.)

We must now ask whether what has been said so far provides a solution to the enigma of classical form, and thereby also of Racine's poetry, in so far as it is possible to speak of solution at all.

When we think back to *Bérénice* we become aware that there has been no explanation at all of emotional effect, so long as one speaks only of emotions. A line which the poet gives to Titus may provide us with the approach to a higher level of view:

Mais il ne s'agit plus de *vivre*, il faut *régner* ... (IV v 1102)

(Observe how the syntactical tension over the caesura emphasises particularly clearly the fundamental idea of contrast.)

What is to be understood by *vivre* is the subject-matter of the whole play: the proximity of the beloved. Without this, life is death. The loss of this love drives the lover consistently towards suicide. We must clearly realize that there is no question of criminal passions here. Each of these three who have been doomed to death may hold openly to his love and regard this as his most sacred possession. And yet it has to yield unconditionally to the opposing force.

The meaning of *régner* is already indicated in the solemn gold background against which the action takes place: the apotheosis of the Roman Empire. The concept *régner* is developed more clearly in a monologue of the young emperor. At first he attempts to brush aside in self-deception the incompatibility of his love and his office, then suddenly realises where he stands:

> ... Titus, ouvre les yeux!
> Quel air respires-tu? (IV iv 1013–14)

Now he hears the spirit of Rome speaking to him:

> Ah! lâche, fais l'amour, et renonce à l'Empire: (IV iv 1024)

(Precisely the counterpart to the basic formula, with 'vivre' replaced by the vulgar expression 'faire l'amour'.)

> ... Depuis huit jours je règne; et jusques à ce jour,
> Qu'ai-je fait pour l'honneur? J'ai tout fait pour l'amour.
> D'un temps si précieux quel compte puis-je rendre?
> Où sont ces heureux jours que je faisais attendre?
> Quels pleurs ai-je séchés? Dans quels yeux satisfaits
> Ai-je déjà goûté le fruit de mes bienfaits?
> L'univers a-t-il vu changer ses destinées?
> Sais-je combien le ciel m'a compté de journées?
> Et de ce peu de jours, si longtemps attendus,
> Ah! malheureux, combien j'en ai déjà perdus!
>   Ne tardons plus: faisons ce que l'honneur exige;
> Rompons le seul lien ... (IV iv 1029–40)

Here we are reminded of the significance of the urge to power in Racine's work. There is no play of his in which the will to power has not played a great part in the light form of service to the whole or in the dark form of a violent terrifying amibition for rule. We have already pointed to the association of 'vivre et régner' as an expression of fullness of life. The brutal phrase 'Mit Claude dans mon lit et Rome à mes genoux' (*Britannicus*, IV ii 1137) expresses the same parallel of love and power. The importance of this cluster of motifs may be seen from this too, that it would be easily possible to compile from Racine's various plays a grandiose and realistic Mirror of Princes. But with this we have still not yet exhausted the meaning of *régner*.

In the following conversation with Bérénice it is transcribed more
sharply into personal terms:

> Rappelez bien plutôt ce cœur, qui tant de fois
> M'a fait de mon devoir reconnaître la voix.
> Il en est temps. *Forcez votre amour à se taire;*
> Et d'un œil que *la gloire et la raison éclaire*
> Contemplez *mon devoir* dans *toute sa rigueur* ...
>
> (IV v 1049–53)

In this quotation *régner* together with its imposing retinue *grandeur,
gloire, honneur, devoir, rigueur,* moves perceptibly in the direction of the
central concept of classicism, *raison.*

Now at last the track becomes clear which points towards the innermost centre of Racine's world: the concept of intellectual and spiritual
alertness. If at this point we wish to penetrate to the depths we must
give sharpened attention to the delicate conceptual mechanism which,
almost imperceptibly, determines the meaning of all the inner action.
All observation up to now has shown us that it is a question of taking
note of the slightest turns in the language.

On the merely psychological plane the dichotomy *régner–vivre* confronts us in the counterpoint of rest–movement. Whereas the Romantic
attaches value to movement, which means for him life, creative
development, the flow of aspiration, while rest signifies on the other
hand inhibition, rigidity and reserve, Racine emphasizes rest as the
positive factor; it means for him reassurance, taming, control, security,
safety and clarity, in contrast to movement which is nothing other than
obscure impulse, restlessness and confusion. The dark world is the
home of such concepts as *trouble, égarement, désordre, transport, agité.*
The world of light is the home of *repos, clarté, raison, ordre, bornes.*
Typical images from the sphere of movement are the rushing torrent,
lightning and storm. The most widely used image is that of the flame:
flamme, feux, éclat, chaleur, brûler. How emphatically this image is a
mere token for the whole concept of this impulse is shown by impossible
combinations such as *flamme noire* (*Phèdre,* I iii 310) and *flammes obscures*
(*Bérénice,* III i 728). An important image from the dark realm of *vivre*
is that of the knot. *Nœuds* is repeatedly rhymed with *feux.* It is not
only a conventional expression for the 'ties of love'. We have already
indicated how Racine in *Bajazet* can play with the most sinister meanings of the word.

The concept of the knot, with its secondary meaning of 'inter-twining entanglement', leads to Racine's central image: the captive. To *captif* belong *esclave, joug, fers, lier, dompter, dépendant, livrer*, etc. Related to this is further the image of the wounded or sick man.

The contrasting theme to all these is the central concept of the realm of the mind: self-determination – coming to oneself, knowing one-self, attaining oneself. *Régner* here acquires its real meaning: self-control. [Here the critic discusses *Phèdre* in this context.]

This desperate striving towards oneself and flight from oneself is the secret 'unrest' in the mechanism of Racine's dramatic work. The issue is everywhere the mind's control over the impulsive powers of life.

But at this point, where we have apparently arrived at the closest proximity to Corneille, Racine's individuality becomes especially clear to us. Corneille, too, knows the conflict between love and honour, between *vivre* and *régner*, but for him there is such an upward-reaching, living force in the will to power that he can, as it were, deflect the counter-current in his direction. Honour and love are fundamentally identical. Ruling means living, and living means ruling. The will directs everything, even love. On that account the Cornelian hero can say:

> Je le ferais encore, si j'avais à le faire . . .

Racine does not know this strong-willed optimism. Life's impulse is too all-powerful and devious for the human will to be able to impel it into its own direction. Man must choose: to live or to rule. The whole paradox of the impossibility and the urgency of this decision is heard in the line:

> Mais il ne s'agit plus de vivre, il faut régner . . .

One cannot decide against life. If one does, one is simply choosing death. Nietzsche's insight 'Mind is life that cuts into its own life' has nowhere been taken with such literal seriousness as in Racine's *Bérénice*.

But how is the dominance of mind shown in the case of those who are swept on by the torrential drive of life? They too are dominated by mind, though not by the mind as will, but as knowledge. All action in Racine's work is exposed to the inexorable illumination of this final authority. The whole daemonic force of *vivre* is displayed under the jurisdiction of *régner*.

It is not until this point that the inner drama of a Racinian character is revealed – in the midst of a fearful submersion in the confusing current of passion, it is a struggle for mental clarity, for the transparency of the self; it is both a conscious self-deception, because truth is not to be borne, and an unconscious urge to truth, because it is impossible to exist without it.

Already in Hermione we see this awareness in ignorance:

> Je crains de me connaître en l'état où je suis ... (*Andromaque*, II i 428)

> Ah! ne puis-je savoir si j'aime ou si je hais? (Ibid. v i 1396)

And in Antiochus:

> Ah! que nous nous plaisons à nous tromper tous deux! (*Bérénice* III ii 798)

And Bérénice:

> Hélas! pour me tromper je fais ce que je puis. (Ibid. III iii 918)

And Atalide:

> Mais qu'aisément l'amour croit tout ce qu'il souhaite! (*Bajazet*, I iv 373)

We now follow breathlessly the alternating movement of vital and spiritual forces. The obscure pressure of elemental impulses is felt all the more threateningly since it is these that violently remove one human being from his conscious and controlled relationship to another. Mind is the connecting, committing and binding factor. Impulse is the isolating element. Nothing makes man lonelier than his feelings. He sinks within them as if in an abyss. A Frenchman does not allow himself to be so easily deceived as a German by vague feelings of interconnection ('Be embraced, O millions . . .'). This instinctive sense of the dissolution of personality and of the obscuring of demarcation-lines is felt with alarm by a Frenchman as daemonic estrangement, as a terrifying moment of pathological abstraction appearing with the suddenness of an epileptic fit.

Fundamentally Racine's drama is the drama of disclosure, because the one supreme thing that a Racinian hero wrestles for is knowledge, the achievement of awareness at all costs. It has been recently demonstrated with great acuity that the issue in each of the plays is nothing other than the revelation of a secret (E. Merian-Genast, 'Die Kunst Racines'). But what might otherwise be merely the mainspring of a detective story, aimed at arousing suspense, is recognised in this newly revealed context in its profound spiritual significance. 'Life is not the highest of

goods. . . .' Unclearness, darkness and obscurity are, however, the
greatest of evils. Now, too, we understand the cruel eavesdropping-
scenes. The whole of Racine's drama is nothing but one long eaves-
dropping. The audience is, as it were, on the watch behind the invisible
front wall to the stage. Like Néron, he has arranged the encounters in
order to snatch from the players their last secret.

The impassioned objectivity appears most purely in the suffering
figures who attempt to enunciate the meaning of their situation with
a cruel sobriety that is close to self-persecution. Let us take the tortured
reply of Iphigénie to her father:

> Mon père,
> *Cessez de vous troubler*, vous n'êtes point trahi.
> *Quand vous commanderez*, vous serez *obéi*.
> *Ma vie est votre bien*. Vous voulez le *reprendre*:
> Vos ordres *sans détour* pouvaient se faire entendre.
> D'un œil *aussi content*, d'un cœur aussi *soumis*
> Que j'acceptais l'époux *que vous m'aviez promis*,
> Je saurai, *s'il le faut*, victime *obéissante*,
> Tendre au fer de Calchas une tête *innocente*,
> Et respectant le coup *par vous-même ordonné*,
> Vous *rendre* tout le sang *que vous m'avez donné*.
>
> (*Iphigénie*, IV iv 1174–84)

The italics are Péguy's. They are intended to demonstrate the
deliberate cruelty of the daughter who, with all her submissiveness,
wishes to put her father in the wrong by means of concealed innuendoes.
Spitzer (see below, pp. 129–31) sees these words as indicating a conscious
restraint by means of objective distancing. We can best show the
significance of this passage by directing attention to all the other
victims in Racine's work. Such a painfully clear vision of the cruelty
of existence is a consequence of their conscious and courageous
assumption of suffering. They are the most living illustration of
Pascal's concept of the 'thinking reed'. 'Quand l'univers l'écraserait,
l'homme serait encore plus noble que ce qui le tue, parce qu'il sait
qu'il meurt.' This taming of fate by knowledge is the secret triumph
of Racine's heroes.

The conflict between corrosive awareness and seething impulse
reaches its greatest intensification in *Phèdre*. Here too the turning-
point occurs which reveals the deepest meaning of Racine's dramatic
work. We stand before the most precipitous heights of his art. The

first triad (*Andromaque, Britannicus, Bérénice*) had achieved classical perfection at the first ascent. The second group of three (*Bajazet, Mithridate, Iphigénie*) is like an exotic interlude. After the deep, quiet notes of *Bérénice* – perhaps influenced by the public's rejection of the work – the poet turned to the crudest and most strident devices. *Mithridate*, like *Bajazet*, demonstrates to us the violence of barbarian and oriental sovereignty. The sexes are exchanged: Mithridate is Roxane, Monime Bajazet. The pressure of the moment is intensified by the fact that Mithridate is a sinking force – an aging man and a threatened prince – and that he is clutching with final desperation at life and rule ('vivre et régner'). Iphigénie leads into the classical world. With her the awareness of suffering becomes vocal (Iphigénie continues the role of the quiet and gentle sufferer Monime); with Phèdre it is the awareness of rage.

In the last triad (*Phèdre, Esther, Athalie*) an unusual change occurs. Up to now the dichotomy of the ravening and the suffering, the beasts of prey and their victims, has predominated. Both are exposed to the devouring, destructive forces of instinct, the first actively, the others passively. The actions of the one group arouse fear in the audience, those of the other group arouse pity. Racine himself describes these two emotions as the 'two great motive-forces' of tragedy. Together they produce what, according to him, drama is about: the impression of 'tristesse majestueuse'. But now this contrast of personages recedes before the final heights. Whether they are suffering or ravening now becomes a matter of indifference in view of the fact that they are all dominated by the judicial authority of mind confronting them objectively, by truth that has become personified in God. The setting now suddenly becomes more alive than the players. The sinister ineluctability of their environment, which terrified us in the earlier plays, now assumes shape and becomes an expression of the omnipresence of God. In *Phèdre* this change appears at first magnified by the myth:

> Misérable! et je vis? et je soutiens la vue
> De ce sacré soleil dont je suis descendue?
> J'ai pour aïeul le père et le maître des Dieux;
> Le ciel, tout l'univers est plein de mes aïeux.
> Où me cacher? Fuyons dans la nuit infernale.
> Mais que dis-je? mon père y tient l'urne fatale;
> Le sort, dit-on, l'a mise en ses sévères mains:
> Minos juge aux enfers tous les pâles humains. (IV vi 1273–80)

'Nowhere', says Vossler, 'do we demand light so intensely as in matters of conscience. In *Phèdre* this is achieved. Now the whole Greek mythology becomes the voice of conscience. There remains hardly an ornament from classical antiquity which may not become threatening as the eternal countenance of the moral law.'

Vossler then goes on to show how tremors of conscience permeate even the narrative of Hippolyte's end, 'that purple patch which would be no more than an academic imitation of the messengers' speeches in Euripides and Seneca, if Racine had not electrified all the characters in his play with the heroine's sense of guilt'. Théramène alone, the 'jovial tutor of the young man', is spared these agonies of soul. But 'it is precisely this balanced man of the world with his healthy and banal reasonableness' who has to witness his pupil's dreadful death. The supernatural, something unknown to him through anxiety of his own, comes before his senses as a roaring monster from the depths. He comprehends nothing of all this except the terror and horror. At the conclusion of his section on *Phèdre* Vossler makes the following perceptive comment: 'The more passionately Racine's characters are aroused, the more disturbed and downcast they are in their outlook, the more they are discountenanced – so much more control and clarity do they achieve in their expression. They are not simply passion and nature, but the spirit of passion and the spirit of nature, temperaments dominated through and through by mind and spirit.'

We should like to emphasize this observation even more strongly by transferring it from the psychological to the metaphysical dimension and making it into a central law of Racine's dramatic work. What is mind or spirit? That absolute authority to which all human activity submits in order to be judged by it. And it is the course of every Racinian play that, beginning in obscurity, it becomes constantly more clarified as light is separated from dark; the more confused the maelstrom is to which man is driven by passion, the more intensely the spiritual clarity grows with which the aberration is condemned. The two factors run parallel – the disclosure of human depravity and the revelation of the judging powers.

If *Phèdre* is still immersed in the confusing and terrifying polytheism of ancient myth, *Athalie* rises above all mists into the clarity of pure revelation. It is here that all Racine's lines reach their end. But the end to which they make their way does not lie in the visible world. The accent is shifted from human activity to divine government. It is from this point that everything has to be explained. For instance, the attempt to describe the figures according to the usual textbook-psychology leads only to the production of quite distorted and impossible character-sketches. These figures do not have their centre of gravity within themselves. The law of their behaviour is their obedience to or defiance of the transcendental power. It is only if we are able to take seriously the placing of emphasis on the transcendental that we can stand at the point of perspective where the lines are disentangled and reveal a clearly defined cosmos. It is from this position that the final clarity illuminates Racine's work.

In *Athalie* revelation becomes visible. All veils are removed, and the immanent resources of the stage disclose the transcendental background of life. . . .

It is the fundamental characteristic of the classical that the tension of universal polarities is not relaxed by soft and tearful complaisance. The violence of the life-impulse is not underestimated, nor is the absoluteness of the judging mind queried. The fact that these people can bear the intolerable strain of the forces of existence makes them great. It is for this reason that their fate moves us. It is not feelings that ennoble men, but men who ennoble feelings. What is at issue here is not only the experience of human beings, but their quality.

Classical man knows with what excess of violence the life-impulse rushes towards the precipice; he knows how slight is the directing force of mind. And yet he does not hesitate in his conscious decision between the realm of *vivre* and that of *régner*. Even if the great act of renunciation in favour of spiritual sovereignty is only achieved in the case of unusual, exemplary human beings – in such cases, only, perhaps, as a hint of an ultimate, other-worldly possibility, as a sacrificial act visible from afar off: 'Servons tous trois d'exemple à l'univers . . .' (conclusion of *Bérénice*) – nevertheless the ordinary person is entrusted with the task of witnessing to the sovereignty of the mind and spirit in every sphere where this rule is possible. If a man cannot control his inner being, let him control his outward self. Hence the bearing of classical man. His restrained demeanour is not a product of convention. It derives from the innermost sources of personality. It stands under the sign of *régner*. If from one point of view the life impulse has acquired its moving tension precisely because it becomes pent up against the barriers of moderation and entrenched custom, from the other point of view classical man achieves his stature by maintaining his attitude in the midst of the torrential flow of the passions.

The great enigma of Racine's biography is illuminated at this point: his definitive renunciation of poetry after the completion of *Phèdre*. All kinds of external compulsion may have played a part, but what poet was ever compelled to silence who did not impose silence upon himself? When the drama of human existence had revealed its last vista in the tragic portrait of the queen with her unhappy and criminal love, was it still necessary to play the same melody over and over again in similar, if magnificent, variations? Would it not then have been a playing on the brink of the precipice? Would not play-writing have become playful observation, mere playing? Racine took the step over into everyday life, into the spheres of family, profession, state and church, with breathtaking simplicity. The younger generation could have maintained disparagingly that he had lost his grip. So much so that after twelve years' silence he created *Esther* and *Athalie* in rapid succession on royal command.

What is known as 'self-control' in man's outward life is called 'form' in the context of artistic creativity. Form too is not a product of convention. All the harmony, moderation, balance and control that man loses in the urgent reality of his life, can be given shape, symbolically and intuitively, in art. Here, and here only, can he rule royally. There is no more tangible sign of the external sovereignty of the spirit than the artist's capacity to mould forms out of recalcitrant wordsounds in which, as in shells of imperishable and costly substance, whenever a human ear approaches them readily, the whole surge of life's waves can be heard infinitely moaning and roaring.

Racine's disclosed secret is indeed terrible. A German may believe in a more reconciliatory solution (like R. A. Schröder in *Racine und die deutsche Humanität*). The last great classicist knows life only in its hostility to mind and spirit; in the midst of the onslaught of the uprising forces of life he holds high the primacy of the spirit with his final effort. But does not his solution lift man wondrously above himself?

Sion a son front dans les cieux. ... (*Athalie*, III viii 1223)

If the lines of life do not meet in the finite world, human existence remains open to the infinite. The light of eternity as it breaks in, through the breaking of the earthly shells, surrounds broken men with a glory that shines more consolingly than all the lustre of fulfilment in this world.

SOURCE: Translated by H. M. Waidson. Abridged from 'Racine, Trieb und Geist', in *Archiv für das Studium der neueren Sprachen*, CLXIII.

JOHN C. LAPP

Racine's Symbolism (1955)

THOUGH the validity of studies of symbolism in Shakespearean tragedy has been long established, in general, critics have shown considerable reluctance in applying the term to French classical literature. This is probably due, in part at least, to the rather considerable truth expressed in Gustave Lanson's dictum concerning the *précieux* theory of language: 'Elle consiste à ne pas traiter les mots comme des formes concrètes, valant par soi, et possédant certaines propriétés artistiques, mais comme de simples signes, sans valeur ni caractère indépendamment de leur signification.' If this means what I take it to mean, Lanson is precisely denying the possibility of symbol in *précieux* writing.

It is, I believe, only because Racine renovates and recreates the language of preciosity that we are able to find symbolism in his work. This process of renovation referred to on several occasions in our *Aspects of Racinian Tragedy*, may be briefly summarized. In the Racinian tragic drama, certain words develop through three stages, none of them chronologically or mutually exclusive: (1) words, which through the influence of preciosity have lost their metaphorical or metonymical quality, function primarily as euphemisms; (2) they become 'demetaphorized', so that they function concretely; (3) they are 'remetaphorized', and they either rediscover an earlier metaphorical meaning, or assume new metaphorical or symbolical force.

Several critics, and especially G. May, have shown how, as Racine's genius matured, words like 'feux', 'yeux', and 'flamme' developed from stage 1 to stage 2. One may, for example, watch the word 'yeux', first as it ranges from the empty metonymy of Créon's words addressed to the dead Antigone in *La Thébaïde* (v vi 1480): 'Et vous-même, cruelle, éteignez vos beaux yeux!' then, as it reaches a painful balance between the euphemistical use and a soupçon of metaphorical quality in Hémon's declaration to Antigone that she ('vos beaux yeux') is his

god and oracle, more powerful than those that Étéocle is consulting
at that very moment:

> Permettez que mon cœur, en voyant vos beaux yeux,
> De l'état de son sort interroge ses Dieux. (II i 317-18)

Finally, in *Andromaque*, *Britannicus*, *Bérénice*, and *Iphigénie*, it begins to
serve a dramatic purpose by revealing the characters' feelings through
fierce or mournful or indifferent glances. The warlike Pyrrhus' eyes
flash, Britannicus is made uneasy by beloved eyes full of sadness, and
Antiochus resolves to escape from

> ... des yeux distraits,
> Qui me voyant toujours, ne me voyaient jamais. (I iv 277-8)

Ériphile, voicing her suspicions that all is not well at Aulis, says firmly
'J'ai des yeux,' and Athalie tells Mathan, 'Vous m'ouvrez les yeux.'

Frequently words participate in at least two of the stages. Thus,
when 'feux' and 'flamme' have regained concrete meaning, this
affects instances in the *précieux* sense when they occur in the same play.
Through the repeated evoking of the scenes of burning Troy, as in the
tableau of Pyrrhus in *Andromaque*,

> ... les yeux étincelants,
> Entrant à la lueur de nos palais brûlants, (III viii 999-1000)

even Hermione's line, 'ses feux que je croyais plus ardents que les
miens', where the word is still firmly in stage 1, takes on heightened
colour, while Pyrrhus' famous conceit, 'Brûlé de plus de feux que
je n'en allumai', if read in the context of fire and devastation, actually
begins to penetrate stage 3.

Through this kind of propinquity, words which may actually have
come from the author's pen as *précieux* euphemisms, can, for the
modern reader, acquire colour and force. Leo Spitzer quite legitimately
discovers a bold oxymoron in Phèdre's 'flamme si noire'. In the same
play, as this critic has shown, the symbolic currents with which
Racine deliberately charges the word 'monstre' flow across into a
euphemistical expression like 'les monstres dévorants', a mere reference
to the dogs that devoured Pirithoüs (unless, as J. Pommier has suggested,
Racine meant them to be more than dogs).

It would be generally agreed that symbol must not only have
metaphorical force, but that it must recur rather frequently in the body
of a work: so, for example, Mallarmé's 'azur', his 'blancheur', his

'fard', his 'chevelure'. Not only do these recur frequently but, unlike the same words in Baudelaire, they began to assume an identity of their own, beyond their basic meaning and even beyond the thing or idea symbolized. In a play, however, a symbol should be first of all a re-inforcement of the theme, and it should remain subservient to it, harmonizing completely with the rest of the structure. Though it is of necessity much less obtrusive in the drama than in lyric poetry, the patient reader who seeks it there will have his reward.

Once Racine has revitalized some key words in the various ways discussed above, he invests them with symbolic significance, both by the frequency with which he uses them, and by linking them closely to the dramatic theme. One such word is 'autel', which beginning with the *précieux* sense of 'veneration' or 'reputation' in *Alexandre*, becomes in *Iphigénie* not only a concrete object, waiting ominously in the invisible scene, but a symbol of love and death toward which the characters are irresistibly drawn.

If we consider briefly how this word develops in three plays, *Alexandre*, *Andromaque*, and *Iphigénie*, we shall be struck, I think, by the fact that the symbolic word in Racine is actually an important vehicle of dramatic irony. In the first of these plays, the word remains within the boundaries of the kind of general conceit of deification addressed to the beloved, a variant of which we have already noted in *La Thébaïde*. The Greek heroes worshiped in India, says Porus, 'ont trouvé des autels' and the gallant Alexandre himself vows that for Cléofile he will 'faire dresser des autels' even among godless savages. In *Andromaque* we can watch the process by which the word takes on various metaphorical accretions. It is first of all the place in the temple where the marriage is performed, and

> Andromaque, au travers de mille cris de joie,
> Porte jusqu'aux autels le souvenir de Troie. (v ii 1437-8)

When Andromaque speaks of herself as 'recevant la foi sur les autels' (iv i 1091), the word suggests not only the place of the marriage rite, but the sacredness of the oath sworn there. Finally, the altar, in one instance, takes on the significance of the scene of sacrificial death, when Oreste pleads with Hermione to be allowed to choose for himself the time and place where he will kill Pyrrhus:

> Laissez-moi vers l'autel conduire ma victime. (iv iii 1210)

It is traditional to point to the 'linear' qualities of the plot of *Andromaque*, with Oreste–Hermione–Pyrrhus–Andromaque as the chain of passion, but this is an analytical statement unrelated to structure, since both Oreste and Pyrrhus vacillate until the end of Act IV. The actual physical movement toward the climax is linked to the altar. Pyrrhus, unguarded, sets out for the temple: 'Sans gardes, sans défense, il marche à cette fête' (IV iii 1218). His inexorable progress toward the fatal goal is also conveyed by the verbs of motion in Cléone's description of the wedding procession:

> Je l'ai vu vers le temple, où son hymen s'apprête,
> Mener en conquérant sa nouvelle conquête;
> Et d'un œil où brillaient sa joie et son espoir
> S'enivrer en marchant du plaisir de la voir. (v ii 1433–6)

Pyrrhus' fatal love-frenzy shows in the combination of verbs of movement like 'entraîner' and 'courir' with 'autel':

> L'un par l'autre entraînés, nous courons à l'autel
> Nous jurer, malgré nous, un amour immortel. (IV v 1299–1300)

All of these meanings – the altar as scene of the marriage rite, as the sacred place of the gods, as the sacrificial table, as the goal of the tragic personage – combine in Hermione's wild imprecations:

> Va lui jurer la foi que tu m'avais jurée,
> Va profaner des Dieux la majesté sacrée.
> Ces Dieux, ces justes Dieux n'auront pas oublié
> Que les mêmes serments avec moi t'ont lié.
> Porte aux pieds des autels ce cœur qui m'abandonne;
> Va, cours. Mais crains encor d'y trouver Hermione.
>   (IV v 1381–6)

In the last scenes, the altar is the point at which the protagonists converge. Oreste runs to the temple, where the Greeks, mingling with the crowd, have secretly made their way to the altar: 'se sont jusqu'à l'autel dans la foule glissés' (v iii 1500). Pyrrhus himself, in a grim echo of Hermione's curses, dies precisely before the altar; after struggling wildly to escape the assassins' blows, 'à l'autel il est allé tomber' (v iii 1520). His triumphal march ends as he drags himself forward to die. Finally, Hermione, who kills herself upon his corpse, commits a sacrificial act related to the altar symbolism.

This symbolism is of course not fully woven into the play, but remains confined to the latter part of Acts IV and V. It is in *Iphigénie* that the altar assumes the full symbolic force that it could not achieve in the earlier plays. Throughout this tragedy, the altar symbolizes death, and the irony derives from its being also a symbol of life and love, the place of man's union with woman. The altar is the goal of Iphigénie's journey both in the pre-dramatic action and in the action proper. Early in the play, Achille points the ironic contrast between the supposed and the actual purpose of her journey:

> On dit qu'Iphigénie, en ces lieux amenée,
> Doit bientôt à son sort unir ma destinée. (I ii 177-8)

This ominous significance of the altar, unknown to the heroine, makes more poignant the famous *quiproquo* in which she questions her father about a projected sacrifice of which she has vaguely heard. When she asks if this will take place soon, the King replies, 'Plus tôt que je ne veux'; and to her request to be allowed to witness the ceremony – 'Verra-t-on à l'autel votre heureuse famille' – he answers painfully, 'Vous y serez, ma fille.'

But the deepest irony springs from the dual symbolism of love and death, love in the minds of Achille, Iphigénie, and her mother, death in the minds of the audience and the other protagonists. Agamemnon attempts to trick Clytemnestre into letting her daughter go alone to the altar by telling her that it is there Iphigénie is to marry Achille:

> . . . Laissez, de vos femmes suivie,
> A cet hymen, sans vous, marcher Iphigénie. (III i 793-4)

In persuading Clytemnestre not to accompany Iphigénie, the King stresses the warlike aspect of the camp, portraying the altar as 'hérissée de dards,' and thus ill-suited to her presence. In III iv, we watch the heroine draw closer to the dread site, serenely confident, and praising her lover's magnanimity in terms the unconscious irony of which strikes at the gods themselves:

> Montrez que je vais suivre au pied de nos autels
> Un roi qui non content d'effrayer les mortels,
> A des embrasements ne borne point sa gloire,
> Laisse aux pleurs d'une épouse attendrir sa victoire,
> Et par les malheureux quelquefois désarmé,
> Sait imiter en tout les Dieux qui l'ont formé. (III iv 871-6)

When Arcas reveals the plot two scenes later, Achille bursts out in anger at the subterfuge:

> C'est peu que de vouloir sous un couteau mortel
> Me montrer votre cœur fumant sur un autel:
> D'un appareil d'hymen couvrant ce sacrifice,
> Il veut que ce soit moi qui vous mène au supplice?
>
> (III vi 975-8)

In the earlier plays, the noun tended to be used in the plural, which emphasizes the abstract at the expense of the concrete. Of the 34 times the word 'autel' is used in *Iphigénie*, it occurs 26 times in the singular, so that it has now acquired greater force as an actual object. Its concrete and symbolic meanings coincide throughout, as they do not in *Andromaque*.

Although Racine could not have found this ironic symbolism in the ancients, who celebrated marriages in various ways, but mainly in the bridegroom's home, the marriage-death irony may have been suggested by Seneca's *Troades*, where it is very fully developed. Helen is required to prepare Polyxena for the sacrifice as if for a wedding:

> ego Pyrrhi toros
> narrare falsos iubeor, ego cultus dare
> habitusque Graios
>
> (864-6)

> [I must forge the tale
> That she shall marry Pyrrhus; I must deck her
> In finest Grecian raiment].

Her speech to Polyxena equivocates between the marriage with Achilles, which means death, and the supposed wedding to Pyrrhus; the word 'thalamus' has throughout the symbolic meaning of death.

Aeschylus may have provided another ironic symbol in the bandeau of Monime in *Mithridate*. It will be remembered how, in the *Suppliants*, when the King first confronts the strange visitors to his land, the Chorus Leader tells him darkly, 'I have headbands and belts to bind my dress; from them I shall seek a wondrous aid.' As Pelasgos answers in puzzlement, 'They are doubtless ornaments proper for women,' irony hangs heavily in the air, for we recall the maidens' earlier threat to hang themselves upon the altar if they cannot, through the help of their hosts, 'escape the embrace of the male'. The similarity between this ironic employment of the bandeau and its rôle in *Mithridate* is evident (it is immaterial whether Racine was inspired by Aeschylus alone, or by the Plutarch of Amyot, where the headband is called 'le diadème ou bandeau royal', or by both). Throughout the play, the headband symbolizes bondage and death as well as royalty; there are repeated allusions to it as the 'gage' or sign of Mithridate's promise to make Monime his queen, and the audience is aware that it will be the instrument of her attempted suicide.

Whenever Monime appears, she is wearing the bandeau, and either she or the other characters mention it. Pharnace's words are typical:

> ... ce bandeau royal fut mis sur votre front
> Comme un gage assuré de l'empire de Pont. (I iii 233-4)

Mithridate, seeing Monime for the first time after his arrival home, drives home again to her its bitter significance:

> ... vous portez, Madame, un gage de ma foi
> Qui vous dit tous les jours que vous êtes à moi. (II iv 541-2)

But a moment later, the 'gage' becomes the ceremonial crown worn by the sacrificial victim – cf *Iphigénie*: 'Mais le fer, le bandeau, la flamme est toute prête' (III v 905) – as the old King cries furiously, 'Vous n'allez à l'autel que comme une victime' (II iv 552). When Monime's attempt at suicide fails with the breaking of the band of which she had tried to make 'un affreux lien', her anguished words sum up the ironic meanings of this badge of royalty which has meant only suffering and death:

> Et toi, fatal tissu, malheureux diadème,
> Instrument et témoin de toutes mes douleurs,
> Bandeau, que mille fois j'ai trempé de mes pleurs,
> Au moins, en terminant ma vie et mon supplice,
> Ne pouvais-tu me rendre un funeste service? (V i 1500-4)

The altar in *Iphigénie* is ominous in part *because* it is invisible and amorphous – in Agamemnon's description, its outlines are broken as it bristles with spears – but the headband, as part of Monime's costume, is a visible symbol of her plight, becoming in a sense a part of the décor.

(Jean Cocteau, in his *Machine infernale*, uses the silk scarf with which Jocaste eventually strangles herself in exactly the same way.)

A symbolism which bears an even closer relationship to stage setting is Racine's use of light. It will be recalled that the opening scene in *Iphigénie*, which takes place before dawn, shrouds in darkness the conversation between Agamemnon and his officer, Arcas. The tragic obligations upon which the helpless King has brooded in silence flow forth in darkness, but as the action progresses the scene grows gradually brighter, until at the end, as Ulysse and Achille burst in, the sun has risen. The light of the sun symbolizes the re-emergence of the King's responsibilities; his forebodings and despair must now retreat before the light of day.

To Racine's use of light, as we have suggested elsewhere, is due the spatial depth of *Phèdre*. The heroine's emergence from the shadows, in surrender to the terrible fascination of the light, also underscores symbolically her struggle with her criminal desires. Before her first appearance, we learn that she has been languishing in darkness, 'lasse enfin d'elle-même, et du jour qui l'éclaire' (i i 46). But the pull of fate is too strong, 'elle veut voir le jour', and she drags herself, a moment after Œnone speaks these words, into the light, only to shrink back in terror: 'Mes yeux sont éblouis du jour que je revoi' (i iii 155). From the light that illumines her criminality she shrinks back toward the darkness of concealment:

> Vous vouliez vous montrer et revoir la lumière;
> Vous la voyez, Madame, et prête à vous cacher,
> Vous haïssez le jour que vous veniez chercher? (i iii 166–8)

This symbolism clarifies the magnificent double image of her dying words, in which her death becomes a purification of the light sullied by her guilt:

> Et la mort à mes yeux dérobant la clarté
> Rend au jour, qu'ils souillaient, toute sa pureté. (v vii 1643–4)

The seventeenth-century stage director, Laurent, prescribed, on the basis of one line of the play, that the scene should be a 'palais voûté', and as recently as 1945, J.-L. Barrault obediently sealed up his heroine in a palace with a vaulted ceiling. But the symbolism of light in *Phèdre*, it seems to me, demands a setting bathed in the brilliant glare of noon, above it the actinic blue of the Grecian sky.

All of the symbols discussed above in some manner support and strengthen the tragic themes, but none with the consistency and range of the symbolism of growth and sacrifice in *Athalie*. The theme of

Racine's last play is the renewal, the revitalizing of the race through divine intervention; beneath its dramatic action we may discern the ancient myth of cleansing and rebirth through the death of the sacrificial victim. The action occurs on the day of Pentecost, the Jewish festival of the harvest. Racine, in his Preface, says merely that the events of the plot were supposed to have taken place on an unnamed holy day, and that he had chosen Pentecost because it enabled him to give some variety to the songs of the Chorus. But these songs celebrate and reiterate God's bounty in bestowing the fruits and the flowers of the earth, and I think we may go beyond Racine's explanation to see a significant link between the sacrifice of the first fruits of the harvest and the killing of Athalie, which assumes ritual proportions. God's intervention is made to depend on the action of the protagonists, the divine power remaining suspended until the victim has been offered up. The people's sacrifices in their customary observation of the law, He has declared perfunctory and inadequate: they must gird themselves for a battle of the faith, to be followed by a sacrifice which will then be full of meaning:

> Du zèle de ma loi que sert de vous parer?
> Par de stériles vœux pensez-vous m'honorer?
> Quel fruit me revient-il de tous vos sacrifices?
> Ai-je besoin du sang des boucs et des génisses?
> Le sang de vos rois crie, et n'est point écouté.
> Rompez, rompez tout pacte avec l'impiété.
> Du milieu de mon peuple exterminez les crimes,
> Et vous viendrez alors m'immoler des victimes. (I i 85–92)

The theme of revival and resuscitation is linked to vegetation symbols. As the action begins, the temple itself, ultimate source of the action, glows dazzling white in the rays of the morning sun. The royal line of Judah has been 'cet arbre séché jusque dans les racines'; the young King – 'fleur d'une tige si belle' – will emerge from the temple where he has hidden for eight years as from the tomb, or in the words of the Chorus, as a lily grows, sheltered from the north wind in a secret vale.

The symbolism of *Athalie* may offer another proof that here, more than in all his other plays, Racine achieved that final synthesis of the Christian and Classical heritage from which he had earlier derived his ironic symbol of the altar.

One of the dangers, of course, in the quest for symbolism in Racine's or any other theatre, is that we may over-estimate the importance of something which is much more the quarry of the reader than of the spectator. This is true of Cleanth Brooks's brilliant essay on the clothes symbolism in *Macbeth*, which strengthens our understanding of the play, but which perhaps tends to obscure the fact that all the elements of structure, the flesh and blood interpretation of rôles, may over-shadow symbols. The striking thing about the symbolism in Racine is that it participates on both the scenic and rhetorical levels; that his symbols, unlike the multi-coloured and multifarious symbols of Shakespeare, are neat and spare, playing their modest part as adjuncts of theme and structure.

SOURCE: Chapter 4 of *Aspects of Racinian Tragedy* (1955), with a con-cluding section from an earlier version published in *Yale French Studies*, IX (1952).

GEORGES POULET

Notes on Racinian Time (1948)

RACINE'S dramatic works open with *La Thébaïde*. But in the very first lines there is posed so urgent and so fundamental a problem that the entire works will do nothing more than restate the question:

> O toi, Soleil, ô toi qui rends le jour au monde,
> Que ne l'as-tu laissé dans une nuit profonde! (I i 23-4)

It is the problem of existence, but posed with reference to the continuation of being, and not directly to its origin. The double reality created and contained by these lines, the first in which the authentic Racinian accent vibrates, is that of a Sun which restores light to the world, and of a world that has deserved that light should not be returned to it. Why does the creative power consent to begin over again a work which has proved defective and monstrous? Why does it consent to prolong for a single present day the series of past days which, of themselves, fell into 'the depths of night'? The problem is the more inexplicable, in that the creation of a new day does not simply imply, like that of the first day, the creation of a being still pure and worthy of God: but this time the invention of a being which has already had an existence and which, by reason of this past existence, far from meriting a present existence, ought to have been 'abandoned to the night'. Unless one can imagine this absurdity – the perpetual creation of a world radically new every time and obliterated in each instant, in order to be 'brought back' in the following instant to the first virginity – then, once the existence of evil has been accepted and the worthlessness of the creature recognised, there is nothing at all for God to do except stop creating, or else to create something that will be continuous, and which will continue precisely this – a past into which evil has been introduced. Before sin and before the fall, God only continued to bring back to the light of day a being which was always the same, always equally worthy of the 'light', and which therefore had no past.

Now, on the contrary, the continued creation of the world implies the creation of a being with a past, whose existence consists not only in living, but in having lived, and lived badly.

Such is the characteristic aspect which the problem of existence takes on for Racine. Like Descartes and like the Jansenists, he lays down as a principle the *independence* of the parts of a duration in which every day God accepts the obligation to bring light back to the world, instead of leaving it to darkness; but on the other hand, he nonetheless feels the absolute *dependence* of each of the new moments upon a past out of which God binds himself to create them, to *co-create* them; so that in the Racinian, as in the Bergsonian universe, what one calls the present is not solely pure and ceaseless invention, but a preservation of the past and a continuation of the past into the present.

It is a continuation, however, which, for Racine, far from having as with Bergson the value of a progress and a promise, has on the contrary the most tragic significance; for it permits of no hope, except the hope that one day, instead of being brought back to the light of day, we shall be abandoned to the night of annihilation. Even God is unable to make the past cease to exist and, therefore, also to make evil cease to continue and repeat itself; not even God can make hatreds cease to be *obstinés* and prolong themselves from times gone by to times not yet accomplished:

> Triste et fatal effet d'un sang incestueux (IV i 921)

the whole Racinian drama is presented as the intrusion of a fatal past, of a determining past, of a past of efficient cause, into a present that seeks desperately to become independent of it.

What is the subject of *La Thébaïde*? It is the story of a man who believes that he can free himself from the past. All the other characters are supremely conscious of continuing into their present a past which is consummated in their hatreds or their terrors of today. What they are is made clear only by what they themselves or their fathers have been:

> Quoi? faut-il davantage expliquer mes pensées?
> On les peut découvrir par les choses passées. (IV iii 1003–4)

Créon alone dreams of a state where, in the endless present conferred by omnipotence, it is possible to free oneself at one stroke from this fatal attachment; of a state in which

> Du plaisir de régner une âme possédée
> De tout le temps passé détourne son idée; (III vi 895–6)

the royal state of a being capable of having no remorse, no memories, no past, and therefore henceforth no destiny; a state in which one could abandon oneself to those transports of joy given by the feeling of living in a naked present, cleansed of all stain and so intensely real that past events left on it no more trace than a dream:

> Ne me parle donc plus que de sujets de joie,
> Souffre qu'à mes transports je m'abandonne en proie;
> Et sans me rappeler des ombres des enfers,
> Dis-moi ce que je gagne, et non ce que je perds ...
> Tout ce qui s'est passé n'est qu'un songe pour moi:
> J'étais père et sujet, je suis amant et roi. (V iv 1453–60)

A strange transport, expressing a feeling believed to be joy, but which is unconscious despair; for the very motion by which the man-living-in-the-present had wished, so to speak, to fabricate himself and to establish his independence, his radical freedom from the past, entails and forthwith completes his dreadful dependence upon the man he has been from his birth, the man he can never cease to be until death:

> Je suis le dernier sang du malheureux Laïus (V vi 1499)

Racinian tragedy is the impossibility of limiting oneself to the present moment. Fidelity to hatred, as in *La Thébaïde*; fidelity to love, as in *Andromaque*; fidelity to custom, as in *Bérénice*; fidelity to blood, as in *Phèdre* – the subject of almost every tragedy of Racine consists in the repetition and the ineluctable continuation of the past into the present:

> Il se déguise en vain: je lis sur son visage
> Des fiers Domitius l'humeur triste et sauvage.
> > (*Britannicus*, I i 35–6)

> Vous ne démentez point une race funeste.
> Oui, vous êtes le sang d'Atrée et de Thyeste.
> > (*Iphigénie*, IV iv 1249–50)

> Fidèle au sang d'Achab ... (*Athalie*, V vi 1786)

Andromaque is, above all, the drama of beginning anew. Here passion is a 'trace' that a man recognizes (i i 86), a 'wound' that he 'reopens' (ii ii 485); its objects are certain figures that he 'remembers', a vanished being which one keeps finding oneself beginning to love again in a living being:

> C'est Hector ... Voilà ses yeux, sa bouche ... (ii v 652 ff)

Furthermore, *Andromaque* is a drama whose characters exist only in so far as they 'represent' (cf ii iv 621) certain beings who exist no longer but who, out of the depths of their past, must come to be 'found again', to 'revive' and be 'recognised' in living beings (1024, 622, 1071, 1512). And if, like Créon in *La Thébaïde*, Pyrrhus is of all the characters in *Andromaque* the most significant, it is because he is the living proof that it is impossible to escape from this *representation* of the past in the present, and that it is no less vain to want to seize in passion an instant that is without commitments and without memories. For it is not possible to resist the double weight of public opinion and private conscience that see in the being that one is, only the prisoner and the executor of the past:

> Ah! je vous reconnais ...
> Ce n'est plus le jouet d'une flamme servile:
> C'est Pyrrhus, c'est le fils et le rival d'Achille ...
> Qui triomphe de Troie une seconde fois. (ii v 627 ff)

Thus the whole drama is only an immense and infinitely complex repetition of a more ancient drama. It is a drama played for the second time – a gigantic phenomenon of memory, in which not only feelings but existences are resuscitated. No work has expressed more completely the endless repetitions of continuous time.

Racinian tragedy stretches back into the past; forward into the future too; enclosed between immensities of time. For if Racine likes to set his characters in distant times, and against a remote background, it is doubtless first because 'the respect the audience has for heroes increases in proportion as they are withdrawn from us' (*Bajazet*, Preface); but it is also because the very withdrawal, and the respect it inspires, have the effect of placing events and personages in a historical perspective and of preventing us from seeing in the action only the brutal image of the immediate.

Andromaque and *Iphigénie* both evoke the historic totality of an epoch, the entire length in time of a great epic subject, and in both plays the subject is the same; but in the one it is situated just before the historic action commences, in the other just after it ends. *Andromaque* is what happens when the *Iliad* is ended:

> Ne vous souvient-il plus, Seigneur, quel fut Hector?
> Nos peuples affaiblis s'en souviennent encor (I ii 155–6)

Iphigénie takes place just before the *Iliad* begins:

> Et qu'un jour mon trépas, source de votre gloire,
> Ouvrira le récit d'une si belle histoire. (V ii 1561–2)

Opening or closing an epic recital, the moment chosen for the dramatic action thus almost entirely loses its proper value, its quality of being the single 'present' moment, its privilege of being for the moment the only moment that is real. Its 'reality' is not rich enough in itself to triumph over a past and over a future, unreal doubtless, but arrayed in all the opulence of history and poetry. And so the Racinian moment becomes the slave of an anterior or posterior duration which sucks it up and attaches it to itself. It becomes the extreme point of a past that is ending, or of a future, a *monstre naissant*; it is as though it were stifled between two walls of events which draw together, which already touch each other. It has not the time to be Time.

The Racinian moment is a point, but in the sense in which one says: 'It is here, at this point, that the drama took place.' The point of fatal encounter between the line drawn from the past and the line drawn from the future – the point where efficient cause and final cause collide and mingle.

Situated at a point without duration, possessed by the action of the moment, Racine's characters nevertheless seem to be endowed with the power of looking at themselves, as it were, historically, as if they were not only themselves but also our contemporaries; they are the prey of the immediate, but at the same time they contemplate both the causes and the remote conclusion of the drama in which they are engaged. They view themselves *in the future* as we view them *in the past*:

> Je n'ai donc traversé tant de mers, tant d'États,
> Que pour venir si loin préparer son trépas?
> (*Andromaque*, V i 1427–8)

Je prévois que tes coups viendront jusqu'à ta mère.
>   (*Britannicus*, v vi 1676)

Je prévois déjà tout ce qu'il faut prévoir.
Mon unique espérance est dans mon désespoir.
>   (*Bajazet*, i iv 335–6)

The Racinian character is like Calchas:

Il sait tout ce qui fut et tout ce qui doit être.
>   (*Iphigénie*, ii i 458)

His foresight does not differ from his memory. It is of the same
nature. It arises, in Racine, from a conception of life which, although
profoundly different from that of the Greeks, is no less fatalistic – only
fatality is no longer external, but internal, and places the determining
forces in the soul itself. They are in the being, they are of the being,
and if at the same time they are hostile and deadly to the being, they
are none the less an evident source of energy whence comes what the
being is in each one of its moments. Prescience, as well as memory,
consists only in referring to this source, whose creative influx may vary
in intensity but never in its nature. *Monstre naissant* or monster complete,
Néron in the past or in the future is always Néron.

It is a foreknowledge which informs the being not only of his actions
but of the particular nuance of emotion which the future reserves for
him. Racinian characters are not content to suffer from their present
ills; they experience suffering in the future:

Dans un mois, dans un an, comment souffrirons-nous ... ?
>   (*Bérénice*, iv v 1113)

An external future, 'coupe affreuse, inépuisable' (*Athalie*, ii ix 839)
from which the damned in the Racinian world know they will continue
to drink hereafter the bitter knowledge of their past:

Ainsi d'une voix plaintive,
Exprimera ses remords
La pénitence tardive
Des inconsolables morts.
>   (*Cantiques spirituels*, 2, 51–4)

The extremity of emotion to which they thus attain has for its
complement the most poignant intensity of poetry: as if, by connecting
certain states of mind separated in the sequence of time, by spreading
their passions over the most immense duration, they invested them with

an absolute significance, no longer that of a sin or misfortune in the present, but of a despair that gives its name to all existence:

> On saura les chemins par où je l'ai conduit.
> (Britannicus, III iii 850)

> Je m'en retournerai seule et désespérée,
> Je verrai les chemins encor tout parfumés
> Des fleurs dont sous ses pas on les avait semés.
> (Iphigénie, IV iv 1306–8)

Self-awareness, in the Racinian being, is that of a man who falls over a precipice, is terrified, and yet looks at himself with detachment and extraordinary clarity, as if his future death were already accomplished, and he saw himself *in the past*.

The Racinian tragedy is an action *in the past*. We see it less in its actuality, in its immediacy, its physical impact, than in the reflective thought and in the affective echo it produces afterward, mediately and almost indirectly, in its victims and in the onlookers. At the moment we take cognizance of it, it has already taken place. It appears in a flash like the lightning one recognizes only when it is gone and has become part of the past. In that respect, the tragedy of Racine differs from all other drama, which by its nature renders the action in a time that is progressive, that is in the course of being. Here, what we are shown is a time completed, and the action it contains being in each of its consecutive parts an action which has taken place and which in each instant is only just past, it seems that we are witnessing the process by which things in the last analysis become 'fatal' in our eyes and force us to recognize that indeed they could not have happened otherwise. Racinian fatality is characterized by this *retardation* of thought following action, and taking from it thereby the leaden hue of the unchangeable; so that each past contingency, even if it be only one instant past, becomes as necessary as the most general law. Racinian fatality is the 'Qu'ai-je dit?' of *Phèdre*. It has the nature of irreversibility.

> Je connais mes fureurs, je les rappelle toutes. (*Phèdre*, III iii 853)

There is no light more intense or more cruel than that projected by self-awareness into the hearts of Racinian characters. The reflective consciousness which leads them to the discovery of their own being, reveals to them not only the kind of being they are, but the kind of continuity or progression in time which has made them become more

and more what they are. The particular lucidity they bring to this
knowledge reaches as far as their past extends. It calls up, in the order
of their development, all the thoughts and actions which have issued
from their very depths to bring them to the extreme situation into
which they are thrown and in which they come to their present
awareness. It even goes back further and seems to search the original
shadows for a primary principle, a prenatal tendency, which, from
before their existence, contained its germ, ready to unfold in frenzies
and passions. Thus the tragic consciousness is here found invested with
the power of contemplating itself through the whole field of its duration: it everywhere recognizes itself as monstrously alike.

But it happens also, in Racinian humanity, that a human being finds
himself provisionally withheld from this fatal knowledge. He is then
mysteriously allowed to remain ignorant of what he is and what he
has been. He lives for a time in a present which has yet no past. And
because of this fact, neither has he yet any destiny; for what is truly
fatal for a human being is the clear-sightedness by which, in dis-
covering what he has been, he finds out what he is going to be; ready
to consummate his ruin and his doom:

> J'ignore qui je suis; et pour comble d'horreur
> Un oracle effrayant m'attache à mon erreur,
> Et quand je veux chercher le sang qui m'a fait naître,
> Me dit que sans périr je ne me puis connaître.
>
> (*Iphigénie*, II i 427–30)

Or again it may happen in the Racinian drama that sudden forget-
fulness follows the recognition of self. There is occasionally a vivid
moment in which, in the very shock of catastrophe, everything is
effaced and collapses; a moment in which there no longer remains
anything in the mind except a sort of blind consciousness of the present
instant. The past is swallowed up, and the being, face to face with the
brutality of the present, feels the sense of his identity tottering:

> Est-ce Pyrrhus qui meurt? et suis-je Oreste enfin?
>
> (*Andromaque*, V iv 1568)

> Qui suis-je? Est-ce Monime? Et suis-je Mithridate?
>
> (*Mithridate*, IV v 1383)

Instantaneous avowals of the human being reduced to the instant, torn
out of duration, which reveal how essentially the Racinian differs from

the Cornelian character. The latter exists only in and for the moment.
In it he finds realization. The instantaneous prompts in him, not a
question, not a *Qui suis-je?* but an affirmation:

> Je sais ce que je suis et ce que je me dois.

With Corneille we are in a universe where God has left something to
the human will. It thrills with the joy of feeling within it the perfect
identity of the moment in which it wills, and of the moment in which
it feels itself will: I will, therefore I am. This single moment encloses it,
completes it, assures it, and gives it fullness of life. But the Racinian
moment, as soon as it finds itself torn out of duration, is then no more
than a shred of existence, a discontinuous being, a sort of fragment, as
if in losing the feeling of being victim and prey, man lost at the same
time the consciousness of the profound unity which, in binding together the different moments of his temporal life, created the sense of
his existence and his true self.

'Racine', says Thierry Maulnier, 'goes straight to what is hardest
and purest in life and death – in destiny.' How is it that one can speak
thus of the *purity* of Racinian destiny, since nothing is less pure or
more horrible than the successive visages it seems to present?

> Que diras-tu, mon père, à ce spectacle horrible? (*Phèdre*, IV vi 1285)

Let us be careful, however, not to confound with destiny the *horrible
spectacle* which makes the consciousness of Phèdre, like the shade of
Minos, shudder; for it is but the spectacle offered to Phèdre by Phèdre,
the light in which she sees herself during the horrible, incessant revolu-
tions of the life of her senses:

> Je sentis tout mon corps et transir, et brûler

experience of the self by the self, situated in the contact and contrast
of two successive moments, only to be replaced immediately by
another presence:

> Je reconnus Vénus et ses feux redoutables,
> D'un sang qu'elle poursuit tourments inévitables. (I iii 277–8)

Upon the horrible, instantaneous spectacle of sensory experience
there is superimposed the consciousness of an eternal, continuous,
supersensible reality which Phèdre *recognizes*: a reality which, as much
by its nature as by its long duration, inspires no longer the horror
called forth by things impure, but the awe engendered by the presence

and persistence of the divine. Immediately the harried consciousness is lifted up to a zone more tragic still, but more serene, in which it even acquires a sort of grandeur; as if, though still feeling itself entangled in the miserable web of impassioned intermittences, of remorse and premonitions in which 'each moment is its death', it saw itself arrayed, at the same time – not indeed as in the romantic poets with the glory of a rebel Titan, but rather with the dignity of a sacrificial victim, in the fulfilment of the rites by which its destiny is worked out. On the one hand it is a being stricken with the palpitation and rendings of a discontinuous time; on the other, it is a person whose destiny is inscribed above the eddies of duration, in the eternal zone of the celestial will – whose destiny is fulfilled in still another zone, in the order of providential temporality, unfolding regularly, inevitably, and serenely the arcana of that will. Hence the existence of three parallel durations in Racine as in the medieval thinkers: the discontinuous time of passions in the present; the continuous time of the fulfilment of the divine will; and finally this will itself in its pure nontemporality.

Close as Racine's superimposition of times comes to the medieval conception, there is a point of difference; and this point is so important that, despite everything, it forces us to place Racine at the very antipodes of the scholastic spirit. Racine's three times are indeed disposed in the stages of the scholastic order; but in Racinian tragedy there is the constant impression that these stages brush against each other; that in some way these planes of existence are liable to unite or merge. The triple existence of things does not stand out with the clarity of line which, in a Saint Thomas or a Dante, allows a distinction to be made, then and there, between eternity and time proper. In Racine, on the contrary, there is something indecisive and turbid which makes the human drama a long, anguished meditation and almost a religious mystery, in which it is no longer a question whether passion is passion, or even if evil is evil, but whether or not the gods themselves are maleficent, or infected by evil; whether, finally, the fatal discontinuity of human realities does not end by reaching upwards and encroaching in some manner even upon eternity. So that this eternal world, dimly descried from amid the harshness of human time, far from having the serenity and purity men fancy, far from guaranteeing, as we could wish to believe, the continuity of a purpose and design to an existence which in itself is rent and perverted – this eternal world would seem

in its turn contaminated or corrupted, becoming a mere reflection of
our tragic condition, projected upon the clouds:

> Barbares, arrêtez:
> C'est le pur sang du Dieu qui lance le tonnerre ...
>
> (*Iphigénie*, v iv, 1696–7)

This cry breathes forth the most authentic religious anguish. Suddenly it is no longer the question of a mother who fears for her
daughter, but of a soul that fears for its God. We are in the presence
here of one of the most indefinable and most profound of the fears
which are at the base of all religions; the fear that in the contact between the divine and the human, which is the essence of religion,
there may be something perilous, not only for the creature but for the
divine itself; the fear lest this the intangible become tangible, the light
become dark, and the purity become corruption. That the thunder
should fall and destroy a sacrilegious creation – this is not the most
terrible risk. For even so the transcendent abides, the divine, which is
alone important, is untouched. The risk is that the thunderclap may be
the signal for an annihilation of Heaven as well.

At the extreme opposite of this terror, and as if Racine had had to
traverse the deepest shadows to emerge into the light, there is at the
very end of that long tunnel which is the tragedy of Phèdre, the
sudden restoration of day:

> Et la mort à mes yeux dérobant la clarté
> Rend au jour, qu'ils souillaient, toute sa pureté. (v vii 1643–4)

The extraordinary beauty of these lines is owing to the double image
of the dawn which they evoke: a dawn, on the one hand, so cruel to
the dying; a dawn, on the other hand, so sweet to the eyes of those
who will continue to live. For the former, the brightness of day is
darkened; for the latter, its purity is restored. In the consciousness of
Phèdre the reality of peace and of purity is perceived only at the
moment when she must bid them farewell for ever. It takes place at
the farthest limit of despair. It *is* that limit. The consciousness of the
pure, of the bright, of the light of day, is achieved by her, as something *interior to her*, only at the moment it leaves her for ever. Until
then the world of daylight and purity had existed only by implication,
as the reverse side of the world of shadows constituting her mind. And

now at the moment of death she *sees* this purity and this brightness, she sees them to be her true nature, but now lost.

The farthest limit of despair, but a despair that implies, though certainly not a hope, at least a discovery and a belief, let us even say a faith: faith in transcendence, in a being whence she has derived her being, in a brightness which makes her shadow to be shadow, in a purity the nature of which, under the stress of an anguish from which she is delivered, she had come to fear that she had irremediably contaminated. This is a purgation by which the consciousness of eternity is attained and which ends therefore in an act of faith: I recognize the eternal; dying, and by my death, I pay it homage.

From this eternity she is doubtless excluded. She knows that fact. She thinks of it only in passing. Her final lot, her eternal destiny is suddenly of very little concern compared with the immense reality in the face of which her humiliation overwhelms her. There is something here that is analogous to the 'pure love' of François de Sales and of Fénelon: 'O my God,' said a mystic of that period, 'how much would I rather not be at all, than that you should cease to be.' 'O my God,' says Phèdre, 'what is it to me that I shall cease to be, since you will not cease to be, and to be he who washes away the stains of the world, but whom the stains of the world do not soil.' An entire disinterestedness of self in the perception of the Being who is light, *le jour*, and supreme purity. Perhaps one might see in this the action of a saving grace; perhaps, after all, Phèdre might be a Christian who did *not* 'lack grace'; perhaps she dies saved, without knowing it; because she has attained, in a transport of absolute humility, the same state of loving self-annihilation at which the great contemplatives arrive. Did not Fénelon say that pure love consists in loving God in indifference to one's own salvation, even if one knows one is going to be damned? Phèdre dies, doubtless not in the divine love, not in *caritas*, but she dies *in renunciation*, in total resignation to the divine will. Her supreme, unique act is an act of perfect abandonment; she dies *esclave volontaire* of God and not *esclave de la mort* (*Cantiques spirituels*, 3, fin.).

In all the plays of Racine, up until the conclusion of *Phèdre*, the dominating idea is that of a world which reveals itself as radically evil, whose very survival seems for that reason to compromise or obscure the notion of a God of Light and a God of Purity. By dint of seeing the continuation of the world only as a repetition of the same crimes and the same passions, the mind ends by perceiving in the dark unfolding of things, only their interdependence. The entire duration of a being is no more in his own eyes than the ceaseless beginning again of what stains and destroys him. Hence the more and more desperate tone of the earlier Racinian drama. But in *Phèdre* and after *Phèdre* a reversal takes place. Suddenly the accent is no longer on the unwearying continuation of being, but on the unwearying act by which it is continued, and on the dependence of the creature on the act by which it exists. Over and above the endless chain of causes and effects which seem to engender duration, we distinguish the presence of a First Cause that mercifully communicates its eternity to the instant; and beyond the despair engendered by the indefinite perpetuity of evil, the soul suddenly discovers in its infinite dependence upon God, a peace which lifts the instant to eternity:

> L'âme heureusement captive
> Sous ton joug trouve la paix ...
>> (*Cantiques spirituels*, 4, 52–3)

And the same *Cantique* has these lines, in which once more the creature is astonished to see the sun *rendre le jour au monde*:

> Et qui suis-je que tu daignes
> Jusqu'à moi te rabaisser? (39–40)

The question is identical to that in the lines of *La Thébaïde* quoted at the beginning of this essay; but here, without abandoning any of its urgency, it has lost its sting. The question is concluded in supplication, in prayer; for what shows through the most intense feeling of human indignity is the feeling, no less intense, of the prodigious dignity which at every instant is conferred on and restored to this unworthy being by the eternal act of Creation. Thus the fatality of the past, seen as cause and as evil, is exorcized by the recognition of a Cause transcending all duration, which is disclosed immediately, almost miraculously, even at the moment of death – the death of Phèdre – since this, like all moments, is the gift of God.

After that, no more remains than to set forth the divine acts of this Providence in the tracts of human time. That is what Racine will do in *Esther* and *Athalie*.

SOURCE: Chapter 6 of *Études sur le temps humain* (1949). Translated as *Studies in Human Time* by Elliott Coleman.

JEAN STAROBINSKI

The Poetics of the Glance
in Racine (1954)

THE hero of Corneille has the universe for his witness. Knowingly
and willingly, he is on view to every people, every age. He invites
the world to look at him; lays before it his admirable, his dazzling self.
In every movement, the Cornelian hero sets out to let it be *seen* what
manner of man he is; any decision, any inner strivings, are immediately
put on show. He may sacrifice himself – give up the one he loves,
give up his life – but he never gives up the right to *show* himself in
the very act of sacrifice, and wins back, in the astonished glance of the
universe, a new existence, transfigured by glory. Through that glance
he receives a hundredfold whatever he has lost.

The Cornelian act is always the assertion of a sovereignty – the
hero confirms his princely nature and his right to rule. For him, to
reveal himself is to establish his greatness; to be seen is to be recognised
as rightful master. The tragedies of Corneille nearly all end in that
instant of dazzled 'recognition', showing the proud purposes of the
individual to be at one with the interest of the community, whose
existence and felicity depend on the lustre of the prince's glory.

Corneille is thus the poet of the dazzled vision – of vision fully
contented and satiated with light. This dazzlement is no illusion:
it confirms the nature and the genuine worth of the beings held up to
admiration. The dazzled eye beholds a peerless greatness, at the point
beyond which brilliance would at once become unbearable, and blind
instead of dazzling; but Corneille never does go beyond. His world
is the realm of evident values, entirely perceptible; each enjoys the
object of desire – both the hero self-displayed, and the glance that
rests upon him; vision and display draw satisfaction each from the
other, soon to lose all separate existence as dazzling figure and dazzled
glance unite in what might be an embrace of lovers. The hero's energy
of will is enhanced by a second force, that of the admiring glances
turned upon him in surrender. The Cornelian *event* occurs at the

meeting of these two. Moreover the hero knows implicitly that he is seen exactly as he shows himself, neither diminished nor deformed. The glances fastened on him confirm him in his being, by their total acceptance and approval. Neither appearance nor the beholder's subjectivity make the truth questionable – misunderstandings will always be cleared away. Appearance brings the hero's ego that confirmation he would have lacked but for being seen by others. For the ego exists fully only by showing itself. And if it never ceases to call the universe to witness, this is because it can only have complete consciousness of itself if it can appear, formally as in a law-court, before witnesses.

In Racine the importance of the glance is not less, but its value and meaning are entirely different. It is a glance lacking not intensity but fullness, unable to hold the object in steady view. The act of seeing, for Racine, remains for ever haunted by tragedy. In the Cornelian world, the dazzled glance reached up beyond the tragic – at the moment when he invited the world's admiration, the Cornelian hero had already overcome his mutilation in the tragic conflict, had won the recognition of his magnanimous rivals or his subjects. Whereas in Racine the glance never ceases to betray frustration and resentment. To see is an act charged with emotion which can never give perfect enjoyment of the object coveted. To be seen implies not glory but shame. As he reveals himself, driven by his passion, the Racinian character can neither approve himself, nor obtain the recognition of his rivals. Most commonly he refuses to contemplate any universal scrutiny, knowing himself condemned by it in advance. What is more, even should he submit to it, he will never show up in complete clarity. However clear in Racine speech may be, it always hints at a psychological bedrock remaining shadowed and invisible. In Racine, behind the seen there lies the half-seen, and further yet again, what we can only sense and never see at all. This dimension of depth in shadow is one of the factors of that impression of truth produced on us by Racine's characters. They exist 'in depth'. And their depth results from their lack of stability and visibility; from something which can be called equally well excess or deficiency, which makes them avoid our glance themselves even while they display to us in vivid light the spectacle of their tragic destiny.

In classical French drama, and particularly in Racine, gesture tends to disappear. Giving place to speech, or so it has been said. And also, we must add, to the glance. His characters do not embrace or strike each other on the stage: they do see each other. Scenes in Racine are *inter-views*. The characters exchange words, and glances. But the glances are the equivalents of embraces and wounds. They say all that the other gestures would have said, with this additional privilege, that they carry further, go deeper, alarm more keenly – they stir the soul.

In this way an aesthetic limitation is turned into a means of tragic expression. The will to style, which turns speech into poetic discourse, at the same time raises all mime and all gesture to the level of the glance. By one and the same transmutation or 'sublimation', the spoken word is refined, and all the body's potential for meaning is concentrated into one language, that of the eye.

The act of seeing gathers up in itself all the gesture abolished by the will to style, giving it symbolical representation, containing all the same tensions and intentions. We should see this undoubtedly as a 'spiritualizing' of the act of expression, in conformity with the requirements of an age of *bienséance* and politeness. It is a way for the passions to find expression within the bounds of decency and chastity, where the body does not obtrude itself unduly. Up to the moment that the blade comes down, the characters never face one another without an intervening gap. The acting-space, almost bare, is abandoned to space – an enclosed space it is true, in which the victims are trapped, before they walk on, by the décor (of arches, colonnades and marble walls) stamped with certain conventional signs of pomp and majesty, not perhaps without a trace of baroque extravagance; but within these bounds a void has been created – a void that seems to exist only to be traversed by glances. So that, now, the distance separating characters permits, in compensation, the operation of a cruelty reduced to the glance alone, striking at souls through their image reflected in the eyes of love or hate. For there exists – in spite of distance and also because of it – a *contact* through the glance. And, where a moment ago we accepted the idea of a spiritualizing of physical gesture by turning it into a glance, so conversely we must admit that of a 'materializing' of the glance, loaded and invested with all the bodily values, all the emotional significance it has assumed. This Racinian glance, heavy with sensuality, is admirably expressed in the famous line:

Chargés d'un feu secret vos yeux s'appesantissent. (*Phèdre*, I i 134)

No transparent glance of appraisal, but a glance of desire and suffering. The Racinian glance meant in the first place, for us, a disincarnation of the emotional gesture; paradoxically, it is at the same time clouded by a turmoil of the flesh which makes it heavy and material. Keen and flashing, turbid with passion – the opposites coexist here, and poetry thrives on the ambiguous mixture of pure and impure. If we study Racine's text with the aid of Leo Spitzer's stylistic analysis (as he has expounded it in *Linguistics and Literary History*), we discover that the verb *voir*, so frequently employed, at times means 'to know', implying an intellectual view – however precarious – of human and divine verities; but at other times *voir* denotes an uncontrolled emotional impulse, the act of desire as it feeds with avid delectation on the presence of the desired, haunted by the imminent approach of disaster and the presentiment of some curse or some punishment attached to this passionate *vue*. The verb *voir* in Racine contains this semantic swing between turbid and clear, between knowledge and infatuation. It is the result of a kind of deep-level interchange – violence becomes weightless and turns into a glance, while the reasonable act of seeing 's'appesantit', becomes material and the conductor of irrational powers.

Certainly the act of seeing contributes to the *magic* of Racine's text – that magic which is usually attributed, a little too exclusively, to verbal melody. The word *voir*, itself almost invisible in its monosyllabic brevity, leads the reader's eye to the core of the essential relationship between characters who are linked, in silence, by the simple exchange of glances. In this way is built up, not on the stage in this case but behind the language, a particular space, a hinterland existing only by and for vision, beyond the verbal structures that conjure it up. In the story which is told us, a drama of glances preceded the drama in the words: the characters saw each other, then loved or hated each other, and only then spoke to tell of their love or hate; but what they say, then, still has reference to the glance – they burn to *se revoir*, they may be doomed never again to *se voir*, they cannot endure the outrage inflicted on them *à leurs yeux*. Speech seems then to exist only to accompany and comment upon the intentions of the glance. It is an intermediary between the silence of the first glance and the silence of the final glances. The modulations of the Racinian melody are drawn to cover these gaps. His beings sing their experiences only while in the movement that takes them towards sight, or takes them away from sight. (This movement does not take place in space alone; they are

deeply immersed in the dimension of time. Man sees before and after
– *il revoit et prévoit*. In Astyanax, Andromaque sees Hector again; all
the past is once more present. Athalie's eyes are haunted by that dream
which showed her simultaneously the past – the death of Jezebel – and
her own death still to come.) The virtue of the glance cuts like a line,
then, drawn through and within the verse itself, and language is used
to show it as a horizon at which speech vanishes. But this at the same
time is the triumph of speech, since it has called into existence what
seems to drive it out – a silence, a space, and visual lines of force
connecting human presences across that silence and that space.

And yet there is nothing less visual than the poetry of Racine.
The glance is not turned towards objects; it takes note neither of shapes
nor colours. It does not explore the world, it asks few or no questions
of nature: it looks only for the glance of others. If it pays little attention
to things, it is because it is turned too exclusively towards the glance
of the consciousness it would question; it is concerned only to have
a hold on someone else, and to know if the eyes it seeks will look
at it or ignore it in their turn. So we must not expect any description of
visible detail: that would show a gaze which was less impatient to
attain one thing only – the existence, the soul of human beings. In
Racine, the act of seeing is always aimed towards the whole of being,
a totality, an essence. No time now to pick out the aspects and charms
of a face: the glance has already passed them by, making for an immaterial prey.

No images, then, or very few. Just as the glance can see only the
essence of human beings, it will see only the essence of the world.
Certain forms highly stylised – horses, forests, shores or sails – are
sketched out. But the visual essence of the material world is simpler
still – the elemental couple of day and night, shade and light. An
almost abstract dualism, in which cosmic reality is immediately brought
down to the human level by the addition of an ethical symbol. The
depth of night cannot connote anything but horror (cf the dream of
Athalie), while purity goes with daylight as of right (cf Phèdre's dying
words). The ethical symbol shows here as a cosmic dimension added to
the glance: light and shade are not only the conditions making sight
possible or impossible; they are themselves a glance or a blindness,
transcendent in nature. In extreme cases, they cease to be things looked
upon, they become possessed of sight. The daylight is not merely what
makes things visible, it is itself, absolutely, a Glance. Phèdre is ashamed

before the daylight and the Sun, which lights her only to condemn her. She knows she belongs to the night, in other words that she is caught in the field of a nocturnal glance directed from the world below.

We read in a youthful letter from Uzès (24 November 1661):

> I went to see the firework display arranged by a man of my acquaintance. . . . All round me there were faces visible in the light of the rockets, against which you would have found it quite as hard to defend yourself as I did.

Faces appearing out of the night, lit up by flames – this seems to have been a favourite theme for reverie with Racine. The Uzès letter describes something which will remain an archetypal situation for him – a figure first seen lighted against a background of darkness. . . . But if we read further in this letter we shall find a second typical element: gay though the tone of the relation may be, nevertheless this sight is under condemnation. It is laid under a ban, it is marked with the sign of sin. It seems to be accompanied by anxiety, or at least insecurity:

> But as for myself, I took care not to think about them; I did not even feel safe to look at them; I was in the company of a Reverend Father of our chapter, who was not much given to frivolity. . . .

The whole scene takes place under the disapproving glance of this priest, who keeps watch over Racine's eyes; they cannot even meet another pair of eyes 'safely'. The imperious, unwelcome glance separates him from the women he desires, literally stealing from him the pleasure of seeing, and leaving him only the shame of having dared to look. Wherever we turn in Racine's tragedies, we shall constantly find this theme of the glance observed. It is rare for an exchange of glances to take place without being overlooked by the near or distant eyes of a third person. If Racine places one of his tragedies in the Seraglio at Constantinople, it is because the Seraglio is the perfect type of a universe where every glance is spied on by some other glance:

Acomat.   . . . La sultane éperdue
   N'eut plus d'autre désir que celui de sa vue.
Osmin. Mais pouvaient-ils tromper tant de jaloux regards
   Qui semblent mettre entre eux d'invincibles remparts?

(Bajazet, I i 141–4)

That letter from Uzès, certainly, is no evidence that this was a
capital event in Racine's biography. And yet it is a fact that the poet
seems to have constantly remembered the situation. It is as if the
moment had brought him, in the world of reality, up against a theme
issuing from the most secret realms of imagination – a personal myth.
There was no need for Racine to come across the seduction and shame
of the nocturnal Glance in the illumination of those fireworks – he
would have invented it in any case. And he will show himself able to
transfigure the fireworks into a conflagration of tragedy.

There are so many examples. Andromaque has never forgotten those
eyes of Pyrrhus, sparkling in the blaze of burning Troy. Néron, by
torchlight, sees Junie for the first time, 'levant au ciel ses yeux mouillés
de larmes'. And in another 'nuit enflammée' Bérénice sees all glances
converge on Titus – those very glances which are to show him that he
may not marry a foreign queen. Each one of these glances in the night
has the value of a primordial event, located before the beginning of the
action to be performed. It is the moment of origin, when fate takes its
birth. Racine's characters know this – everything began with these
meetings in darkness. What sealed their fates was to have seen those
eyes, and never again be able to escape their image.

It is of course part of the rhetoric of love that passion should be
born of a single look – at first sight. To be in love is to be the captive
of a glance. And this rhetoric is still in force in Racine. But what added
gravity he gives to the sorcery of a glance! To assign its birth to the
darkness of night, lit up by torches and surrounded with arms and
burning buildings, is to link it with maleficent powers, to make it
responsible for a destiny. Even where the scene does not take place at
night, the act of seeing still possesses a sacred or sacrilegious violence.
It worships, or it violates. In the midst of the carnage of a conquered
city, a conqueror eyes his prisoner (Andromaque), or a prisoner
(Ériphile) her bloodstained conqueror – glances which, between
enemies, should never have been exchanged, giving birth to a love
that forgets or betrays the love of country. Each time, it would have
been better not to have seen, the sight was a *forbidden* one. By the law
of the Seraglio Roxane should never have seen Bajazet; for simply
setting eyes on him, she deserves death. All the misfortune of Phèdre
stems from the day when she saw Hippolyte: the first glance meant
the immediate violation of the ban of incest and adultery:

> Athènes me montra mon superbe ennemi.
> Je le vis, je rougis, je pâlis à sa vue.
> Un trouble s'éleva dans mon âme éperdue.

Phèdre's glance is darkened, night falls within her:

> Mes yeux ne voyaient plus, je ne pouvais parler. . . . (*Phèdre*, I iii 272-5)

Thus the act of seeing, by its very violence, produces darkness. This scene has no need to take place in a nocturnal setting: the darkness gathers within the tragic personage. And that image of torches in the night, which we found in *Andromaque*, *Britannicus* and *Bérénice*, we now find internalised and reversed. Against a background of daylight and sun, Phèdre's passion burns like a flame of darkness:

> Je voulais en mourant prendre soin de ma gloire,
> Et dérober au jour une flamme si noire. (*Phèdre*, I iii 309-10)

This darkling blaze, this sombre something over against the daylight, is Phèdre herself – and yet she belongs to the race of the Sun, and her Greek name means 'the Shining One'. Darkness lives in the glance of Phèdre as it lives in the eye of Athalie – to be confronted with the killing, purifying light of day.

The glance in Racine is avidity and frustration. Satisfaction is always withheld; it remains unsatisfied. Not without cause has Racine borrowed from the Ancients this 'digestive' metaphor: 'se rassasier d'une si chère vue'. But surfeit is impossible. Eyes seek out eyes, and even when they obtain the hoped-for response, something is lacking. They have to look again, return to this disappointing pasture, in pursuit of a happiness never finally to be obtained. The lovers must never cease to see each other again and again. They find themselves bound to the treadmill of reiteration – endless beginning again, valueless reassurance. Their happiness is somehow akin to an interminable death agony. They obey the behests of passion with weariness and exhaustion, and the weight of fatigue in the glance of their desire becomes a new weapon of love.

We said a moment ago that the act of seeing, in Racine, was aimed at a single primordial essence. But it must be added that this essence, always seen in part, aimed at, desired, is for all that never achieved, never possessed. What desire so passionately hoped to attain – the depths behind the glances of others – eludes its every grasp; desire hurls itself on its prey, to find nothing but pain – its own pain – which is only deepened by its unflagging efforts; and so turns to destructive fury. What it discovers next is only in fact its own elusive depths, its lack of all internal support, its tragic delusion. As the hero sees others and cannot reach them, so he sees himself and cannot reach himself. He finds his own inner turmoil, but nothing beyond. The glance turns back upon itself, and becomes stupor and incomprehension – 'Que vois-je?' The question can of course receive no answer. This happens at the moment when the hero faces the most violent of his ordeals, and finds in his path something unnatural, monstrous. But what is monstrous is not the thing that meets his glance, is not in front of him; it is the glance, in its stupefaction, in that vain questioning in which eyes open only to fill with the terror they themselves create (as Phèdre's eyes fill with darkness). This terror is accompanied by no images, though sometimes it becomes hallucination. Thus Oreste in his delirium recovers Hermione and is aghast at her 'affreux regards': his final vision is the vision of her glances, ending a tragic story which began when first those glances met his own.

But before it becomes that questioning turned inwards upon itself, the Racinian glance is an unquiet questioning that thrusts deeply into the souls of others. The common characteristic of love and hate, in Racine, is that both use the interrogative form. To convince ourselves of this we have only to read over some of his great scenes. The characters face each other with ceaseless questionings; this is their way of seeking out and hurting one another (seeking out in order to hurt). Often question meets question; a new question ripostes instead of answering: challenge against challenge. The famous Racinian cruelty finds its favourite weapon in the question. Quite literally, the characters apply the question to one another. (Torture had its charm, we remember, to the Dandin of *Les Plaideurs*:

> N'avez-vous jamais vu donner la question?

To which Isabelle replies:

> Hé! Monsieur, peut-on voir souffrir les malheureux?

And Dandin:

> Bon! Cela fait toujours passer une heure ou deux.) (III iv 848 ff)

The glance turned question has a double purpose: it tries to seize the truth, and at the same time to possess as a lover possesses. The double purpose changes into a single act – to hurt. To bring tears to the eyes of the creature one desires, is at once to acquire knowledge and possession. The prize which had obstinately eluded capture seems to be at one's mercy. Tears are a clear confession of pain: if the victim does not yield in love, it yields at least in suffering. And the lover, turned executioner, finds pleasure in operating against this glance which will escape him no more, will ignore him no more. The tears he makes flow will prove to him that he exists at last in the eyes of her he loves. He holds now a certainty he lacked before: but this certainty is only that of being more than ever rejected. For this, in Racine, is what happens to the glance turned question – it aims at the possession of others, it penetrates even to the source of tears; but the more it strengthens its hold on the glance it desires, the more it excludes itself. It attains the knowledge it sought; but that knowledge is intolerable, for it announces clearly the pain of being separate, rejected, banished into bitter solitude. The keenest pain is here the executioner's. When Junie 'lève au ciel ses yeux mouillés de larmes', Néron suffers no less than his victim. He made those tears flow; but Junie's glance turned away from him to the skies. The persecutor knows his strength and knows it to be useless; eyes filled with tears hurt more than they are hurt, and the question now is turned back upon Néron. Accused by this reproachful glance, he finds no other answer than to increase his violence until he makes it lethal, by turning still more and more to evil. As love is inflamed, the monster is born and grows in this man, as if by some external fatality. For in the victim's glance is a provocation to ill-treatment – a deliberate challenge to cruelty, heaped on former cruelties. It suggests a secret joy in continually increasing the persecutor's guilt, inflaming his suffering and driving him to extremes. So that Néron cannot but go to the ultimate violence, defrauding himself each moment more completely of the response he desires. Haunted even on his sleepless couch by the sight of Junie's tears, he will seek the death of that glance and endeavour to quench the sparkle he cannot possess. This is the meaning of the famous scene in which Néron, in the character of a murderous *voyeur*, hides and spies on the interview between Junie and Britannicus:

Madame, en le voyant, songez que je vous voi. (*Britannicus*, II iv 690)

Nowhere do we see more clearly the sadism which Racine always attaches to situations involving the overlooking glance. Secretly watched by Néron, Junie's eyes will be prevented from saying anything to

Britannicus. By a single glance Néron puts to death the exchange of
glances by which their love was fed. He enjoys that strange optics by
which the rays of suffering converge towards his hiding-place. The
concealed *voyeur* holds in his hands the happiness of those he envies,
and transforms it into despair. But the despair is directed back at him
and pierces him in his turn. The more visible the misery he causes, the
greater will be for Néron the certainty that he is not loved. At the point
where the rays unite in this optics, after passing through the extinguish-
ed glances of the victims, pain reaches it peak and the *voyeur's* pleasure
is destroyed. Cruel and effective though the overlooking glance may
be, its cruelty is the measure of its failure. It will never attain that inner
essence it desires. The sparkle of the tears it makes flow reflects back its
own cruelty, amplified. What it knows from now on is not that other
consciousness that it sought to possess, but its own limitation, the point
it is forbidden by destiny to pass, which it cannot even break through
by dying or by inflicting death.

　　Having said this, we can define more clearly the significance of these
two fundamental situations of the Racinian being – to look and to be
looked upon. The act of seeing includes a fundamental failure; he
comes up against a hidden refusal, and discovers his own impotence.
Not that the glance lacks clarity, but this clarity, unlike what we see in
Corneille, can never be changed into firm will or effective act. The
glance in Racine is not so blinded that it cannot discover the truth.
But it is worse for it not to be blinded; every truth that it discovers is
baleful, every avowal it extorts – and with what difficulty – will
have mortal consequences. Racine's characters are clear-sighted enough
to realize that their very violence is a weakness beyond remedy. They
know that they are being dragged onward in spite of themselves and
can do nothing to escape their doom. A clear but useless knowledge,
since the view it gives is of uncontrollable turmoil. A keenness of
vision that, far from ending the tragic error, only increases it. The
truth it discovers brings no salvation in any case: 'J'ai des yeux,' proclaims Ériphile, but when she knows her own identity, she will discover
that she is condemned to death, and take her own life in a fit of fury.
No better example could be given to confirm the principle which is
endlessly repeated in the tragedies of Racine – that, if illusion and
blindness can be done away with, it will lead to the imposing of a
truth that kills. Thus the progression of the tragic turmoil coincides
with the progress of knowledge.

The act of seeing, in all its violence and possessiveness, contains this weakness and the knowledge of this weakness. To be seen, conversely, will be to discover, at almost the same moment, one's guilt in the eyes of others. The hope of a character of Racine was for the caressing glance, the gentle conquest of love: what he discovers in reality is his own guilt. Instead of the felicity of being looked at, the misfortune of being seen in the posture of guilt. Not merely because, like Néron or Pyrrhus, he has turned himself into an executioner to seize what can never be seized; but because, in every glance of desire, there is a future transgression, the violation of a ban, the beginning of a crime. He discovers it as soon as he meets the other glance, and from thenceforth can no longer escape that crime; the glance, quite literally, fixes him in his guilt.

As if to stress it still further, Racine brings in, above the tragic debate in which the characters are engaged, another downward glance – a final court of appeal – falling from a greater height, or a greater distance. It only needs a few allusions, scattered here and there in the poem – all Greece has its eyes on its ambassador Oreste and King Pyrrhus (in *Andromaque*); Rome watches the loves of Titus (*Bérénice*); Phèdre knows that she is seen by the Sun; and the religious plays unfold under the eye of God. In every case the guilt of the characters piles up under the supreme glance of this transcendent witness – or, sometimes, Judge. Every glance exchanged by the human heroes is spied upon by this inexorable eye, which judges and condemns. All, busy with the satisfaction of their passions, thought they could escape from the community, or the Sun, or God; all tried to elude that accusing glance. But sooner or later it catches up with every one of them. Anyone who essays to analyse the evolution of Racine's drama would do well to consider how this accusing downward glance, after first representing some collectivity (the people, or the nation), took on in the later plays a religious significance – God, the Sun, absolute supra-tragic powers, overruling and guiding the tragic action from above. However this may be, man in Racine, when he is not the chosen interpreter of the divine Glance (like Calchas or Joad), is mercilessly exposed to the wrath of the Judge. This wrath sometimes results in a death sentence, but, more often, does no more than establish Guilt, and leave man at grips with it.

Weakness and guilt: such, constantly present and almost indistinguishable, are the significations attached by Racine to the act of the looker and the state of the looked-upon. The only glance without weakness – that of the transcendent Judge – has its source on the hither or the yonder side of the tragic universe. As for man, he never emerges from the tragic universe, in other words from weakness and guilt. He receives no help from outside. If he feels on him the down-ward glance of the Judge, the result will be to increase, and not to heal, the rending of his nature. There is no peace for him whose eyes are open, nor for him who knows that he is seen.

The poetics of the glance, the weakness and the guilt of the glance, presumably originated in the encounter between Greek tragedy and Jansenist thought. The least we can say is that this poetics, if it was born of Racine's imagination, finds in Port-Royal and Euripides an ideology to match it. The Christian tragedy of Guilt comes together with the ancient tragedy of Error; and the persecuting god of Euri-pides' plays becomes that God whose glance no man can meet without feeling himself to be a sinner.

But we are in the theatre, not before the judgement seat of God. The theatre, whose existence and function are a source of scandal, since the poet and the audience usurp the office of the Judge's downward glance, and presume in their turn to overrule and judge. In that strange architecture of vision built of glance behind glance, the poet sets up the last glance of all – a reasoning glance over unreasoning passion, a pitying glance over pitiless destiny. The crowning vision is poetry. From poetry all proceeds, to poetry all returns. But it still contains a turmoil and an anxiety that nothing can efface. For the audience, the tragic knowledge is the strange pleasure of knowing man to be weak and guilty. And, as a final proof that to look is to hurt, this pleasure causes tears: tears that there is nobody now to see.

SOURCE: Translated by R. C. Knight. 'Racine et la poétique du regard' (1961), in *L'oeil vivant* (1961).

LUCIEN GOLDMANN

The Structure of Racinian Tragedy (1962)

THERE is one word in my title on which I would dwell for a moment before passing on – the word structure.

I think we are today at a turning-point, not only in the study of literary works, but in the sciences of man in general, in the study of any historical or social fact; it is a turning-point which we have seen coming for more than a century, and which is proving ever more important in teaching and research. Its distinguishing character is the idea of structure – the fact that no human reality presents itself to the researcher as an isolated element side by side with others, but as part of a whole possessing a significant character.

I can mention here only a few, adding that most of the important advances made by psychological, social and historical science during the last decades seem to me capable of being seen, whatever the divergences between the different schools, as advances effected in this new approach.

Now Hegelianism and Marxism first, then psycho-analysis, Gestalt psychology, phenomenology, the work of Lévi-Strauss in France (remarkable work despite reservations I cannot go into here), and that of Piaget in Geneva, all have this, if nothing else, in common – that they are essentially and fundamentally structuralist.

I shall base what I have to say on a few incomplete findings of a wider inquiry, concerning the possibilities of genetic structuralism in the particular field of literary history. Let me say at once that structuralism comes up, not only against hallowed traditions – habits which still dominate the study of literature in particular and the sciences of man in general – but also against what may be called administrative realities – the traditional dividing lines of our studies, which have been called into question by the new approach.

May I point out, before coming to Racine, three of the many methodological consequences of genetic structuralism.

The first is that, if the structuralist approach is valid, there can be no autonomous history of literature, since this, like the history of philosophy or art, or what you will, ceases to have an object of its own. To use an analogy, it is exactly as if biology, to explain the evolution of species, studied nothing but the evolution of animals' heads. What evolves is a total structure, in our case the whole social reality. One work does not beget another autonomously; it is linked with the general structure, the social environment, the human reality into which it was born and of which it is a part. If later we find a transition to a different type of literary work, this implies precisely, if it is to make sense, that there was a total change in this environment. To study a series of literary or philosophical works as an autonomous sector of human reality, is to study an artificially delimited object which is not itself a structure. Thus to understand the work of Racine and Pascal, we must consider the genesis and internal structure of the Jansenist group.

The second consequence is to eliminate the concept of influence as an explanation of the genesis of literary, artistic or philosophical works. Influence explains absolutely nothing, for the simple reason that at every moment, theoretically speaking, hundreds of influences are possible, while only one or two operate in fact. Moreover, if we study for example the influence of Montaigne on Pascal, we find that the Montaigne read by Pascal is not the real Montaigne, but a purely sceptical Montaigne derived from a distorting interpretation. And this is true in every case where the traditional history of literature or thought speaks of 'influence'. We could cite that of St Augustine on the Jansenists. It is not the real St Augustine, but St Augustine as they read him. Now the choice of a master or a partner in a dialogue, and his influence on the author or thinker under discussion, can only be explained by analysing the structures of the latter's consciousness. The problem may be stated thus: why did Montaigne influence Pascal; and why did Pascal, in order to undergo this influence, distort Montaigne in this or that way? It is significant that in revealing analogous structures in the works of Pascal and Kant, we have found that each argues with two interlocutors, a rationalist and a sceptic respectively, whom they invent when they cannot find them in reality. Pascal can see a sceptical Montaigne to the extent that the mental categories of the writer 'undergoing the influence' determine what that influence shall be, as well as the distortions this involves.

So our approach has to be reversed. Influence explains nothing; at most, it creates problems.

The third consequence is this. We must pass over one level, still important of course but nevertheless secondary, in the author's consciousness. Naturally we must, when we study a work like Racine's, ask what the poet intended to do; but we must not assume that what he intended coincides with what he has done. It is even probable that the difference will be considerable, for the work is created with mental structures of which the author is almost never conscious; so that when we want to know what Racine wrote, and what is the objective meaning of his work, we must look at the work itself, and not his intentions.

I am slightly embarrassed in Racine's case, because in starting from the work we can explain the biography so readily that it would be wrong not to take it into account. But it may happen in other cases that the life is entirely different from the work, and we are led to put it aside.

I have said this much to show how a genetic–structuralist approach alters the traditional way of understanding and studying human facts in general and literary works in particular. So I now come to the subject of my paper: the structure of Racine's dramatic works.

In a structuralist approach it is already almost wrong to limit ourselves to the study of this drama, for while it has a clear-cut structure, it is one that must be seen as a part of other structures by which alone it becomes comprehensible; so that if here I put forward an analysis centred mainly on Racinian drama, I had first to see that drama in the context of the wider structure of Jansenist thought, and link it with that of Pascalian thought – which has proved to be so closely related that I was able to study the *Mystère de Jésus* as a commentary on *Phèdre*, and *vice versa*. At first sight these texts are of course quite different, and there is nothing Christian in *Phèdre*, but collective mental structures may be as readily transposed into a religious as a secular work.

Then too, Jansenism itself must be seen in the context of the totality of relationships between social groups constituting French society at a given period in the seventeenth century. I should add that since the publication of my book, research into these structures has made great progress.

I shall therefore start here from the concept of tragic vision – the product of a whole body of structurally inspired research. It denotes a mental structure of which I will explain the principal features, and try to show what an understanding it gives of Racine's drama. I add that it is this same mental structure that we find in Pascal's *Pensées*, and in the 'extremist' form of Jansenism, itself a part of the wider structure of Jansenism as a whole.

The vision is distinguished by three fundamental elements, which – since we are talking of drama and dramatic works – I shall call three characters (with all the approximateness implied in the term). The relation between the three, already worked out in Jansenist theology, and particularly in that of the extremists, will give us, transposed and secularized, the key to Racinian drama. The three characters are God, man and the world. Not, of course, any god, any man or any world; the structure of Racinian drama depends on a specific relationship between the three, characteristic of what I call tragic vision – and I would make it clear that it would probably have to be modified to fit the tragedy of Shakespeare.

What distinguishes tragedy, if we give the word its strict sense, is the fact that its conflicts are essentially insoluble – and not merely non-resolved; for there may be plays where conflicts are not resolved for accidental reasons. (Thus in Racine a play like *Bajazet* is not tragic, since if the conflict is not resolved it is on account of an accident, the discovery of a letter, but it is not insoluble in essence.)

In Jansenist thought, however, in Pascal's *Pensées* and in Racine's tragedies, conflicts are insoluble by reason of the fact that one of the three characters, man, approaches the world with a demand that is unrealizable – the demand for the absolute. The demand is distinguished by a mental category which I shall call 'all or nothing'. Pascal formulated it once in one of his writings by saying that adding finite to finite makes no difference in relation to infinity.

Now in reality, in this world which is part of the structure to which we give that name, there are obviously only differences of degree. To attain, approximately, certain values we have to make concessions; and on the other hand, certain desires and certain values never advance beyond the stage of aspirations. Over against this world which we shall call the world of the relative, stands tragic man with his demand for the absolute, judging the world by the category of 'all or nothing'; for him, whatever is not all is thus nothing. And as the world is *never* all, it can only be nothing. In other words, in tragedy, the conflict between the hero and the world is radical and insoluble.

Tragic man finds himself pitted against a relative world, in which his values are unattainable; in relation to this world they show themselves necessarily as a cause of scandal. And on the logical or moral plane, what is scandalous is contradiction. And indeed, in the world, the values of the tragic character are *contradictory*.

If we place ourselves on the literary plane – for I cannot carry the analysis very far here – we shall find in all the tragedies of Racine properly so called, two strictly contradictory demands which demand to be satisfied together – to remain loyal to Hector and also save the life of Astyanax, or to save Britannicus' life and save his relationship with Junie, or to reconcile the glory of empire with love for Bérénice, or else the *gloire* of Phèdre, as queen and wife of Thésée, with her love for Hippolyte.

This, be it said in passing, explains why Pascal's style, at the moment when he also has reached positions that are tragic – the moment of writing the *Pensées* – becomes of necessity paradoxical; for, from this point of view, one can only say things that are true by attaching the same subject to two contradictory predicates, which is the very definition of paradox.

On the plane of the tragic play, then, the problem is posed in this way. Over against a world with its own laws, in which we can only live by choosing (Andromaque can save the life of Astyanax if only she will marry Pyrrhus; or she can save her loyalty to Hector if only she will give up Astyanax), a world whose laws force us to choose, to fulfil one's values approximately, to save what matters most by giving up what matters less, tragic man calls for rejection of all compromise and all choice, because choice for him is the essence of evil or sin. The structure of Racine's work is distinguished by the fact that the two terms of the contradiction matter equally. Each attempt to save one by giving up the other becomes thereby a major crime, a deadly sin. This then is one constituent of the structure – the tragic relationship, the insoluble conflict, between man and the world.

But there is still the third character, God. Not any god, but a very particular god resulting from this relationship, this rupture, so that I could just as well have begun my analysis with the relationship between God and man, and shown in the second place how it engenders the man–world relationship I have been analysing. Indeed the unattainable demand set up by man against the world appears to man as a demand greater than himself, a transcendental demand for absolute values, a law. In Racine it is represented by concrete characters like Hector and Astyanax, the Sun and Venus, etc. But I prefer to give it the name it had in Jansenist theology, since it was from this starting-point that Racine took it and secularized it – the name of God.

And this god has a particular characteristic: he is an onlooker-god, watching, demanding, judging, but never revealing to man what he should do. If there were a divine revelation that it is better to be loyal to Hector than to save Astyanax, or to save him rather than be loyal to Hector, tragedy would disappear; man would be either weak enough not to obey the divine law, or strong enough to obey it, but nothing paradoxical or tragic would remain. In tragedy however there is no solution – God demands both protection of Astyanax and loyalty to Hector, both resistance to Néron and protection of Britannicus, both empire and union with Bérénice, both the queen's *gloire* and her love for Hippolyte. And he will never tell how to reconcile one with with the other. He is a strictly silent god, always present *qua* demand, always absent *qua* counsel or enlightenment – the opposite of the providential gods we find, for instance, in *Iphigénie*.

There is in fact, in this same *Iphigénie*, a moment when the opposition between these gods is clearly expressed. The structure of the play includes two different universes – Ériphile's tragic universe, where the gods never speak and knowledge of the truth implies the hero's death, and the universe of the other characters with its providential gods. So, the moment the priest, proclaiming that Ériphile is the one that is to die, makes ready to sacrifice her in the name of these last, Ériphile will be heard to cry:

> Arrête ... et ne m'approche pas.
> Le sang de ces héros dont tu me fais descendre
> Sans tes profanes mains saura bien se répandre ...
>
> (v vi 1772–4)

The contrast could not be put more strongly. The gods of providence are petty and profane for the gods of tragedy; we are at the meeting-place of two radically different universes. The tragic god is a silent god who presents himself to man as the demand for the unattainable. The gods of providence act, and thereby relieve man of responsibility for his acts; this of course is why, in a work of literature using characters and not concepts, the tragic god is almost always double – Hector and Astyanax, the Sun and Venus. In every Racinian tragedy he is a god with two faces, or, if we prefer, two contradictory demands creating the structure of the universe.

This then is the fundamental situation. One thing more must be added, if we would understand the tragic structure – a third concept, that of tragic man. Up to now we have seen the world, vain and visible, valueless but present, and God, the only authentic value but remaining always silent, an onlooker, present only as a demand, the Hidden God.[1] These are two parallel realities, entirely alien one to the other. And the only intermediary between them is tragic man, great and petty at once (here I am using Pascal's words to gloss Racine, and this can be done for all his tragedies), great by his awareness, because he knows what he must demand, because he knows the only authentic value; petty, because he can never attain it. Now value is not simply wishing to save the life of Astyanax and wishing to remain loyal to Hector, it is doing it. And not to do both – even if it is impossible – constitutes a major crime, the only crime that exists in the universe of tragedy, that of the tragic hero who cannot, in the world, attain his values. As for the world, it is too vain and insubstantial to be at fault with regard to the divinity; we may say it is simply transparent and inexistent.

Describing the tragic god, Lukàcs once wrote: 'In his eyes only miracle exists, and the miracle is clarity.' In other words, the god can neither see nor judge the world with its ambiguities; nothing exists for him except tragic man, whose greatness consists precisely in his clear and unequivocal awareness. And it is precisely this clarity of vision that makes tragic man aware of his permanent state of guilt, a state all the more grave because involuntary, because it consists in the impossibility of attaining, in the world, the demands of God.

Here I may perhaps bring in another Pascalian image: the tragic hero knows that the world is crushing him, but he is greater than the world because he knows he is being crushed, and the world does not.

I come to another example of transposition from Jansenist tragic thought into the secular world of Racine's plays. It is that of the priest representing God in the world, but not God's will concerning this or that act, only his law in general terms. Herein lies the whole problem of Jansenism, as shown for instance when Barcos writes to the Abbess of Port-Royal that at the very moment when her nuns were facing the bitterest persecution by refusing to sign the Formulary[2] they may have been in a grave state of sin because they could not know the will of God.

And in the same way, in *Bérénice*, where one of the faces of the divinity is represented by the Roman people, Titus asks Paulin what is this people's will, and Paulin can tell nothing but the tenor of the general law forbidding the Emperor to marry a queen. And we shall see Titus rightly complain that this is not enough; for he knows the law as well as Paulin, and what he wants to know is the exact reaction of the Roman people, not to the general problem but to the precise case of his marriage with Bérénice. And as his question will eternally remain unanswered, he will have to reconcile the divinity's two general, contradictory, demands – separation from, and union with Bérénice.

Another concept at the centre both of Jansenist theology and Racinian tragedy is one I shall describe by the theological term of conversion.

Conversion should be understood as a radical, absolute and timeless break with a man's previous life. There is no transition from life in the world to tragic consciousness. There may be a progressive psychic process taking place in time, for the outside observer of a conversion; it is possible to reconstruct the psychology of the convert: but it is *another* that does this. For the tragic character, there is a sudden moment of realization, creating an impassable gulf between what there was before and what there is after. For the universe before conversion was regulated by a different mental category, that of the world, of 'more or less', 'better or worse' – of the relative, in short. In the universe of God, of tragedy, there is only 'all or nothing'. I add that the two viewpoints can be distinguished in another way, inasmuch as the historian tries to apprehend the psychic process of conversion, while for tragic man there is no psychology possible, conversion being timeless.

There has always been talk of the psychology of Racinian characters; but there is no psychology except for the non-tragic characters. To enter tragedy abolishes all psychology since it abolishes time.

In the same way history books speak of the conversion of Mère Angélique as taking place on a given date, whereas she, even in her latest years, would end some of her letters with formulas such as '. . . and pray God to grant me conversion'. It is not a reality taking place at this or that instant, it is a timeless reality, an eternal problem. If we read the *Écrit sur la conversion du pécheur*, we may look on it simply as a work with certain passages missing, but the curious thing is that the interruptions appear just as we expect that time will make its appearance, and the work remains timeless; for conversion is, precisely, an exit out of time. This is the starting-point from which I wish to pose the problem of time in Racinian tragedy.

Over against a world of vanity in which it is impossible to attain authentic values, there is only one attitude valid for tragic man, rejection of the world, rejection of life. For this reason time in Racinian tragedies is reduced to a moment, coinciding with conversion to the tragic universe. The one exception, *Phèdre*, takes place in a time which is paradoxical, circular, and in the last resort timeless. The play ends with a return to the starting-point, the realization that life is impossible. There is one line which recurs in every tragedy by Racine and expresses its whole message:

Junie. Et si je vous parlais pour la dernière fois! (*Britannicus*, v i 1546)

Titus. Et je vais lui parler pour la dernière fois. (*Bérénice*, II ii 490)

Bérénice. Pour la dernière fois, adieu, Seigneur. (Ibid. v vii 1506)

Phèdre. Soleil, je te viens voir pour la dernière fois. (*Phèdre*, I iii 172)

So that the problems posed for Racine by the rule of the three unities are systematically the opposite of those posed to Corneille. Where the latter came up against the difficulty of confining in one day a sufficient number of events to show the greatness of his hero, Racine's problem was to fill five acts with a timeless action occupying no more than an instant.

In this paper I have no space to analyse the tragic universe further, nor to go deeper into the relations of Racine the individual with Port-Royal, and the influence of these on the genesis of his drama. For all these questions I may be allowed to refer the reader to studies I have published elsewhere. Let me simply say that a drama of this kind could only be written by someone in the exceptional position of being steeped in Jansenist thought and yet having broken with the Jansenists; since no 'friend of Port-Royal' could devote himself to that vain worldly activity, the writing and production of plays. Nothing but the combination of a whole cluster of special circumstances, and more particularly a man whose whole mental structure had been determined by Jansenism, but who had left Jansenism, lived in the world, and turned to literary activities, could have produced, out of the literary, secular, transposition of the thought of Port-Royal, the miracle of Racinian tragedy.

Let me now show in outline how the different modalities of this tragic structure found expression in his plays.

The first (almost) tragic play to be born of this transposition was *Andromaque*. I emphasise the word almost, for reasons which will become apparent.

The opening scenes have exactly the kind of structure that I have described. In transposing a religious vision on to a secular stage the hardest problem was this – how to fill an evening's entertainment with a timeless subject dealing with no more than the instant of rejection; or, to put it another way, how to obtain a series of dialogues in a play where, as we have seen, the basic pattern involved those three characters – the world, man, and God – between whom there never is dialogue; where, to use an expression of Georg Lukàcs, the thing that distinguishes the central character, tragic man, is the absolute aloneness of a life reduced to one 'dialogue in solitude', since he unceasingly and exclusively addresses a God who never answers.

Racine turned first towards the simplest solution. It consisted in putting the world in the foreground, as a collective personage which could be formed of a number of individual characters, who could hold dialogues and so make the play possible. *Andromaque* – and, as we shall see in a moment, *Britannicus* – are plays written to this pattern. The front of the stage is occupied by the wild beasts of the passion of love, Pyrrhus, Hermione, Oreste, over against whom, in the background, stands the tragic – or more exactly the quasi-tragic-character, Andromaque. Above them, the paradoxical two-faced divinity whose demands are both absolute and irreconcilable – Hector with his demand for loyalty, Astyanax with his demand for protection.

If, for all that, the play is not strictly a tragedy, if in mid-career it veers towards drama, it is because, instead of finding the dilemma insoluble, Andromaque works out a solution which does satisfy the moral demands of the divinity – to protect Astyanax she will marry Pyrrhus, to remain loyal to Hector she will kill herself at the moment of the marriage.

I need hardly say that Racine was a great enough poet to feel that

this veering towards drama necessarily entailed a change in the natures
of the characters. If there is a solution for the hero, God has ceased to
be silent, he is no longer the tragic god, onlooker and hidden, but the
god of drama. So Racine is forced by this structural exigence – or
aesthetic exigence, when it operates in the work of literature – to make
Hector speak, in defiance of all verisimilitude. Three lines in Act IV,
scene i, tell us explicitly that it was Hector who gave the solution:

> Ah! je n'en doute point: c'est votre époux, Madame,
> C'est Hector qui produit ce miracle en votre âme. (1049-50)

And a little later:

> Voilà ce qu'un époux m'a commandé lui-même. (1098)

I need hardly say, also, that this veering deprives the denouement of
all inevitability; which is why we shall see Racine hesitate, and change
it. In drama, a whole spectrum of possibilities remains open, whereas
in tragedy all is inevitable.

Later Racine went back to this form of tragedy, but gave it a more
strictly conceived structure, and we had *Britannicus*. But between the
two plays comes the comedy *Les Plaideurs*, easy to account for if we
connect it with Jansenist thought. The *solitaires* were mostly ex-
members of the judicial bodies called *parlements*, judges who had
given up the world and refused to judge. Racine mocks the judge who
remains in the world and insists on judging come what may, even if
he has only a dog to sentence. From the point of view of the pattern
in his mind, *Les Plaideurs* may be a necessary, or at least a useful,
transition between *Andromaque* and *Britannicus*. In the first, the world
still keeps a certain value: Hector has spoken, the conflict is not
insoluble. *Les Plaideurs* are precisely the description of the world as
the Jansenists saw it, totally valueless and turned by the absence of the
tragic character into a subject for comedy.

In *Britannicus*, Racine goes back to the tragic pattern of *Andromaque*,
but this time carries it out consistently.

Néron and Agrippine, the wild beasts of passion – political passion
this time, mixed with that of love   occupy the front of the stage, with
the puppet Britannicus. Britannicus is in any case not the principal
character, as I will attempt to show. Let me however say a few words
about him.

We met in *Andromaque*, as forming the world opposed to the tragic

hero – the world which does not exist for the god – the wild beasts of
the passion of love, closely related to those moved by political passion
in *Britannicus*; but the world is made up also of puppets, characters
weak, passive, and above all inaccessible to truth. Britannicus is easily
defined – he is the man who always believes falsehood and always
mistrusts truth. He defines himself when he tells Narcisse:

> Narcisse, tu dis vrai . . .
>
>   Mais enfin je te croi,
> Ou plutôt je fais vœu de ne croire que toi. (I iv 339 ff)

The statement exactly matches his behaviour throughout the play.
It is moreover what distinguishes him from the tragic character, Junie,
who has only been twenty-four hours at court and can see at a glance
what sort of world surrounds her:

> Je ne connais Néron et la cour que d'un jour;
> Mais si j'ose le dire, hélas! dans cette cour
> Combien tout ce qu'on dit est loin de ce qu'on pense!
> Que la bouche et le cœur sont peu d'intelligence!
> Avec combien de joie on y trahit sa foi!
> Quel séjour étranger et pour vous et pour moi!
>
>   (v i 1521–6)

To show how close is the relationship between the ground-plans of
Andromaque and *Britannicus*, let me quote the lines marking the decisive
moment in each – the first meeting between the tragic character and
the world, between Andromaque and Pyrrhus, Junie and Néron.

> *Pyrrhus.*   Me cherchiez-vous, Madame?
> Un espoir si charmant me serait-il permis?
> *Andromaque.* Je passais jusqu'aux lieux où l'on garde mon fils.
>
>   (*Andromaque*, I iv 258–60)

> *Néron.* Vous vous troublez, Madame, et changez de visage.
> Lisez-vous dans mes yeux quelque triste présage?
> *Junie.* Seigneur, je ne vous puis déguiser mon erreur:
> J'allais voir Octavie, et non pas l'Empereur.
>
>   (*Britannicus*, II iii 527–30)

The two scenes are identical. There is no contact, and never will be,
between the tragic character and the world.

Let me finally, for lack of space, emphasize one element only in *Britannicus*, the dénouement; for from Racine's day until our own it has always called forth the same criticisms, which are these:

(*a*) The play goes on after the death of Britannicus, and this is said to violate its unity.

(*b*) It is extremely improbable, and in any case contrary to historical truth, that a girl of twenty could have entered the Vestal Virgins, and that the Roman people could have prevented Néron entering their temple.

These objections seem to me to show complete failure to grasp the tragic structure of the play. The first would be valid if Britannicus were the principal character; whereas he is really only one of the numerous figures representing the world. The tragic character, set up over against the world, whose conversion and radical rupture with the universe constitutes the conclusion of any Racinian tragedy, is here Junie; which is why the play cannot end until she has entered the universe of the divinity.

As for the second objection, it is equally unjustified; for when she leaves the world Junie enters God's universe – and there tragic man ceases to be alone, making contact with the community.

In Racine's plays God's universe and the People are synonymous. That is why we shall find a chorus surrounding the hero in the plays where God is present, *Esther* and *Athalie*; and this chorus is already prefigured in the People surrounding Junie as soon as she finds His universe. As for the impossibility for Néron and Narcisse to enter it, this is one of the structural data of the tragedy: there exists no link, however slight, between the world of puppets and wild beasts, and that of God.

Britannicus is the tragedy of Racine – tragedy in the strict sense – in which the world occupies the front of the stage. And it is a distinguishing mark of his drama that he never repeats the same structural type (except where he fails to attain full consistency the first time, as in *Andromaque*, corrected in *Britannicus*, and *Esther*, corrected in *Athalie*). So he passes to another, where the hero himself is in the forefront. But this type set him a fairly difficult literary problem; for the tragic hero is the secular transposition of the *solitaire* of Port-Royal. The very structure of the tragic universe as we have described it implies that there is no dialogue between him and the world, which for him is nothing but an abstract negative, a non-value having no essential relation with him. On the other hand, as we have said, he has only 'solitary dialogues' with God, since God never answers.

So it was not the easiest thing to write a play and fill five acts with a hero lacking any active interlocutor. The result was that Racine wrote one containing two tragic heroes, Titus and Bérénice; what is more, he had to invent a situation making possible dialogue between them.

The play takes place in the time elapsing between the conversion of Titus and that of Bérénice. The world (which in the play becomes the court) is represented by a single character, Antiochus; the silent god of paradox, by the double demand for empire and for union with Bérénice. I add that Paulin completely corresponds to the function of the priest in the Jansenist universe: he is there to tell Titus the divine will – in the play this is the will of the People – which the visible world of vanity prevents Titus from achieving directly. But he transmits only this will in general, not the particular will of a god who is quite as hidden from him as from other men.

The subject of the tragedy is Titus' attempt to bring Bérénice to understand and accept the necessity of their material separation, which alone will enable them to carry out both the god's contradictory demands, the glory of the empire and the union of the two heroes; and the play ends the moment the conversion of Bérénice creates, by separation and solitude *jointly accepted*, the inexorable universe of tragedy. Antiochus' final 'Hélas' points out to the audience how far removed the world of vain hopes and futile regrets remains from the majesty of what has come to pass.

After *Britannicus* and after *Bérénice*, a third version of the tragic universe was open to Racine; but its correspondence to the categories of Jansenist thought was only implicit, inasmuch as it concerns behaviour which must have appeared essentially blameworthy to Port-Royal. This is probably why we only meet it in Racine at the moment when it does correspond to the experience, if not to the ethics or theology, of the *solitaires*.

It is the version in which the tragic hero still thinks he can reconcile the god's contradictory demands in the world, and only discovers this hope to be vain on his conversion at the end of the play. In historical reality, Port-Royal had thought it possible to be reconciled with the world and live a Christian life in it, but the *Paix de l'Église* soon ended and the persecutions began once more. The beginning of the play shows Phèdre as a similar figure to Titus or Junie, who know that in the world of choice and partial solutions there is no reconciling the contradictory demands of tragic greatness; but she lets hereslf be lured by the false hope of authentic life, and regains her initial awareness and initial greatness only at the close.

As the history of an attempt to attain values *in this world*, the play makes no separation between the plane occupied by the world and that of the tragic character; both are at the front of the stage under the eye of the silent two-faced god – the Sun, and Venus.

The world is made up entirely of puppets. There is Hippolyte, who defines himself at the rise of the curtain by the first words he lets fall, 'Je pars, cher Théramène,' and will do nothing but run away from reality through the whole play. A few lines further on he says it again:

> Et je fuirai ces lieux que je n'ose plus voir. (I i 28)

In the same way, his first words after Phèdre has declared her love will be 'Théramène, fuyons' (II vi 717). Then there is Aricie, the convent schoolgirl who asks Hippolyte, in the crisis of his life, whether he intends to marry her properly; Racine has invented her simply to show the difference between the greatness of tragic solitude and the weakness of the worldling. Finally there is Thésée, a kind of older Britannicus or Hippolyte, who asks only to be deceived, and will live to the end in fear of the truth.

To end this paper, let me say something about a line which has often been quoted by critics as an example of pure poetry, independent of content:

> La fille de Minos et de Pasiphaé,

and, with the reader's permission, quote the whole sentence:

> Tout a changé de face
> Depuis que sur ces bords les Dieux ont envoyé
> La fille de Minos et de Pasiphaé. (I i 34–6)

It seems to me, quite on the other hand, that the content of this line is extremely rich, since it sums up the sense of the tragedy on three different levels – the opposition between the traditional, linear order in which worldlings live and the new ethic of tragedy, which is an ethic of totality and the combination of contraries, while Phèdre, who embodies that ethic, combines in her person by her very ancestry a goddess of heaven and a god of hell (for the play was written for a

Christian public who took it in this way); and while, moreover, the goddess in heaven represents sin, the god in hell represents righteousness.[3] Add to this the contrast in sound between the airy lightness of the 'a', 'é', and 'ph' of 'Pasiphaé' and the tight block of the other name, Minos.

A complete account of Racine's drama would have to mention *Athalie*, but this fourth and strictest version of the pattern is no longer strictly tragic: it is the play where the god is present and victorious, and thereby exceeds the limits of this examination. My hope in closing is that this short sketch, in spite of its schematic character, may have shown some of the new possibilities opened up to the objective study of works of literature by a method based on the concept of genetic structuralism.

SOURCE: Translated by R. C. Knight. From *Le Théâtre tragique*, ed. J. Jacquot (1962).

NOTES

1. [*Editor's note.*] The phrase, which is the title of L. Goldmann's book, comes from Isaiah xlv 15 ('Verily thou art a God that hidest thyself' – A.V.). It had been used by Pascal (*Pensées*, 242, 585, ed. Braunschvicg).

2. [*Editor's note.*] A document that the nuns were called on to sign in 1664, stating that the 'five propositions' condemned by the Church were in fact to be found in the *Augustinus* of Jansenius, and condemning them in the sense intended by the author.

3. [*Editor's note.*] There is some confusion here; the goddess representing sin is presumably Venus, but there is no goddess in the genealogy of Phaedra.

LEO SPITZER

The Muting Effect[1] of Classical Style in Racine (1928)

Il rase la prose, mais avec des ailes.

WHAT the present-day reader, and especially the present-day German reader, again and again finds inhibiting about Racine's style, hindering direct approach to the heart of this poetry, so deeply embedded in its language, is the frequently sober, muted quality of this style, rational, cool and formulistic, which then often, suddenly and unexpectedly, makes a transition for some moments into poetic song and form realised in experience, after which, however, an extinguisher of rational coolness quenches the shy beginnings of the reader's lyrical expansiveness. Racine, the particular Racinian quality, is indeed neither mere formula nor mere lyrical singing, but the sequence and enmeshing of both elements. As Vossler rightly says: 'To conform to custom and to remain unobtrusive is the ideal of this style, a negative and flatly prosaic aim. Racine's poetic language has no strong features. It is a secularised style, formed from worldly conversation, which attains its heights and its solemnity essentially through the renunciation of what is sensuous, rough and brightly coloured. Just as renunciation of material happiness is the guiding star of his poetry, so it is also of his language. A worldly, other-worldly chastity and apartness without equal, an inwardness and restraint which appear poor and tedious to a barbaric taste, but noble to a refined one.' 'To this strained and high-flown manner [of the images in Corneille] Racine's language brought rest in motion, gliding smoothness, and a cradle-soft descent to the proximity of earth.' 'Word-order, rhythm and rhyme work together in his case, to introduce flow and harmony into the factual, indeed sober, colloquial speech of the personages in the drama. From the point of view of the history of style, Racine has also taken over these means from Corneille and to some extent from Rotrou. ... It would perhaps be attractive to follow in detail these modest attenuations and to demonstrate them by means of comparisons.'

In what follows I should like to trace the muting effects in the style of Racine (not merely in word-order, rhythm and rhyme), not with reference to his predecessors, as Vossler suggests, in which case Racine would appear too much as a satellite of other stars, but rather as a star in his own right, a cosmos of stars which I see as self-contained, as I usually do the objects of my stylistic investigations. I leave to other scholars the task of delineating and comprehending historically in relation to their models, these muting effects which I have considered in isolation. For this reason I have added the umbrella-word 'classical' in the title, because it is precisely this muting element in Racine's style which gives the impression of refined, self-contained, exemplary and historical-seeming restraint which we, bearing German works like *Iphigenie* [*auf Tauris*] in mind, designate as classical. The expression readily suggests a piano pedal – the damper, not the other pedal which sustains and strengthens, and which is meant in the familiar image of the remark that French is a 'piano sans pédale'.

As a first muting effect in Racine's style, I would mention de-individualisation by means of the indefinite article (or in the plural through *des*). In the following passage Andromaque wishes to repudiate the advances of King Pyrrhus:

> Captive, toujours triste, importune à moi-même
> Pouvez-vous souhaiter qu'Andromaque vous aime?
> Quels charmes ont pour vous des yeux infortunés
> Qu'à des pleurs éternels vous avez condamnés?
> Non, non: d'un ennemi respecter la misère,
> Sauver des malheureux, rendre un fils à sa mère,
> De cent peuples pour lui combattre la rigueur
> Sans me faire payer son salut de mon cœur,
> Malgré moi, s'il le faut, lui donner un asile,
> Seigneur, voilà des soins dignes du fils d'Achille.
>
> (*Andromaque*, I iv 301–10)

She is aiming now at effacing her own person as much as possible: after the self-absorbed lyricism of Hector's widow has made a fleeting appearance in the triad of appositions (... *importune à moi-même*), already in the second line the proper name (*qu'Andromaque vous aime*)

features with an atmosphere of remoteness; and from this point onwards everything is said by excluding the individual case and referring
to general principles. It is no longer a question of Andromaque, but
of *un ennemi* whose misfortune Pyrrhus is to respect, of *des malheureux*,
not of the specific Astyanax, but of *a* son who is to be given back to his
mother. Or at least that is how it is supposed to seem, as if it were
not a question of the individual case; for the listener realises that
Andromaque is after all concerned about herself and her child's fate,
not only from the situation but from the relapse into the first person
(*malgré moi*). Andromaque is speaking *pro domo* and at the same time in
general terms – her feeling springs from deep within her nature; we
can sense it fermenting and storming deep within her, but almost all
that ventures 'beyond the fence of her teeth' is the general, one might
even say the juridical aspect of her case: here is *an* enemy (masculine,
not feminine!) whose wretchedness commands respect, a son who has
rights to his mother – a muted, unlyrical, mode of expression! On
the other hand the repressed feeling takes control of the linguistic
expression and strengthens the dynamic of those articles *un* and *des*
which are in principle so cold; something that invokes and insists
on the law with declamatory rhetoric can be heard in spite of all the
modesty and reserve. Feeling that has been held back and silenced,
avenges itself by making the verbal expression dynamic, by a counter-
pressure against the verbal pressure that weighs upon the feeling. Thus
we have a muted state that is laden with tensions, and at the same
time an example of the way in which Racine's language is not 'dead'
but filled with what might be called a subterranean, dammed-up
animation. I only need now to show how characteristic of Racine
this stylistic device is by various references to *Andromaque* and the later
plays. Withdrawing modestly behind the principles involved in his
case, Oreste says:

> J'abuse, cher ami, de ton trop d'amitié;
> Mais pardonne à *des* maux dont toi seul as pitié;
> Excuse *un* malheureux qui perd tout ce qu'il aime,
> Que tout le monde hait, et qui se hait lui-même.
>
> (Ibid. III i 795-8)

The indefinite article causes a certain alienation and withdrawal,
distance in fact, to appear with regard to the interlocutor. This is
all the more remarkable when within a speech this distance is, time and

again, slightly removed, and time and again brought back; the personages thus move in an atmosphere of their own, from which they sometimes deign to approach their interlocutor, while at other times they alienate themselves from him:

> A de moindres faveurs *des malheureux* prétendent,
> Seigneur; c'est un exil que *mes* pleurs vous demandent.
>
> (Ibid. I iv 337–8)

At first Andromaque proudly insists on the rights of the unfortunate generally; with the vocative *Seigneur*, she addresses Pyrrhus, the lord of her fate, personally, thereby providing the transition to a more intimate form of utterance in which her own *personal* wish may be enunciated (... *mes pleurs vous demandent*). The alternation of pride and humility in Andromaque's character is reflected in the alternation between the non-individual and individual modes of expression.

One of the finest examples of this effect of the *un*, which brings about a sense of distance in a modest, but decisive manner, is to be found in *Mithridate*, when Monime is speaking to Mithridate:

> Et le tombeau, Seigneur, est moins triste pour moi
> Que le lit d'un époux qui m'a fait cet outrage,
> Qui s'est acquis sur moi ce cruel avantage,
> Et qui, me préparant un éternel ennui,
> M'a fait rougir d'*un* feu qui n'était pas pour lui. (IV iv 1350–4)

d'un feu = *de mon amour* – but the addition of the relative clause makes it possible to insert in this clause, as if in passing and as a matter of course, an absolute refusal, concealing a dagger-blow beneath the gracefully held train of the period. It is difficult to imagine a more perfidious grace or a more graceful perfidiousness.

The de-individualised indefinite article, with its expressive muting effect (as one might put it), appears of course especially where the ego aims at concealing itself and none the less at laying claims to its rights:

> *Hermione.* Le croirai-je, Seigneur, qu'*un* reste de tendresse
>   Vous fasse ici chercher *une* triste princesse? (*Andromaque*, II ii 477–8)

or where fortuitous aspects of a relationship might have obscured what is fundamental:

> *Andromaque.* Voilà de mon amour l'innocent stratagème:
>   Voilà ce qu'*un* époux m'a commandé lui-même. (Ibid. IV i 1097–8)

'*A* husband', even though Andromaque's husband Hector is meant;
Hector has commanded *qua* husband. Although there is talk of one
particular husband, he appears in his dignity which belongs to the
abstract conception. So again:

> *Cléone.* Mais vous ne dites point ce que vous mande *un* père. . . .
> *Hermione.* Mon *père* avec les Grecs m'ordonne de partir.
>
> (Ibid. II i 405, 408)

> *Roxane.* Ne désespérez point *une* amante en furie,
>   S'il *m'*échappait un mot, c'est fait de votre vie.
>
> (*Bajazet,* II i 541–3)

These two lines are shorthand for: 'Do not drive me to despair, for
I am a lover mad with rage.' One detects a general experience, indeed
an aphorism, behind the *furioso* of the expression: 'One should not
drive to despair a lover mad with rage.' In the next case the aphorism
is specifically uttered:

> Est-ce qu'en holocauste aujourd'hui présenté
> Je dois, comme autrefois la fille de Jephté,
> Du Seigneur par ma mort apaiser la colère?
> Hélas! *un fils n'a rien qui ne soit à son père.*
>
> (*Athalie,* IV i 1259–62)

which could give, without much difficulty, in Racine's style, *Est-ce
qu'en holocauste . . . un fils doit apaiser. . . .* Or again:

> Votre mort (*pardonnez aux fureurs des amants*)
> Ne me paraissait pas le plus grand des tourments.
>
> (*Bajazet,* II v 687–8)

where the enormity of what is uttered (the jealous person is prepared
to acquiesce even in the death of the beloved) has to be mitigated by
the appeal, in a parenthesis giving a muted effect, to what lovers
commonly experience. . . .

A muted effect, which weakens the direct quality of the emotion,
is also obtained by what I should like to call the distancing use of the
demonstrative; pointing is in fact an involuntary, very primitive
impulse of every speaker who would wish to direct the attention of
his interlocutor to a matter or to a set of circumstances. Racine understands how to transform an appeal to the senses into an intellectual
instruction and to introduce a certain distance between the man who

shows and that which is shown. In a Racinian *ce* we see not so much a
finger pointing to something close, as a signpost directed into the
distance. How does this arise? From the fact that Racine causes attention
to be directed to things which are already there – by which means
they are already put at a distance. Someone who says not 'your son'
but 'this son' no longer allows us to feel the living warmth of the
possessive adjective, which as it were enfolds mother and son once
more in one body, but puts him at a distance and regards him as an
autonomous phenomenon, separate from her:

> ... je viendrai vous prendre
> Pour vous mener au temple où *ce* fils doit m'attendre;
> Et là vous me verrez, soumis ou furieux,
> Vous couronner, Madame, ou le perdre à vos yeux.
> *(Andromaque,* III vii 973–6)

Pyrrhus does not as yet fix his attitude to Astyanax; the latter will
not have any significance for him until Andromaque shows herself
compliant to Pyrrhus, and for the time being he is still 'this son',
who may be brutally slaughtered. All the hardness of which the
barbarous lover is capable is contained in the coldly neutral demonstrative, with its overtones of officialdom and general principle.

A confidante is more likely than the heroine to see 'objectively';
absence of passion is often in Racine's work the dubious privilege of
menial souls:

> Je sais de ses froideurs tout ce que l'on récite;
> Mais j'ai vu près de vous *ce* superbe Hippolyte.
> *(Phèdre,* II i 405–6)

This almost sounds as if ironical inverted commas had been provided
('This reputedly so proud Hippolyte'); only the sceptical Ismène talks
thus.

It is no wonder that the narrative of Isaac's sacrifice demonstrates
how Abraham

> Leva sans murmurer un bras obéissant,
> Et mit sur un bûcher *ce* fruit de sa vieillesse ...
> Et lui [à Dieu] sacrifiant, avec *ce* fils aimé,
> Tout l'espoir de sa race, en lui seul renfermé.
> *(Athalie,* IV v 1440 ff)

The filial relation, so to speak, is designated by the word *fils*, but the

intimacy and the self-evident tie between father and son is removed by
the distancing effect of the demonstrative; this Isaac is almost more
the *fruit de la vieillesse d'Abraham* than *fils aimé*. The demonstrative
raises the personages and happenings up to the level of the supra-
personal action of history, as the historiographer Racine indicates:

> [Faut-il vous rappeler]
> Près de *ce* champ fatal Jézabel immolée,
> Sous les pieds des chevaux *cette* reine foulée . . . ?
>
> (*Athalie*, I i 115–16)

> Nous regardions tous deux *cette* reine cruelle . . .
>
> (Ibid. II ii 416)

Athalie has become a 'spectacle', an object of historical observation,
remote from us. From the mouth of a ruler or diplomat, the emotional
coldness of the great lord who treats individuals and whole peoples as
means, as the objects of politics, is cutting in its effect:

> *Acomat.* D'ailleurs un bruit confus, par mes soins confirmé,
> Fait croire heureusement à *ce* peuple alarmé
> Qu'Amurat le dédaigne . . .
> Surtout qu'il [Bajazet] se déclare et se montre lui-même,
> Et fasse voir *ce* front digne du diadème.   (*Bajazet*, I ii 243 ff)

The possessive would have a quality of empathy (*notre peuple, son front*);
the demonstrative remains in cool neutrality that refuses to anticipate.
If someone refers to himself (to his body, etc.) with the demonstrative
he becomes estranged from himself, and this can have either an effect
of candid modesty or of cold objectivity:

> Mais, hélas! il peut bien penser avec justice
> Que si j'ai pu lui faire un si grand sacrifice,
> *Ce cœur*, qui de ses jours prend ce funeste soin,
> L'aime trop pour vouloir en être le témoin.
>
> (Ibid. III i 837–40)

> . . . si tu ne veux qu'un châtiment soudain
> T'ajoute aux scélérats qu'a punis *cette* main . . .
>
> (*Phèdre*, IV ii 1059–60)

Here too, as with the indefinite article, something protesting and
imploring, rhetorical and elevated can be heard in the use of the
demonstrative: 'This heart which has borne so much', 'This hand that

has chastised so much'; Racine knows how to place coolly at a distance
and yet again to evoke 'subterranean movement'. . . .

The displacement from the personal to the general cannot be better
expressed than through the personification of abstract nouns which
appear in lieu of personages; in Racine's work it is, as it were, not the
characters who act, but abstract forces that propel and give life to the
characters. The example provided by

> Zu Aachen in seiner Kaiserpracht
> Saß König Rudolfs heilige Macht
> [At Aachen in his imperial splendour
> sat King Rudolf's holy power]

could be exemplified dozens of times on every page of Racine, as for
instance:

> [Hermione] Semble de son amant dédaigner l'*inconstance*
> Et croit que, trop heureux de fléchir sa *rigueur*,
> Il la viendra presser de reprendre son cœur.
>
> (*Andromaque*, I i 126–8)

The mode of expression deflects us from what is direct and close
(which would have been: 'Hermione despises her inconstant admirer',
'happy to win her') and contains within itself a kind of justification by
appealing to principle: *Hermione dédaigne l'inconstant parce qu'il faut
dédaigner l'inconstance*, etc. It is no longer a question of an attitude
towards a person, but towards a human attribute.

> Ah! Seigneur! vous entendiez assez
> *Des soupirs* qui craignaient de se voir repoussés.
> Pardonnez à l'éclat d'une illustre *fortune*
> Ce reste de *fierté* qui craint d'être importune.
>
> (*Andromaque*, III vi 911–14)

Even in this scene, where she makes the greatest efforts to prevail
upon herself to meet him half-way, Andromaque does not permit her
interlocutor Pyrrhus to come close to her: his wishes and efforts can
only be shattered against the walls of personified abstractions (*éclat,
fortune, fierté*); not Andromaque, but only her pride *craint d'être
importune*, and it is not she but the brilliance of her former lot that
begs forgiveness. And even her own humanly frail utterances, the
sighs (not 'my sighs') have been made abstract and have been personified by the *craignaient de se voir repoussés*. In a similar way Phèdre, in

the passage to follow, is not depicted as a suffering woman but as the incarnation of various forces of suffering which act on her behalf (just as the independently acting Œnone, the nurse, is only an incarnation, separated from Phèdre, of Phèdre-like desires):

> *Un désordre éternel* règne dans son esprit.
> *Son chagrin inquiet* l'arrache de son lit.
> Elle veut voir le jour; et *sa douleur profonde*
> M'ordonne toutefois d'écarter tout le monde.
>
> (*Phèdre*, I ii 147–50)

An undefined power is explicitly denoted as the originator of an action:

> [Pyrrhus] me renvoie; et *quelque autre puissance*
> Lui fait du fils d'Hector embrasser la défense.
>
> (*Andromaque*, II ii 513–14)

Thus not 'he defends Hector's son', but 'an (obscure) power causes him to take over the defence'.

Consequently we arrive at a whole ceremonial of circumlocutions which cause what is personal to be blurred into the abstract:

> Oui, *mes vœux* ont trop loin poussé leur violence
> Pour ne plus s'arrêter que dans l'indifférence;
>
> (*Andromaque*, I iv 365–6)

> Sa grâce à *vos désirs* pouvait être accordée;
> Mais *vous* ne l'avez pas seulement demandée.
>
> (Ibid. III vi 909–10)

(In the first line *vous* would be as appropriate as in the second.)

> Il se souvient toujours que son *inimitié* [the Sultan's]
> Voulut de *ce grand corps* retrancher la moitié.
>
> (*Bajazet*, I i 39–40)

> Quoi! tu crois, cher Osmin, que ma gloire passée
> Flatte encor *leur valeur*, et vit dans leur pensée ... ?
>
> (Ibid. I i 49–50)

> Je crois que *votre haine*, épargnant ses vertus,
> Écoute sans regret ces noms qui lui sont dus.
>
> (*Phèdre*, II ii 471–2)

> Cependant je rends grâce au *zèle officieux*
> Qui sur tous mes périls vous fait ouvrir les yeux.
>
> (*Athalie*, I i 65–6)

> Josabeth livrerait même sa propre vie
> S'il fallait que sa vie [Éliacin's] à sa sincérité [Josabeth's]
> Coutât le moindre mot contre la vérité.
>
> (Ibid. III iv 1004–6)

There are classical models. Racine transforms a *divum inclementia* of Virgil into *pour fléchir l'inclémence des Dieux* (*Iphigénie*, I ii 187), as Mesnard has shown (*ad loc.*). Cicero says: *Suffragiis offendebatur saepe eorum voluntas*. Silver Latin provides even more 'sumptuous' paraphrases by means of abstract nouns, for instance *ubertas lactei roris* instead of 'mother's milk'.

It is well known that such modern titles as 'Your Majesty, Excellency, Eminence' have a similar origin to, for example, *leur valeur* above. With these titles as with Racine's abstract formulations, however, we can observe the tendency towards personalisation; they are no longer wholly abstract, they are on the way to becoming personal designations. We have here again one of those majestic intermediate forms between personal and official diction which have not as yet become hardened into lifeless formal pomp but nevertheless encase the soul of the personages with an armour of abstract unapproachability.

Even a locality or a specific day can appear as the originator of some action which it witnessed; not that the day or the place is 'to blame', but that it was then, or there, that the action occurred. In classical antiquity, familiar as it was with local deities and gods of the days and the hours, the personification of place references and measures of time corresponded to a living effect, almost like a formula, or at most like the reflected splendour of an inscrutable fate:

> Qui l'eût dit, qu'*un rivage* à mes vœux si funeste
> Présenterait d'abord Pylade aux yeux d'Oreste?
>
> (*Andromaque*, I i 5–6)

> *Le jour* qui de leurs rois vit éteindre la race
> Éteignit tout le feu de leur antique audace.
>
> (*Athalie*, I i 95–6)

Racine frequently permits the personification of the powers of fate, but in general he only allows a very gentle hint at fate's being the author; the personification is almost, but not entirely formalised.

> Jusqu'ici *la fortune et la victoire mêmes*
> Cachaient mes cheveux blancs sous trente diadèmes.
>
> (*Mithridate*, III 5 1039–40)

In the *mêmes* there is a hint of the mythical character of these powers (cf Rudler's comment: '*Mêmes*: en personne: prenaient soin de. Emploi tout latin (ipsae)'; and earlier '[un naufrage] Que Rome et quarante ans ont à peine achevé', ibid. II iv 570).

We have already discovered that in *soupirs*, *désirs* there is one of those contour-blurring plurals of abstractions, which inhibit too sharp a definition of the emotions of the characters. Such genuinely Racinian plurals as *amours*, *fureurs*, *flammes* are well known; for example,

> N'allez point par *vos pleurs* déclarer vos amours.
>
> (*Bajazet*, I iv 411)

> Je connais *mes fureurs*, je les rappelle toutes,
>
> (*Phèdre*, III iii 853)

But yet other emotional states are shown in unrestricted plurality:

> [L'ingrate] Apprend donc à son tour à souffrir *des mépris*
>
> (*Andromaque*, II i 400)

> Dissipez ces indignes *alarmes*! (Ibid. 401)

> Dans *ses retardements* si Pyrrhus persévère (Ibid. 406)

(instead of the simple *son retard*, which could not be put into the indefinite plural like the more abstract *retardement*).

> *Les refus* de Pyrrhus m'ont assez dégagé. (Ibid. II ii 512)

> *Tous mes ressentiments* lui seraient asservis. (Ibid. III viii 1011)

> [Je tremble qu'Athalie] N'achève enfin sur vous *ses vengeances funestes*
> Et d'un respect forcé ne dépouille *les restes*. (*Athalie*, I i 23–4)

Where a metaphor or figurative usage is employed, the plural is a weakening of the sensuous content: the indefinite plural blurs the sensuous outline of the image. The eighteenth century objected to the plural in:

> Il n'a plus aspiré qu'à s'ouvrir *des chemins*
> Pour éviter l'affront de tomber dans leurs mains.
>
> (*Mithridate*, V iv 1569–70)

('Un seul chemin tout ouvert suffisait pour éviter l'affront.') But *un chemin* would have been taken literally: the reader would imagine a road, whereas 'way' is intended to be equivalent to 'means'. Similarly *soin* would represent too palpable a care: an extended and impalpable plural of particular shapelessness is provided by *soins*:

>Déjà, trompant *ses soins*, j'ai su vous rassembler (*Athalie*, IV iii 1344)

(*ses soins* = 'her'), when compared with the singular:

>Aurais-je perdu tout *le soin* de ma gloire? (*Phèdre*, II v 666)

There is the famous quotation from *Britannicus*:

>La fameuse Locuste
>A redoublé pour moi *ses soins* officieux (IV iv 1392–3)

where these words replace 'prepared the poison'. Truc rightly says: 'Les *soins officieux* disent tout sans rien préciser et laissent dans une manière d'ombre la noire besogne.' We see a dark bustling of accomplices behind Narcisse, who is on the stage; the paucity of figures on Racine's stage is redeemed by the figures we sense dimly in the shadows.

Charmes in the plural also has a less palpable effect than the singular: 'the attractions', of a woman for the most part, leave the imagination free, whereas 'her attractiveness' would give the impression of too close a definition. (Compare Hofmannsthal's remark: 'One advantage of the French language – it can form plurals without effort from the sensuous abstract nouns: *Les fatigues, les vides, les noirs.*')

Indeed Racine has used the same word of a man (*Bajazet*, I i 138). He could do so, because by the plural the physical aspect is somewhat concealed. . . .[2]

The above material seems to me to explain why in spite of all secret lyricism and all psychological penetration we always feel something chilling, distanced and muted, and why maturity and a particular understanding of the reserved and chaste modes of expression are required in order to feel the recondite passion in Racine at all. Every reader will have noted too that single lines of our poet quoted out of context have a much more lasting effect than when they are left in their smoothly flowing setting: for instance, if one goes through the Des Hons collection of quotations[3] (which the latter only compiled at the suggestion of *his* master, Anatole France)! This experience may be explained by saying that the mass of Racine's accumulated muting devices, taken in context in the speeches of his characters, affects the listener far more strongly than the isolated display of single 'jewels' of well-tried emotional value. It can now be objected that I have in fact only analysed those elements of Racine's style which are un-poetical and repellent to us, and that the fine dust of what is infinitely great and timeless has slipped through the meshes of the stylistic-grammatical butterfly-net.

My answer to this is yes and no. 'Yes', in that I have not succeeded in providing an analytical explanation of the beautiful intertwining of the musical, syntactical, lexical, rhythmical and intellectual elements (the limitation of analysis is in fact that it isolates components which yield their specific effect precisely in their synthesis). And 'No' in that the stoical Racine must have attached at least as much importance to the muting devices of his classical poetry as to the lyrical-elegiac and directly musical utterances of his inner self, so much more pleasing to our aesthetic taste that still likes to romanticize. As Fubini rightly says, Racine was 'one of the serenest poets that ever sang'.

It is highly characteristic that the French explicators of Racine (Rudler, Roustan) make a habit of choosing those passages where one Racine character deceives another with cunning calculation, not, as would seem more obvious to me, a passage such as Phèdre's declaration of love or Esther's prayer; it is precisely in those 'scenes of intrigue' that the rational, rhetorical devices predominate which are easy to analyse, the 'mathematics of the soul', as Rudler says. For *l'explication française*, like all explanation of the poetic, though to an even higher degree than with us in German, is the rationalisation of the irrational.

It is significant that Péguy, in *Victor Marie, comte Hugo*,[4] emphasises in Racine just the quality of cruelty (which for Péguy is an indication that Racine, in contrast to Corneille, does not live and work in a state of grace) and that he would like to regard the word *cruel* (*cruelle*) not merely as a linguistic remnant of preciosity in Racine, but as a leitmotif, 'le mot même de la révélation du cœur'. According to Péguy this cruelty is deeply rooted in Racine's characters: 'Tout est adversaire, tout est ennemi aux personnages de Racine; les hommes et les dieux; leur maîtresse, leur amant, leur propre cœur.' And by the use of italics he proves from a speech of Iphigénie, that creation of the 'tendre Racine' who is known to be so 'delicate', the 'filial cruelty' of this 'daughter of Agamemnon and Clytemnestra':

> Mon père,
> *Cessez de vous troubler*, vous n'êtes pas trahi.
> *Quand vous commanderez*, vous serez *obéi*.

Ma vie est votre bien. Vous voulez le *reprendre.*

Vos ordres *sans détour* pouvaient se faire entendre.

D'un œil *aussi content,* d'un cœur aussi *soumis*

Que j'acceptais l'époux que *vous m'aviez promis,*

Je saurai, *s'il le faut,* victime *obéissante* [I would also italicize *victime*]

Tendre au fer de Calchas une tête *innocente,* [I would also italicize *une*]

Et respectant le coup *par vous-même ordonné*

Vous *rendre* tout le sang *que vous m'avez donné.* (IV iv 1174–84)

Péguy writes in this context: 'There is not a word, not a line, not a half-line, not a clause, not a conjunction, there is not a word that does not carry to put the opponent (the father), in the wrong. Racinian dialogue is generally a fight ... in Racinian dialogue the interlocutor is generally, constantly, an opponent; the characteristic of the Racinian character is that the Racinian character constantly speaks to put the opponent in the wrong, which is the very starting-point, the first principle of cruelty ... Racine's victims themselves are crueller than the executioners in Corneille' (p. 423). I believe that we may ascribe the 'cruelty' not so much to Racine's individual characters as to his view of the world, which is indeed that of someone who has fallen from grace, and which time and again observes and objectifies the human condition not merely from the position of a suffering human being, but from a rational, objective viewpoint. In the above passage Iphigénie enunciates (*a*) her submission to her father's will, (*b*) the revolt of the objective being against her father's will. She speaks with double tongue (in the most literal sense), with the tongue of Iphigénie and with that of someone objective and rational who has transcended the position of Iphigénie. In fact she gives a 'réponse terrible à son père, d'une sourde cruauté tragique', but only because the gentle tones of Iphigénie sound at the same time as the harsh reproaches of objective Reason. The putting of the 'opponent' in the wrong is looked after by the 'second voice', which Péguy, the friend of mysticism and the enemy of the political, has noted especially well; it is the voice of Reason which repeatedly in Racine drowns the voice of feeling, turning away towards the interlocutor to argue, and resulting for the listener in a 'cruel' dissolving of the emotion he has felt. All the words and phrases underlined by Péguy are indeed a constant indictment of the father (they can all be reduced to an indignant 'vous l'avez voulu, vous!'), but in fact less the complaint of an 'I' than the indictment of a 'You'; but the indictment, as in regular legal proceedings, must pay attention to the rules of reason. And a Phèdre is differentiated from an Iphigénie only by the fact that she herself is the defendant; the self-lacerating lucidity of the Racinian passionate heroine has always been emphasised. And as for the 'double exposure' to which Vossler refers in connection with *Athalie*, does it not also mean this ability to see a character in human aberration and at the same time measured against what is reasonable? Racine does not let himself be swept away either for or against Athalie, he looks at her soberly ('avec des yeux de gentilhomme ordinaire du roi', Mauriac says, recalling Nietzsche's master-morality); and he allows this sobriety to permeate her manner of speech which does not merely alternate between:

> Cette paix que je cherche et qui me fuit toujours (*Athalie*, II iii 438)

and

> Je jouissais en paix du fruit de ma sagesse (Ibid. II v 484)

but which frequently – in Racine's usual way – creates at once quiet and unrest, understanding and agitation, reflection and lyricism. . . .

SOURCE: Translated by H. M. Waidson. Abridged from 'Die classische Dämpfung in Racines Stil', in *Romanische Stil- und Literaturstudien* (1931).

NOTES

1. [*Translator's note.*] The German word *Dämpfung* and its cognates are associated in this essay with the action of the damper-pedal of a piano. I have translated 'muting' or 'muted' ('effect', 'device', 'state', etc.) as the context required.

2. [*Editor's note.*] Other features of Racine's style noted by the author in this long article, which we have been obliged to abridge drastically, include the use of: *on* (for *il*, *vous*, etc.), e.g.

On peut vous rendre encor ce fils que vous pleurez (*Andromaque*, III vii 948)

si (e.g. 'des discours si charmants'); proper names, e.g.

Pouvez-vous souhaiter qu'Andromaque vous aime? (Ibid. I iv 302)

savoir, oser, etc. + infinitive (instead of simple verbs), e.g.

Daignez m'ouvrir vos bras pour la dernière fois (*Iphigénie*, V iii 1664)

evaluating adjectives and adverbs (e.g. 'juste colère', 'avec regret'); ornamental epithets (e.g. 'heureux hyménée', 'désordre funeste'); proleptic adjectives, e.g.

Ne souviendrait-il plus à mes sens égarés . . . (*Phèdre*, I i 103)

transferred epithets (e.g. 'noble poussière'); rhetorical figures such as oxymoron, antithesis, and other repetitions or symmetrical patterns of words; and conventional metaphors (revived by various means).

3. [*Editor's note.*] G. des Hons, *Anatole France et Jean Racine* (1927) – a catalogue of Racinian echoes in A. France's prose.

4. In *Œuvres complètes* (Gallimard, 1916) IV.

R. A. SAYCE

Racine's Style: Periphrasis and Direct Statement (1952)

THE existence of two differentiated, even opposed, forms of expression in Racine has often been recognized, or suspected. Voltaire distinguishes between his prosaic simplicity and his poetic elegance:

> On a trouvé une grande quantité de pareils vers trop prosaïques ... Mais ces vers se perdent dans la foule des bons; ce sont des fils de laiton qui servent à joindre des diamants.

It is impossible to ignore Sainte-Beuve's famous dictum, which may be quoted in full:

> ... Racine, quand il y a doute, péril, ou même qu'il n'y a pas nécessité de haute poésie, rase volontiers la prose, sauf l'élégance toujours observée du contour.

Mesnard seems to have a similar difficulty in mind when he says:

> Racine, comme Corneille, mêle à l'élévation du langage la simplicité familière, mais avec une transition plus insensible de l'une à l'autre.

Spitzer also sees two sides in Racine, the uninhibited poetic outburst and the sober restrictions imposed by reason:

> ... the frequently sober, muted quality of this style, rational, cool and formulistic, which then often, suddenly and unexpectedly, makes a transition for some moments into poetic song. ... (see above p. 117).

Rudler makes a distinction between a *style d'action* and a *style de l'émotion*, the former bare and prosaic:

> Il ne rase pas la prose, comme disait Sainte-Beuve, il y est en plein;

the latter sinuous, poetic, musical. Mornet finds in *Andromaque* two kinds of simplicity, the pure and the noble, and notices that in moments of greatest passion noble ornament tends to disappear.

The object of this study is to pursue the matter further, to examine the mechanism of this Racinian dichotomy in its extreme manifestations, periphrasis and direct statement, and to inquire whether it can be resolved, whether in brief there are two styles or one.

Of all rhetorical figures periphrasis is perhaps the most difficult to circumscribe. In one sense, indeed, it does not exist, since it is impossible to express the same thought with the same connotations in other or fewer words. It is easy, however, in practice, to arrive at a working definition and to recognize examples:

> A cet instant fatal le dernier de nos Princes,
> L'honneur de nostre sang, l'espoir de nos Provinces,
> Ménecée en un mot, digne Frere d'Hémon . . .
>
> (*Thébaïde*, III iii 631–3)[1]

Racine himself draws attention to the single word, which forms the direct statement of the thought and the true subject of the sentence. Round it are grouped four periphrases, each of which could (with a sacrifice of meaning) be reduced to the same single word. Not all cases are as sharply divided as this and the two terms, periphrasis and direct statement, must probably be regarded as differing in degree. Between them, much of Racine's verse gives a periphrastic impression, without offering tangible periphrases, but this hardly comes within the scope of the present study.

The most obvious use of periphrasis is as euphemism, to disguise what is held to be beneath poetic or tragic dignity. An example is Aman's gibbet:

> D'un infame trépas l'instrument execrable. (*Esther*, III iv 1132)

But though often thought characteristic of French classical tragedy, such disguises are not very common in Racine, at least in a pure state without contributory motives. (Brunot, *Histoire de la langue française*, iv 303–5, gives three other examples, but these also are much more than mere disguises.) When Phaedime addresses Monime:

> Hé quoy! vous avez pû, trop cruelle à vous-même,
> Faire un affreux lien d'un sacré Diadême?
>
> (*Mithridate*, v i 1455 6)

we have a euphemistic account of Monime's attempt to strangle herself, but the contrast emerging from the periphrasis, between the sacred diadem and its unlawful use, seems much more important in the final effect of the lines.

The main purpose of this periphrasis, and of those that accompany it, seems, however, to be narrative. The lines occur at the beginning of the act and the audience must be told what has happened in the interval. This narrative use is perhaps the principal function of periphrasis in Racine. A few examples will suffice. When Clytemnestre changes from rhetorical argument to narrative (and from present to past tenses) she seems to fall naturally into periphrasis, of which there are three instances in two lines:

> Avant *qu'un nœud fatal l'unist à vostre Frere*,
> Thesée avoit osé l'enlever à *son Pere*. (*Iphigénie*, IV iv 1281–2)

It is therefore particularly frequent in the mouths of confidants, who are so often charged with the duty of explaining events to the audience, for example, Arsace:

> Vous portastes la mort jusques sur leurs murailles.
> Ce jour presque éclaira vos propres funerailles . . .
> (*Bérénice*, I iii 111–12)

With this narrative function is connected, almost indistinguishably, an expository function. Phaedime (again a confidant) tries to persuade Monime that Xipharès is alive:

> D'abord, vous le sçavez, un bruit injurieux
> Le rangeoit du party d'un Camp seditieux . . .
> (*Mithridate*, V i 1469–70)

This is not strictly narrative, since we already know it (cf IV vi), but it is a step in the argument, with no special emotional content or dramatic force. Similarly Paulin tells Titus that Rome

> . . . ne reconnoist point les fruits illegitimes,
> Qui naissent d'un Hymen contraire à ses maximes.
> (*Bérénice*, II ii 379–80)

Again periphrasis is used to convey indispensable argument.

If these cases are typical (and other examples, I hope, will show clearly that they are) we are confronted with the paradoxical conclusion that periphrasis is used mainly to carry narrative and argument, that direct statement is expressed mainly by indirect means. The simplest explanation of this would appear to be that in such passages, of limited interest in themselves, necessary supports rather than part of the drama, Racine felt the need for ornament which would have been superfluous where the poetic or dramatic tension was higher. It was an attempt to give artificial poetic colouring to what was essentially plain. This explanation seems partly true, but a great poet creates opportunities from the difficulties imposed by his medium, and in Racine periphrasis of this type is usually more than superficial ornament.[2] It serves above all to introduce the wide background which was excluded from the stage by the conventions of the period. A minor example of this is given by Acomat:

> Pour moy, j'ay sçû déja par mes brigues secrettes
> Gagner de nostre Loy les sacrez Interpretes.
>
> (*Bajazet*, I ii 233–4)

The spectator is given necessary information, but at the same time, by means of the periphrasis, he catches a glimpse of the fanaticism which lies outside the gates of the seraglio. A major example occurs in Théramène's report to Hippolyte:

> J'ay demandé Thesée aux Peuples de ces bords
> Où l'on voit l'Acheron se perdre chez les Morts.
> J'ay visité l'Elide, et laissant le Ténare,
> Passé jusqu'à la Mer, qui vit tomber Icare.
>
> (*Phèdre*, I i 11–14)

Here periphrasis expands a simple narrative statement until it embraces vast regions of classical mythology. In this way it may be regarded as a counterpoise to the narrowness of the décor and the restrictions of the unities.

A second main function of periphrasis is to be found in the expression of irony and of deceit, conscious or unconscious. Irony is seen in Néron's

> Quoy Madame! est-ce donc une legere offence
> De m'avoir si long-temps caché vostre presence?
>
> (*Britannicus*, II iii 539–40)

This, it must be admitted, is not specifically Racinian: periphrasis is perhaps a normal form of irony. Racine is no doubt distinguished by a superior and pitiless precision.

In this example we have deliberate concealment of thought beneath verbal complexity. There are more interesting cases where the concealment seems unintentional, where periphrasis reveals a conflict between open expression and secret feelings.

> Je sçais en luy des ans respecter l'avantage, (*Mithridate*, I i 19)

says Xipharès of Pharnace. Cold and formal expression here corresponds closely to a formal and perfunctory respect and suggests that (as we soon discover) the speaker's deepest feelings are very different. When Phèdre says:

De son fatal hymen je cultivois les fruits, (*Phèdre*, I iii 300)

the periphrasis (almost the only one, after the first four lines, in this long *tirade*) betrays an antipathy, or at least indifference, to the children of Thésée. The tone in this line is very unlike that used to express the violent emotions of the remainder of the passage.

Have these two main types, which might be called the periphrasis of statement and the periphrasis of concealment, anything in common? Clearly, though they are in some ways opposed, both appear when there is a drop in poetic or dramatic emotion: when necessary information is to be given or when a character expresses feelings which, whether sincere or not, do not come from the centre of his being. The second type too, it will be observed, becomes in the hands of Racine more than an ornament. In the examples quoted it is an instrument for the recording of emotional and dramatic nuances.

Direct statement, it is not surprising to find, performs the contrary function of expressing more than itself. It is found at the moments of greatest structural significance or of greatest emotional stress. The former occurs as early as the *Thébaïde*:

Mais il veut le combat, il m'attaque, et j'y vole. (II iv 572)

The point of highest dramatic interest in the act is emphasized by colloquial simplicity of language, though there is perhaps a suspicion of rhetorical arrangement in the ternary division, unmistakable in

C'en est fait, j'ay parlé, vous estes obeïe. (*Bajazet*, III iv 941)

This objection, however, can hardly be made with regard to a similar case in *Phèdre*:

Phèdre. Tu le veux. Leve-toy.
Œnone. Parlez. Je vous écoute. (*Phèdre*, I iii 246)

Here the language is completely prosaic and ordinary and it is used to mark the moment of supreme decision, not only in the act but in the play, from which the rest of the action is inexorably derived. It is indeed followed by new hesitations, but they seem to be made for form's sake. The crucial point of the play, structurally speaking, is here.

It is true that the line is adapted from Euripides (see Mesnard's note), but Racine lays still greater stress on the importance of the moment by means of the four short sentences and the two imperatives lacking in the original.

The use of direct statement to convey deep or violent emotion can be seen in Andromaque's

> Et quelquefois aussi parle-luy de sa Mere, (*Andromaque*, IV i 1118)

(the end of this line presents a minor periphrasis, but the impression given by the whole line is direct); or in Antiochus's

> Pourray-je sans trembler luy dire, Je vous aime? (*Bérénice*, I ii 20)

Sometimes structural and emotional elements are combined, as in:

> La Reine vient. Adieu, fay tout ce que j'ay dit. (*Bérénice*, I iii 134)

Antiochus has seen Bérénice, and the emotional key changes as a result. At the same time action is substituted for discussion. A more powerful example is

> Neron est irrité, (*Britannicus*, III vii 959)

which dominates a whole scene, dramatically and poetically. On a larger scale we have the *récit de Théramène*, which is remarkably free from periphrasis. This is narrative but of a different kind from that studied earlier. It is not expository, a preliminary to the action, but the heart of the denouement and a poetic climax. The difference is accentuated by the fact that present tenses are most frequently used.

So far we have considered the two forms of style in isolation, in order to establish their functions clearly. In fact many of the examples quoted are set in surroundings which include both forms, but it would have been impossible to demonstrate this without quotations of inordinate length. To discover the relations between them it will be necessary to examine particularly passages where both occur in close juxtaposition, which may also afford confirmation of the tendencies already indicated.

The most interesting, common enough to make a distinguishing feature of Racine's style, are those in which there is both a direct and a periphrastic statement of the same idea. Either may, of course, precede. Hermione says first of all:

> Mais, Seigneur, cependant s'il épouse Andromaque?

and then:

> Songez quelle honte pour nous,
> Si d'une Phrygienne il devenoit l'époux. (*Andromaque*, II ii 570–2)

The direct statement is the immediate, unguarded expression of dismay, the periphrasis contains calculated second thoughts, an attempt to retrieve the slip. Again there is a significant change of tense. It is a splendid example of the use of periphrasis to carry (probably intentional) deceit. And, although the psychological interest is fully maintained, there is an unmistakable drop in what may be called the tragic temperature. A slightly different and more complex case occurs in *Esther*:

> *Asaph.*   Seigneur, puisqu'il faut vous le dire,
>   C'est un de ces Captifs à perir destinez,
>   Des rives du Jourdain sur l'Euphrate amenez.
> *Assuérus.* Il est donc Juif? (II iii 566–9)

Here we have one familiar aspect of periphrasis. Asaph proposes a transparent enigma which the reader or spectator has the pleasure of solving just before Assuérus announces the solution. This, however, is secondary. Asaph, the confidant, gives a specimen of narrative periphrasis, devoid of emotion, though complicated by the wish to disguise a disagreeable fact. At the same time he (or rather his creator) introduces a picture of epic breadth in lines of almost unlimited poetic resonance. Finally Assuérus translates all this into a statement of extreme simplicity and brevity, which yet contains the emotion lacking in what has gone before. (The question in its turn becomes the basis of a rhetorical repetition (571–2), but this is delayed and does not affect the directness of the first impact.) A last example hardly requires commentary. Again the double statement is divided between main character and confidant.

> *Phèdre.*   Tu connois ce Fils de l'Amazone,
>   Ce Prince si long-temps par moy-même opprimé.
> *Œnone.* Hippolyte! Grands Dieux!
> *Phèdre.*   C'est toy qui l'as nommé.
>   (*Phèdre*, I iii 262–4)

The periphrasis this time is one of concealment (Phèdre's passion is still under restraint) and the mechanism is familiar. It is not indeed fundamentally different from the *Ménecée en un mot* of the *Thébaïde* quoted above.³ But the division between two characters and all the attendant circumstances make the device here more dramatic.

Almost identical are the cases in which periphrasis, instead of being opposed to direct statement as in the last two examples, serves as a preparation for it, as earlier in the same scene:

> ... au Fils de l'Etrangere,
> A ce fier Ennemi de vous, de vostre sang,
> Ce fils qu'une Amazone a porté dans son flanc,
> Cet Hippolyte ... (*Phèdre*, I iii 202-5)

Here we have the same arrangement as in the last example, and almost the same words (the next words of Phèdre and Œnone continue the parallel). It is a first version of the later passage, an unsuccessful attempt at discovery, in which the two points just miss coming into contact. In spite of the close similarity, however, the difference in dramatic function is reflected in a difference of style: the periphrasis here prepares for, rather than contrasts with, the final direct statement. Nevertheless, it appears that one of the most moving scenes in Racine is built largely on a double use of the same device.⁴

The use of this type may become clearer if we take an isolated example:

> Pourriez-vous n'estre plus ce superbe Hippolyte,
> Implacable ennemi des amoureuses loix,
> Et d'un joug que Thesée a subi tant de fois?
> Venus par vostre orgueil si long-temps méprisée,
> Voudroit-elle à la fin justifier Thesée?
> Et vous mettant au rang du reste des mortels,
> Vous a-t-elle forcé d'encenser ses Autels?
> Aimeriez-vous, Seigneur? (*Phèdre*, I i 58-65)

Four questions come in succession, each with the same basic meaning, revealed in naked purity only in the last. (It is unnecessary to analyse the wealth and variety of suggestion in the periphrastic questions: earlier examples show in what direction they lie.) The first three prepare the mind for the last and throw it into relief by the contrast of expression which accompanies the similarity of sense. The effect may be compared to that of a sword drawn from its sheath, or, as Spitzer puts it: 'It is as if the tutor had penetrated the manifold wrappings and reached his charge's soul.'

A case of the same kind, though less extended, is to be found in
Athalie:

> Mais quand l'astre du jour
> Aura sur l'horison fait le tiers de son tour,
> Lorsque la troisiéme heure aux prieres rappelle ...
>
> *(Athalie*, i i 153–5)

This is of limited importance, but it furnishes an example of a periphrasis of time, common in sixteenth-century poetry but rare in
Racine, perhaps because the passage of time is not usually a prominent
element in his plays. (But cf 'Les ombres par trois fois ...' *Phèdre*, i iii
191.) Here the double statement serves by emphasis to focus the attention on the moment of the catastrophe.

This periphrasis of preparation is perhaps more effective when it
is not the exact equivalent of the following statement, which offers a
contrast of thought as well as of expression:

> Oui, cruelles, en vain vos injustes secours
> Me ferment du Tombeau les chemins les plus courts.
> Je trouveray la mort jusques dans vos bras même.
>
> *(Mithridate*, v i 1497–9)

Here again the convolutions of the first two lines prepare for the
immediacy of the third, and the tension seems to rise as more direct
statement approaches; but now the closing of the paths of the tomb
and the finding of death are sharply contrasted. However, this is not a
certain case, as *en vain* gives both parts the same logical significance,
and *trouveray la mort* is itself a minor periphrasis. The finest and clearest
examples occur in *Britannicus*. In v i most of Britannicus's opening
speech is periphrastic and it is the account of an illusion, the bene-
volence of Néron, very probably an attempt at self-deception of a
type already examined. Junie's reply brings the direct statement, which
contains the harsh truth and intense emotion:

> Je l'ignore moy-même,
> Mais je crains. (1503–4)

Earlier in the play she says:

> Dans un temps plus heureux, ma juste impatience
> Vous feroit repentir de vostre defiance.
> Mais Neron vous menasse. *(Britannicus*, iii vii 983–5)

The first two lines, not perhaps a true periphrasis but periphrastic in character, are in cushioned language and they express something not essential, a preamble which reserves rights in a dubious future. The last line is direct and terrible, the sword is drawn from its sheath. The contrast is heightened by the change of tense from conditional to present and by the prominence of the verb in the last line, whereas in the first two lines the substance is contained in adjectives and abstract nouns (this seems to be generally typical of the two forms).

A different type, so frequent that it may afford another distinguishing characteristic of Racine's style, is the Alexandrine couplet divided into one hemistich; and then three, joined by *enjambement*. Usually, though not quite always, the first hemistich contains a direct statement, the remainder an equivalent periphrasis:

> Que tarde Xipharés? Et d'où vient qu'il differe
> A seconder des vœux qu'authorise son Pere?
>
> (*Mithridate*, IV i 1131-2)

> Oui, Seigneur, nous partions. Et mon juste courroux
> Laissoit bien-tost Achille et le Camp loin de nous.
>
> (*Iphigénie*, III i 767-8)

> Mon Pere la reprouve, et par des loix severes
> Il défend de donner des Neveux à ses Freres. (*Phèdre*, I i 105-6;
> cf *Mithridate*, V i 1453-4, and *Iphigénie*, II ii 531-2)

The initial statement conveys, as succinctly as possible, information about an event of importance for the action. It seems most likely that the periphrasis is a pause, which gives the spectator time to appreciate the information while throwing heavy emphasis on it. A more trivial explanation does indeed suggest itself: once the important announcement was made, it was necessary to fill out the rest of the couplet, which was done by diluted repetition. This is perhaps true, but again the great poet is distinguished by the way in which he exploits technical necessity for other purposes.

> Il fallut s'arrester, et la rame inutile
> Fatigua vainement une mer immobile. (*Iphigénie*, I i 49-50)

To the bare statement is added a picture of oars beating the waves. It will be noticed that the first part contains two verbs and very little else, and that the effect of the periphrasis depends almost entirely on two adjectives and an adverb. Moreover, the periphrasis is still narrative,

as well as pictorial, and whatever dramatic emotion there is in the
couplet is concentrated in the verb *fallut*.

> Mon mal vient de plus loin. A peine au Fils d'Egée
> Sous les lois de l'Hymen je m'estois engagée . . .
>
> (*Phèdre*, I iii 269–70)

Here the connexion between the two parts is less complete, the periphrasis is of a pure narrative type and the poetic quality lies mainly in
the direct statement. *Mon mal vient de plus loin* is another example of
what I have called unlimited resonance. The reader or spectator does
not yet know how far this ill extends, since the comparative is essentially indeterminate. His imagination is free to return to the legends
of Crete which Phèdre has just evoked, beyond them to the sun and the
origins of the world and of evil and pain (it would be interesting but outside our purpose to speculate on the effect of the three nasals). The function of the periphrasis is to stop this resonance, to limit it to the immediate occasion of Phèdre's anguish, which appears shortly afterwards:

> Athenes me montra mon superbe Ennemi. (272)

This is achieved mainly by the sense of the periphrasis, but also by the
contrast between general and precise language. A formal rhetorical distinction seems in this case to reveal something of the secret music of Racine.

Two single cases should be mentioned for the sake of completeness,
though they cannot be called types. One is simply a variation on the
last device:

> Le dessein en est pris, je pars, cher Theramene,
> Et quitte le sejour de l'aimable Trézene. (*Phèdre*, I i 1–2)

Here the division of hemistichs is 1:1:2, the second hemistich contains
the direct statement and the second line the periphrastic expansion. I
have not found any other examples, and the stylistic significance does
not seem to differ from that of the examples just discussed.

Greater complications arise in a case where, although the general
pattern is similar, periphrasis and direct statement are mixed in each
half of the couplet:

> [S] [P   ]
> Aricie à ses loix tient mes vœux asservis.
> [P   ] [S?   ]
> La Fille de Pallante a vaincu vostre Fils.
>
> (*Phèdre*, IV ii 1123–4)

a vaincu vostre Fils is itself a periphrasis, but it appears as a direct statement by contrast with the preceding line. Here we have once more a repetition in the second line, but now the two lines balance in a pseudo-chiasmus, and it cannot be said that one is an expansion of the other. Here, it will be observed, Hippolyte is telling the truth but he is constrained by respect, and the impression given to Thésée is of deception. The mixture of the two forms seems singularly appropriate to this ambiguous effect, though in the absence of corroborative examples it is difficult to speak with assurance.

The main conclusion which emerges from all these passages is that direct statement is used by Racine to carry the weight of supreme dramatic and perhaps poetic emotion and that periphrasis is used for a variety of purposes – narrative, psychological analysis, epic description, but always at a lower tension. Before we attempt to formulate our conclusions more exactly, it will be as well to consider some possible exceptions and objections.

In the soliloquy of Jocaste:

> Me feront-ils souffrir tant de cruels trépas,
> Sans jamais au tombeau précipiter mes pas? (*Thébaïde*, iii ii 593-4)

periphrasis, here combined with paradox, seems to express a moment of intense emotion and it is not balanced by simple statement in the rest of the speech. This is undoubtedly an exception to our general principle. But (perhaps for this reason) Jocaste's complaint to the gods never rises above the ordinary. A comparison with Phèdre's soliloquy (iii ii) will make this difference clear. At the time of *La Thébaïde* Racine's style was still in the formative stage.

A more serious case is Hermione's superb series of periphrases, beginning

> Est-il juste aprés tout, qu'un Conquerant s'abaisse,
> Sous la servile Loy de garder sa promesse? (*Andromaque*, iv v 1313-14)

The presence of strong and genuine emotion here cannot be contested. But in fact the paroxysm is only reached later, in direct statement (separated from this by Pyrrhus's reply), the speech which begins

> Je ne t'ay point aimé, Cruel? Qu'ay-je donc fait? (1356)

and ends

> Va, cours. Mais crains encor d'y trouver Hermione. (1386)

(This is not quite so simple as it looks, since the effect depends partly on the repetition of *va* in the preceding lines, but it is not periphrastic.)

The abbé Bremond chose as the embodiment of pure poetry a Racinian periphrasis:

> La Fille de Minos et de Pasiphaé.

This line seems to contain a good deal of dramatic meaning, as well as a peculiar poetic intensity. However, when examined in its context, it does not differ radically from other examples:

> Cet heureux temps n'est plus. Tout a changé de face ...

This is direct statement and true.

> Depuis que sur ces bords les Dieux ont envoyé
> La Fille de Minos et de Pasiphaé. (*Phèdre*, 1 i 34–6)

This is mostly periphrasis and is untrue, or at least it is not the central explanation of Hippolyte's change of mood. At the same time it is used to suggest wider horizons.

An objection which is much more difficult to meet, and which may be opposed to any attempt to characterize an individual style in a period governed by fairly rigid conventions, is that these features are perhaps not confined to Racine, that they may belong to the tragic style in general. If so, their value is not thereby diminished. However, though it would be all but impossible to prove the negative proposition that none of these stylistic forms exist in Racine's contemporaries, it does seem that not indeed the elements but the modes of combination are his alone. (Mornet gives some examples of simplicity charged with emotion in Thomas Corneille and Quinault, but when considered in their context they bear no real resemblance to the passages analysed here.)

The passages examined throw some light on the evolution of Racine's style. The features which seem characteristic of him hardly appear in *La Thébaïde* and *Alexandre*. They are, as Mesnard has pointed out, most numerous in *Phèdre* which seems to be the peak of his development (from this point of view). In *Esther* and *Athalie* examples are again rare, probably because Biblical influence produces new forms of expression.

On the other hand, there is not much differentiation of character. Apart from the natural predominance of narrative periphrasis in the language of the confidants, it seems that the most striking instances of direct statement expressing the strongest emotion are all spoken by female characters. This tends to confirm the general view of Racine's women.

The examples discussed show that there is in fact a contrast of two styles in the plays and that their appearance is not fortuitous. Each has clearly differentiated functions. We may indeed be tempted to reverse the judgements of Voltaire and Sainte-Beuve. It seems that Racine is usually most poetic when he comes nearest to prose (though we cannot leave out of account changing attitudes toward the nature of poetry). This view would, however, be incomplete. Racine's poetry is essentially dramatic and in spite of their different functions the two forms are closely integrated. Their relations in such cases as

> Mon mal vient de plus loin. A peine au Fils d'Egée . . .

or Asaph's periphrasis and the reply *Il est donc Juif?* are approximately those of a melody and its accompanying counterpoint. The direct statement gives the theme, round which harmonic variations are built. Most of the examples chosen are, it is true, particularly favourable to the argument, since we find the two in juxtaposition, but the same unity can be observed on a more extensive scale, as in the two speeches of Hermione or the great scenes from *Britannicus*.

So far we have considered these features only from a poetic and dramatic point of view. However, they may also be regarded as the expression, in poetic and dramatic terms, of a problem which exercised the minds of other men of the period, devoted to more purely intellectual investigations. In the second *Meditation*, Descartes shows the difference between a piece of wax as it appears to the senses, assuming totally different forms with changes of temperature, and as it appears to the mind in its permanent essence, and he goes on to say (in the French translation):

> Mais ce qui est à remarquer, sa perception, ou bien l'action par laquelle on l'aperçoit, n'est point une vision, ni un attouchement, ni une imagination, et ne l'a jamais été, quoiqu'il le semblât ainsi auparavant, mais seulement une inspection de l'esprit . . .

Racine's perception, a poet's, is on the other hand a vision, a touching, and an imagination, but to these normal constituents of poetry is added the 'inspection' of the mind: and direct statement and periphrasis correspond approximately (in general direction if not always in particular cases) to these two forms of mental activity.

This may become clearer if we consider the distinction made in the sixth *Meditation* between imagination and intellection or conception. Descartes illustrates the distinction by means of the triangle, which can be imagined (pictured in the mind) or conceived (analysed in terms of abstract properties, with no picture), and the chiliagon, the thousand-sided figure, which cannot be imagined but only conceived. Now it seems obvious that direct statement corresponds to imagination, in the Cartesian sense, since the object is immediately apprehended, and periphrasis to intellection or conception, where it is described and analysed. It is the balance between the two processes which appears to be characteristic of Racine and perhaps of his contemporaries.

A similar, though not identical, duality may be found in Pascal. In his essay *De l'esprit géométrique* he recommends, as one of the central principles of geometrical method, the regular substitution of the definition for the thing defined (which is normally a single word). This substitution is essentially periphrastic. On the other hand, we have the *esprit de finesse*, which disdains this cumbersome process and again seizes the heart of the problem without passing through the intermediate stages of definition and conscious ratiocination. When the necessary allowances have been made for the transposition from the realm of philosophy to that of art, we may see a similar distinction between the two versions of Hermione's reflection on the possible marriage of Pyrrhus and Andromaque. And it may be suggested, indeed, that French classical literature is in the last resort founded on such a union of the *esprit de géométrie* and the *esprit de finesse*.

SOURCE: *The French Mind: studies in honour of Gustave Rudler*, ed. W. Moore, R. Sutherland and E. Starkie (1952).

NOTES

1. [*Editor's note.*] In quoting Racine Dr Sayce keeps the original spelling, punctuation and use of capitals, because in discussions of style every detail may have some importance.

2. '... l'emploi de la périphrase ... n'est pas qu'une façon éloquente et noble de parler. Chez Racine, elle a presque toujours une valeur descriptive; elle évoque des attributs de l'objet, parmi les plus chargés d'émotion.' (M. Cressot, 'La Langue de *Phèdre*', in *Le Français moderne*, X (1942) 172.) But, as we see, this does not exhaust the functions of periphrasis.

3. Cf also *Mithridate*, III v 1059–61, and Rudler's commentary (*L'Explication française* (Paris, 1948) pp. 149–50).

4. This is no doubt equally true of Euripides, whom Racine follows closely in both these passages (see Mesnard's notes). It will be observed that in the first example he adds a periphrasis absent in the Greek:

Ce Prince si long-temps par moy-même opprimé.

This does not diminish his debt, but we are entitled to consider his choice of details from his source as evidence of his own stylistic methods.

E. VINAVER

Action and Poetry in Racine's Tragedies (1960)

(For Henri Jourdan)

WHO does not recall the brilliant case, so persuasive and so disturbing, made by the Abbé Bremond in favour of Racine the 'pure poet'? 'Being at once a poet and a dramatist,' he says, 'two claims, the pure and the impure, dispute his allegiance; onward! cry the rules of drama, *semper ad eventum festina*; while poetry would have him hover in all but motionless flight. Martha and Mary, action and contemplation, discourse and melody. Should he let himself become absorbed by the progress of the plot, his inner lyrical gift will soon fail; but this lyricism will keep the action from advancing. He must then satisfy each of the two claims – advance and hover at the same time, bustle with Martha, and yet not interrupt the contemplation of Mary. A programme impossible, if not absurd. Yet Racine has carried it out, and seemingly without trying.'

We know the aesthetic doctrine that inspired these words. Its starting-point is the desire to isolate poetry from any essence other than itself, and to demonstrate that it begins at the precise point when everything but itself ceases to exist. In the quietude imposed upon our senses there then unfolds the pure poetic mystery, ineffable, irreducible to the solid state; and the Mallarmean swan, till then a prisoner, is delivered from 'l'horreur du sol où le plumage est pris'.

Is this deliverance a gain? Has it served poetry or betrayed it? We think of another swan, the bird that Baudelaire saw, escaped from its cage and 'de ses pieds palmés battant le pavé sec'. If we deliver poetry from all that is not itself, are we not exiling it from its native lake and dooming it to drag its plumage along the ruts of the road? For this rigid division the partisans of purity would make between poetry and all that is not poetry is proclaimed also by a certain trend in scholarship – not, it is true, for the sake of basking in the poetic ray, but the better to withstand it. Thus there has arisen a tacit agreement between students of opposite approaches, all equally determined to dissociate the *essence* of the work from its *situation*, so that one group may concentrate on what is considered not to be poetry – structures, traditions or technical devices – while the others enjoy in its purity the splendour of the poem. In the eyes of the pure aesthetician, *Phèdre* is a melody rising clear above the dramatic work – a few verses or groups of verses through which the current passes, in which we catch the vibrations, 'obscures, paisibles et silencieuses', of the poetic incantation. The melody is spoken of most often as residing in a select cluster of sound-images detached from the text; *Mais tout dort, et l'armée, et les vents et Neptune. . . . Souveraine des mers qui vous doivent porter. . . . Ariane, ma sœur* – dead butterflies on pins. Moréas, who used to greet people, so it is said, with the Racinian salutation *La fille de Minos et de Pasiphaé*, loved the line in isolation, as a thing intrinsically beautiful, like a colour glowing in its own vibrations. Was he so much the victim of an illusion of our age, as not to realize that this line reached him through the image of Phèdre herself, that he heard it with all the harmonics belonging to the work in which it is embedded?

In theoretical writing, the illusion hardens, and the misapprehension turns into a system; a system which requires – to quote Bremond once more – that we should strip the masterpieces of all in them that is not pure poetry. What wonder if the criticism of scholars, in its turn, proceeds by elimination, but in the opposite direction, anxious to high-light that which does not fall into the domain of poetry? Racine emerges from this loaded with all the non-poetic ingredients his work contains: the psychological subject matter, the analysis of sentiments, the use of discursive speech in monologues or dialogues, and 'style' with all its adornments, noble and *précieux*. And as none of these is original in the seventeenth century, as everything can be found in the contemporaries and immediate predecessors of our poet, the whole effort of scholarship is directed, in the final analysis, to what in Racine is not Racine. He is of course left with the title of poet; but this very title has only a negative force; it denotes what does not interest scholarship, as his title of tragic poet or author of *Phèdre* signifies that there is in him something which does not interest the purists. If we look closely we discover that, despite the abyss that seems to divide them,

purists and scholars start from the same principle, and take their stand
on the same side of the great watershed – since each faction depends
equally on the analytical method, which considers any study of a text
as a series of subtractions made from material in which each element
can be studied in isolation.

Whereas it is sufficient to have a little familiarity with works of
poetry to know that both ideas are equally illusory – that of a poem
which can be grasped through its *situation* alone, and that of the
essence of a work perceptible in its pure state. For on the one hand, as
Valéry puts it so well, 'to make a poem which is only poetry is impossible'; and on the other hand, no poet works by *additions*, as did the
illuminators in the Middle Ages when they inserted miniatures into
frames left blank by the scribe. The moment we substitute the
notion of superimposed elements for that of a continuous tissue of
relationships, we disintegrate a structure of which each 'moment'
only exists by the support of the rest; we create a fictitious picture, like
the picture given by physical analysis of a universe irreducible to its
laws. The essential interdependence of these successive 'moments'
makes it impossible for us to consider any one of them apart from the
rest, and forces us from the outset to find a functional relationship
connecting all of them.[1] For this reason no poet, at a certain level of
consciousness, would accept that his poetry could be treated as if it
were detachable from his work. In the preface to *Bérénice*, Racine states
that he has been able to hold 'durant cinq actes *ses* spectateurs par une
action simple, soutenue de la violence des passions, de la beauté des
sentiments et de l'élégance de l'expression'. Who would venture to
pick out from that formula those terms which alone have a right to
the name of poetry? If we set up the 'poetic' in opposition to the rest,
to 'beauty of sentiments', or 'elegance of expression', the discursive
monologue or dialogue, we are in danger of refusing it what, in
Racine's eyes, was its birthright. For him, though not all discourse is
poetry, all poetry is discourse, and all dramatic poetry, noble discourse.
He would certainly not have understood the first word of the subtle
dilemmas posed by Bremond – contemplation or bustle, hurried
advance or motionless hovering. But eloquence *is* advance, if not
bustle, and eloquence may *also* be contemplation.

The dichotomy appears no less false if we pass from the dramatic
eloquence of the seventeenth century to remoter models. The tragic
art that Racine had admired in the Greeks necessarily implied a

continuous movement inherent in the poetry itself. We perceive its
nature and its progression if we think of the successive phases of the
song of the Danaïdes, or the long lament of the Theban Maidens:[2]
that lament which passes from terror at the foreign menace to a great
sweep of triumph, checked at once by mourning over the double
fratricide – an action almost devoid of matter, sketched out by a
rhythm which gradually infects the audience, the movement of a
soul in the grip of fate. And when the chorus of Aeschylus abdicates
its supremacy and allows individualized characters to have their say,
the tragic trance passes to the speaking actor, and henceforth the
responsibility is his for maintaining it. The very logic of the genre
calls forth the same kind of movement as before, which is the onward
march of life, placed under the sign of poetic incantation. This it is
that Racine means by the 'beauty of sentiments' which 'upholds' the
action, and 'cette tristesse majestueuse qui fait tout le plaisir de la tragédie'.
Neither hasty advance nor hovering. Neither Martha nor Mary.
Whether we think of *Bérénice* or *Phèdre*, it is in vain that we try to
pluck out of the moving flood some verbal felicity, some motionless
'talisman', as it is also in vain to try to think of this poetry which
refuses to 'hover' as if it were a mere bustle devoid of poetic movement.
Neither is movement divorced from melody, nor melody from
movement; each is expressed by a voice so pure that its echoes linger
on through the intervening silences, and no one can tell whether the
tragic action shapes its inflections or the voice itself describes the line
of the action. To become aware of this poetic essence *en situation*, of
this reality in its Becoming, this is the true problem we have to face –
a historical problem *par excellence*, which by definition resists any
attempt to analyse it inorganically.

A play, in Racine's age, is thought of as a series of dynamic encounters, enabling the characters to exert constant pressure upon each
other. Each scene must be, as Marmontel expressed it, 'un nouveau
moyen de nouer et de dénouer', a new way of forming and resolving
complications; each group of scenes must show a conflict between
speaking characters. In d'Aubignac's formula, the speeches made on the
stage are 'comme les actions de ceux qu'on y fait paraître' – and no
other kind of action is permitted in 'regular' drama. Thus it is that
dramatic discourse is looked on as a kind of offensive and defensive
weapon. 'Parler, c'est agir', d'Aubignac goes on – by which we are
to understand: act *on others*.

It was not the ancient world or the renaissance, but a more recent tradition that gave speech this orientation. It is the work of the French *moralistes* of the first half of the century, those who had founded in France the doctrine of speech as a form of action, eloquence in the service of world conquest. Gabriel Naudé says that he 'knows nothing exempt from its sway'. It is speech, he says, that causes the most unjust wars, veils and justifies the foulest acts, soothes and allays the most violent of seditions, or excites rage and madness in the calmest breast. This comes near to being the whole programme of oratorical tragedy from the pre-classical era onwards, be the tone violent or tender, heroic or gallant. Guez de Balzac distinguishes between two kinds of eloquence, one 'pure, libre et naturelle', the other 'toute peinte et toute dorée, plus propre pour les fêtes que pour less combats'. But true eloquence gives to her works not merely countenance, grace and beauty like Phidias, but heart, life and movement like Daedalus. She is willing to adorn herself if necessary, but is less concerned with her ornaments than her weapons: her function is to range arguments 'in battle array' and launch them against the adversary. Like war, eloquence calls for 'strength and courage, no less than arms and skill'. Arms and skill come to the speaker or writer from schooling, from the study of rhetoric, for, says Balzac, 'la bonne éloquence doit recevoir instruction de la bonne philosophie'; but 'Aristotle is powerless without the stars'; so there must be added something 'celestial and inspired', an art to make speculation accessible to the senses, to turn knowledge into action, and words into *choses* going straight to the heart of the listener. 'Born to authority and sovereignty, most potent and full of vigour,' eloquence is an arm that never fails, able not only to ensure victory to the advocate's pleading, but to confer on the ruler dominion over his subjects, and on the humblest of subjects, 'with no sceptre and no material crown', absolute power over the greatest princes in the world.

Who can fail to recognise in this cult of the spoken word the creed of the Cornelian hero, trusting to the influence of speech alone as, clear-eyed, his courage screwed to the sticking point, he overcomes misfortune and distress? In this vigil of arms, echoing already with footfalls of future victory, is it not the exultant word that conjures up the prodigious vision of a conquest over fate? It has been said that in Corneille the heroic act has its place, not on the plane of reflexion, but on that of the unforeseeable, spontaneous movement; that so soon as the hero becomes the narrator and interpreter of his act, we have moved from drama to the psychology of drama, from acts to talk about acts, from the lists to the *salon*. But the true lists of combat are surely just that zone of light wherein, with sword sheathed, the hero proclaims both his will to win and his will to be, his double conquest of self and of the universe. Surely it is just this moment of active reflexion that in fact produces acts of heroism, and exalts the protagonist to the heights of his glory and his kingship?

The same moment can be transposed with perfect ease into the non-tragic mode, where self-exaltation is replaced by hyperbolical self-assertion. Every character in high comedy aspires to this moment and strives to attain it. 'Mais enfin je prétends discourir à mon tour,' exclaims the irrepressible Madame Pernelle, thus establishing on the comic plane the prerogative of the speaking character. And if, in tragedy as comedy, each speaker has the floor until the end of his argument, it is because the aim is to give every play the character of a rhetorical contest, the rhythm of a duel. In tragedy this rhythm spreads to dominate every phase of the action. From about 1640 attempts are made to abolish those monologues that Chapelain had condemned ten years before;[3] Corneille hardly uses them after *Rodogune*. In the second half of the century, apart from Racine's works, we know no tragedies in which scenes without dialogue are not severely restricted. Everywhere the struggle is without breathing-space, unless in order to lay out arguments in preparation for a new encounter, without respite, unless to give greater force and brilliance to the speech. At the decisive moment, the carefully whetted blade, always poised over the action, descends victoriously to hasten its advance.

On a stage thus transformed into a battlefield, how should the tragic muse make her voice heard? Everything else seems unpropitious – the cult of speech as action, the arrogant confidence of language used as a means to victory, and the very rhythm of the actions, which banishes the inward-looking glance. Foreign as it is to every form of tragic vision, can this drama admit the rarest and most unmanageable form of all, that which lays in the hero's own consciousness the springs of his misfortune and destruction? And yet Racine's drama combines these two requirements, at first sight so incompatible – on the one side, characters who discover the horror of their condition, whether remorselessly dragged towards absolute clarity of vision, or led out of the illusion which preys on them into a sudden awakening which is death and silence; and on the other, a language made for battle, 'born to sovereignty', bearing within it a promise of victory. This is the language that leads or misleads them, reveals to them the weight of their destiny. How can it accede to this new function which it alone can fulfil? And when the avenging deities resign to it their power to confound and humble man, what miracle enables it all at once to take over the ruthless work of fate?

The conclusion we must reach is that this language which, without forgetting its origins, is capable of giving birth to the Racinian sense of the tragic, abolishes the dichotomy between essence and situation and forbids us to think of any poetic substance in a pure state. Far from struggling against the structures that imprison it, it strives to enter them and become essential to their life and being. It enables the work to enjoy full possession of its forms, to subjugate a refractory material to its intentions; it prevents the components from falling apart. It is poetry, which can recreate in its own image every form it inherits, and so give discourse access to tragedy, and tragedy the aid of discourse. Impure poetry, whose very impurity provides the whole pleasure of tragedy.

A glance at the plays should suffice to convince us of its presence.

When Oreste comes to tell Hermione that he has carried out her order and Pyrrhus is dead, she turns on him and disowns him. This famous scene has been held up as an example of realistic observation, a *situation-type* drawn from nature – that in which a woman punishes the man that obeyed her. Others see in it one of these furious exchanges of mortal blows so dear to the seventeenth-century public; others again, the recurrence of a theme of the *précieuses*: 'Is it better to know one's lover dead or false?' We know indeed that the 'Hermione case' was put on the stage at least twice before Racine – by Quinault and by Boyer. Each time it was the same vengeance or attempted vengeance followed by the same despairing regrets, and the same anger against the man who had undertaken to avenge the jealous mistress:

> Quoi, ses beaux jours aux miens par l'amour enchaînés,
> Par ta rage barbare ont été terminés? (*Amalasonte*, III iv)

So, in Quinault, Amalfrède upbraids Clodésile. The same fury is seen in Boyer's Arsinoé,[4] and the same in Hermione. In the true tradition this fury of an 'insensate mistress', this 'amour en colère', is turned against her avenger; and the fury of Hermione *seems* indeed to turn against Oreste, born 'pour être du malheur un modèle accompli'. But what does she say?

> Va faire chez tes Grecs admirer ta fureur,
> Va, je la désavoue, et tu me fais horreur.
> Barbare, qu'as-tu fait? Avec quelle furie
> As-tu tranché le cours d'une si belle vie?
> Avez-vous pu, cruels, l'immoler aujourd'hui
> Sans que tout votre sang se soulevât pour lui?
> Mais parle. De son sort qui t'a rendu l'arbitre?
> Pourquoi l'assassiner? Qu'a-t-il fait? A quel titre?
> Qui te l'a dit? (*Andromaque*, v iii 1535-43)

Every word, here, has a double impact, thanks to the prominence given to the most wounding elements of the speech, which are those directed against Hermione herself – what cries out at the thought of having sealed Pyrrhus' doom is *her* blood; the fury and barbarity she denounces in Oreste are her own. Amalfrède and Arsinoé only accused their accomplices. The words of Hermione strike at herself – each moment, in her mind, the consciousness of what she has willed fights against her refusal to admit it. And when at last she cries:

> Pourquoi l'assassiner? Qu'a-t-il fait? A quel titre?
> Qui te l'a dit?

we see the same process in her mind break the customary links of logic, and replace the normal speech order with a poetic disorder, subordinating in characteristic fashion the parts of the sentence to the laws of rhythm. Proust writes somewhere that in these two verses the circling, broken line of the thought does in a measure obscure the prosaic, and enhance the poetic, sense of the sentence. We recognise with pleasure here, he goes on, the living syntax of the seventeenth century, 'the very forms of that syntax, laid bare, respected and embellished by Racine's bold and delicate chisel'. This is what moves us in 'these turns of phrase, familiar even to singularity and audacity'. Nothing could be truer; but what moves us is not the singularity and audacity with which *Qui te l'a dit?* is separated from its logical antecedent ('Who told you to [assassinate him]?') and the normal, prosaic order of the questions inverted; rather is it the conformity between the line described by the bold, nervous chisel of the poet, and the secret movement, lyrical, irresistible, that rises out of the profoundest

levels of being and can find manifestation only through poetry. Hence
the pitiless light which, at this very moment, reveals to Hermione
the whole horror of the desires she had formed: a sharp flash severing
the thread of her destiny.

This then is the end of the habitual discipline of dialogue, of the
traditional use, by the dramatists of the period, of the resources of
ratiocinative discourse. No more formal fencing. The mortal wounds
are now not those received from others, and even fury loses its victorious crown of light. The traditional structure has remained intact,
but it is put at the service of the poetry of tragic discovery. And as if
to bind it better to its purpose, this poetry takes over its shapes, builds
on its well-tried foundations. It goes further still – working within
the fixed patterns of discursive speech, it absorbs them and brings
them into its own movement, as a man's expression may transfigure
the features wearing the expression, or melodic units the intervals and
rhythms on which they are based.

In *Phèdre* we find this metamorphosis at each turning-point of the
action. It will be enough to study it in two great scenes – that of the
'déclaration' in Act II, and that at the beginning of Act IV, when
Thésée hands Hippolyte over to the vengeance of Neptune. In one
Phèdre reveals her love to Hippolyte; in the other Thésée condemns
an innocent son to death. How are these things brought about? What
extorts the avowal from Phèdre, and the curse from Thésée? How
comes it that Phèdre, who could scarcely find the courage to confide
her secret to Œnone, Phèdre who shunned the daylight and trembled
at the very thought of disclosure, tells Hippolyte what her whole
being is bent on keeping from him? The report of Thésée's death has
nothing to do with it, though it provides her with a pretext, that of
pleading for a son defenceless before his enemies. There is no thought
of an avowal. We should expect then to see the poet look to the
dialogue for means to bring Phèdre to her confession. What happens?
From the opening lines, fate takes a hand:

> Le voici. Vers mon cœur tout mon sang se retire.
> J'oublie en le voyant ce que je viens lui dire. (II v 581-2)

This last line in its simplicity, its candour of self-revelation, upsets the
plan of her speech by its very harmony; it blots out both the scene
and the business in hand. It states a theme which emerges enriched

each time it is repeated by the faltering voice of Phèdre, more powerful, more penetrating, until at last it blossoms into a dream and a confession. The dialogue begins with a subterfuge:

> On dit qu'un prompt départ vous éloigne de nous,
> Seigneur. A vos douleurs je viens joindre mes larmes. (584–5)

But no subterfuge can restrain this voice, though Hippolyte hardly notices it:

> Jamais femme ne fut plus digne de pitié
> Et moins digne, Seigneur, de votre inimitié. (607–8)

Joined with this suppliant voice we hear another, firm, incisive, impassive, which, far from helping the scene to develop into a confession, seems to be striving to stifle the very thought:

> Madame, il n'est pas temps de vous troubler encore.
> Peut-être votre époux voit encore le jour.
> Le ciel peut à nos pleurs accorder son retour. (618–20)

And the two voices converse without replying to each other, as if the dialogue had renounced its right to turn every exchange into a hand-to-hand struggle and a reversal of the action. They come together for a mere instant. Hippolyte has spoken of the 'prodigious effects' of Phèdre's love for Thésée, and she, like a distant echo, says:

> Oui, Prince, je languis, je brûle pour Thésée.
> Je l'aime . . . (634–5)

The confession which falls from her lips a few moments later springs from a vision that lures her to total surrender, from a dream shaped out of her words, borne on the sinuous line of the speech. Everything here is food for poetry, determined by poetic values, although everything is said as if Phèdre, in replying to Hippolyte, was taking up his words, weighing them and expanding them. In that line which she seems to hear rather than utter – *Oui, Prince, je languis* . . . – what she says acts on her and transcends her intention. On the literal, simple sense of the sentence is superimposed a poetic sense which blots out the final words – *pour Thésée* – enhancing those warm, caressing, irresistible sonorities, *Prince, je languis, je brûle*. This strange metamorphosis engenders another as the legend of Theseus and Ariadne

is little by little displaced by a legend of Ariadne and Hippolytus, then
by that of Hippolyte and Phèdre:

> Par vous aurait péri le monstre de la Crète
> Malgré tous les détours de sa vaste retraite.
> Pour en développer l'embarras incertain
> Ma sœur du fil fatal eût armé votre main.
> Mais non, dans ce dessein je l'aurais devancée … (II v 649–53)

Borne on by the cherished vision, beguiled by the melody of her own
words, she sees herself supplanting Ariadne – the dream proceeds from
the myth and is supported by it, as Phèdre's voice is supported by the
movement of the speech. She thrusts aside the last vestige of the old
legend, the clew which might still keep her apart from Hippolyte.
She is at the brink of the precipice:

> Un fil n'eût point assez rassuré votre amante.
> Compagne du péril qu'il vous fallait chercher,
> Moi-même devant vous j'aurais voulu marcher,
> Et Phèdre au labyrinthe avec vous descendue,
> Se serait avec vous retrouvée, ou perdue. (II v 658–62)

That final line, bent on perdition, forms a cadence symbolising the
abyss opening before her, an abyss of rapture, despair and shame.

A cry of horror halts her, and brings the action back to a plane forgotten by her dream-dazzled eyes:

> Dieux! qu'est-ce que j'entends? Madame, oubliez-vous
> Que Thésée est mon père, et qu'il est votre époux? (663–4)

Brought back from unreality, speech reasserts itself and resumes its
ordinary rhythm, turning away from the beckoning quarry it had
pursued. It chooses another, innocent and reluctant:

> *Hippolyte.* Ma honte ne peut plus soutenir votre vue.
>   Et je vais …
> *Phèdre.*   Ah! cruel, tu m'as trop entendue.
> Je t'en ai dit assez pour te tirer d'erreur.
> Hé bien, connais donc Phèdre et toute sa fureur. (669–72)

This outburst, and the new turns in the action that follow, had to be set
in motion by a speech and an act of Hippolyte, just as Phèdre to
expiate her crime seizes Hippolyte's sword and tries to inflict on herself
the death he refuses to give. The logic of the dialogue assumes the duty

of bringing about the event required by the economy of the work.
But through this event, and through the dramatic action reviving like
a freshly stoked fire, there lingers on the magic of the myth in which
Phèdre had been moving, a myth which remains for ever present and
irreversible, fatal in the Racinian sense of that word. The movement
in which it is inserted takes from it an absolute significance, which
now is not that of a *péripétie*, an instantaneous deed, but a relentless
glance into the dark ways of destiny.

The scene between Thésée and Hippolyte describes a similar curve,
and it too reaches, as if by a spontaneous effect of symmetry, two
climaxes of unequal height. In Euripides, Phaedra left a letter of accusation before her death; and Theseus cursed his son and delivered him
to the vengeance of Poseidon on reading that letter, even before the
entrance of Hippolytus on the stage. The curse preceded their encounter and could not therefore be caused by it; it constituted an
immediate unreasoning reflex, unconnected to any preparation. And
it is this lack of preparation in the first place that Racine attempts to
make good from the moment that Thésée appears in the third act.
Sharing, he knows not why, the terror he inspires, Thésée recoils
before the 'funeste poison' that he senses all around him. At the
beginning of Act IV, we see him with Œnone who has brought her
charge against Hippolyte. The evidence is overwhelming – the distress
of Phèdre, the sword left in her hands; what more is needed to stir to
action the impetuous and fearless hero who has just returned from
purging the world of the tyrant of Epirus? Yet Thésée does not act.
Hippolyte appears, a dialogue begins between them, a violent, terrible
dialogue following which Thésée dooms Hippolyte to perpetual
banishment. The exchange of thrust and counterthrust in this scene
conforms at every point to the traditional pattern. Nothing is lacking
– neither the logical progression of the speeches, nor the ever increasing
violence of the attack, nor the sense of forward movement in the
language, which is the infallible sign of oratorical mastery. And yet
we know that this encounter prefaces not Hippolyte's exile, but his
death. What in fact takes place? Hippolyte asks his father what is the
'funeste nuage' that has disturbed his countenance, and at once the
fury of Thésée breaks out:

> Perfide, oses-tu bien te montrer devant moi?
> Monstre, qu'a trop longtemps épargné le tonnerre,
> Reste impur des brigands dont j'ai purgé la terre. (IV ii 1044–6)

From the first words of this tirade we feel ourselves in the climate of irremediable evil, 'des crimes peut-être inconnus aux enfers'. Each line is a ground swell pressed upon by others, and the appeal to Neptune springs spontaneously, even more passionate and direct than the appeal of the Greek Theseus because fed by a long pent-up distress. The speeches exchanged afterwards between father and son, the rancour of the one and the respectful but firm resistance of the other, all this cruel fencing is but the prolongation of that curse. What is then the secret power that causes the murderous gesture of Thésée, the blind force that makes him sacrifice his child? We see him struggling desperately against it when he commands Hippolyte to flee his wrath in hopes of warding off the blow of fate:

> Fuis, traître. Ne viens point braver ici ma haine,
> Et tenter un courroux que je retiens à peine. (1053–4)

He seems to contemplate Hippolyte's exile, an exile which would remove the danger of an irrevocable punishment. Such is the apparent, literal sense of Thésée's words, after which a tragic act would be almost inconceivable if poetry did not give them an entirely opposite value. Poetically, what dominates is the horror they bespeak, the 'horrible aspect' of a polluted son which they bring before the outraged father, the infamy to be washed away by the victim's blood alone – obsessive thoughts that call for and justify the curse, precipitating the very act the discourse seemed to condemn:

> Fuis. Et si tu ne veux qu'un châtiment soudain
> T'ajoute aux scélérats qu'a punis cette main,
> Prends garde que jamais l'astre qui nous éclaire
> Ne te voie en ces lieux mettre un pied téméraire.
> Fuis, dis-je, et sans retour précipitant tes pas,
> De ton horrible aspect purge tous mes États. (1059–64)

And this poetic charge, always at work in the depths of Racinian verse, this time submerges all that withstands it:

> J'abandonne ce traître à toute ta colère.
> Etouffe dans son sang ses désirs effrontés.
> Thésée à tes fureurs connaîtra tes bontés. (1074–6)

This is the moment of essential truth; one more triumph of a sovereign art – the art which neither rejects, nor subordinates itself to any artificial device; an art which the gods of antiquity would themselves have recognised as their equal.

There we must consent to leave the question, now that we have caught the sound of those voices which can bend speech to the secret cadences of melody, and elicit melody from the most fleeting movements of speech. A double barrier divides us from them – the illusion of Racine the 'pure poet', unconnected to the traditions of the age in which he works, and the other illusion of a writer speaking through what is not himself, summing up in himself the essential of his age, and distinguished from it only by a greater mastery in the domains of language and of stagecraft. Is it attempting the impossible to try to see him in the plenitude of his nature, to hold in one and the same view the sheer approaches to his work, the towering heights which it shares with its period, and the privileged retreats that shelter the creative energy of the poet? Not, indeed, to enter in, but to descry them from afar, point them out with a respectful finger, and take no further liberty than to contemplate them with humble awareness.

Source: Translated by R. C. Knight. 'L'Action poétique dans le théâtre de Racine', the Zaharoff Lecture for 1960.

NOTES

1. This reproduces almost literally the definition by M. Merleau-Ponty of the limitations of mathematical language (*La Structure du comportement*, nlle éd. (Paris, 1949) p. 153). For the 'presence of each moment at every other' see the same chapter, pp. 147 ff.

2. In the *Suppliants* and *Seven against Thebes* of Aeschylus.

3. For the history of the monologue in the seventeenth century, see J. Scherer, *La Dramaturgie classique en France* (Paris, 1950) pp. 256 ff. Scherer's statistics, and the contrast they disclose between Racine and contemporary tragedians, pose a problem which deserves a thorough study to itself.

4. *La Mort de Démétrius ou le rétablissement d'Alexandre roy d'Épire* (performed 1660) v iii

> Cruel, mon repentir a prévenu ta main,
> Et si ma jalousie en forma le dessein,
> Barbare, as-tu bien cru qu'un amour en colère
> Aux dépens de mon cœur se voulût satisfaire?

Cf the case of Araxie in *Arsace, roi des Parthes* by De Prade (1662, published 1667).

R. C. KNIGHT

Racine and Greek Tragedy (1951)

> *L'Abbé.* . . . . Cependant nous avons parmi nous des auteurs très excellents
> et très célèbres qui avouent hautement qu'ils doivent aux anciens ce
> qu'il y a de meilleur dans leurs ouvrages.
>
> *Le Chevalier.* Il faut bien le croire, puisqu'ils le disent; mais je suis persuadé
> qu'ils ont encore plus d'obligation aux modernes, quoiqu'ils ne le
> disent pas.   (*Parallèles des Anciens et des Modernes*)

RACINE was still alive when Charles Perrault posed in these terms the
question I should like to return to here.

The indignant Boileau retorted: 'Pouvez-vous ne pas convenir
que ce sont Sophocle et Euripide qui ont formé M. Racine?' For a
long time critics were content to repeat his assertion with embellish-
ments; and only in our own time have a few people, after taking the
trouble to read through Racine's rivals and immediate predecessors,
realized how closely he is bound up with his own century and its
drama, neither of them particularly Greek.

Was Perrault altogether wrong?

There is no denying that from the Renaissance to the neo-classical
movement of the eighteenth century, between Budé and Caylus,
Ronsard and André Chénier, Greek influence was halted in France,
allowing art and thought time to throw off their dependence on the
ancient world. Peiresc (who died in 1637) was the last Frenchman to
take all knowledge for his province. The great scholars of the seventeenth century were specialized researchers, such as Du Cange, Baluze,
Bochart, Saumaise, or the Benedictines of St-Germain-des-Prés. The
'doctes' who sought to shine in literature as well were all second-
rate – Ménage, Chapelain, d'Aubignac, Huet. The average educated
man (and the species was multiplying) left school after learning Greek
'juste assez pour avoir le prétexte de dire tout le reste de *sa* vie que le
grec s'oublie facilement'.

It was becoming possible for men to be looked on as *beaux esprits,*

poets, philosophers or critics, without having any classical culture. To
such, with their natural tendency to decry beauties beyond their own
ken, the cult of antiquity seemed a sort of fetish worship, or worse, a
cabal of pedants jealously defending a vested interest. This attitude
was one of the reasons for the 'Querelle des Anciens et des Modernes'.

And the public, ill-served by critics, destitute of any general notions
of what distinguished ancient history, civilisation and literature, and
cheated by translators who garbled the prose authors of Greece and
almost completely ignored its poets,[1] the public for whom seventeenth-
century literature was composed – Racine's public – had no real
knowledge of any society except the one it lived in, never reflected
that there had been others, and in general condemned everything in
antiquity which it considered incompatible with its own patterns of
behaviour.

The novel was only using the ancient world as a façade to mask
contemporary allusions. All the playwrights, up to but not including
Racine, had been through the school of tragi-comedy, and all, Corneille
as much as any, from about 1650 claimed the unfettered privilege of
rewriting history and legend in the interests of *bienséance*, and distorting
fact in the interests, not of verisimilitude, but of romance. It was a
good thing to have a historical source, but not a good thing to follow
it too closely.

In spite of appearances, the Greek drama had ceased to influence the
Paris stage. Its forms and usages interested at most two or three
theoretical writers, its subjects attracted nobody. True, the Latin
tragedies of Seneca still served from time to time as sources, if no
longer as models: but of plays produced in Paris between 1600 and the
beginnings of Racine which are essentially Greek in their inspiration,
we can count precisely three – *Alceste*, a tragi-comedy of Hardy, and
Rotrou's *Antigone* and *Iphigénie*. And no Greek tragedy had appeared
in translation during the period.

Among tragedians, Corneille and Rotrou may have known Greek,
but they made little use of their knowledge. The same is true of
Gilbert – of all the *Hippolytes* composed in France before *Phèdre*, his
is the only one to borrow a few details from Euripides, while at the
same time it is the version that mangles the essential data the most
deplorably. Quinault's classical reading cannot have gone further than
Ovid. Pradon never mentioned antiquity except to boast of correcting
its 'grossièreté'.

In every walk of literature many of the leading spirits – such as Descartes, Pascal and Molière – were turning their backs on the past. Among the avowed champions of the ancients, we find La Fontaine, who expresses affection for Plato but according to Racine's son was incapable of reading Greek; La Bruyère, who read it less well than he professed to; Boileau, who did indeed translate Longinus (though the translation is not very scholarly) but otherwise owes Greek literature only some of the worst of his work – a would-be Pindaric ode, and the unconvincing polemics of the *Remarques sur Longin*. Bossuet appears to have read Plato and Aristotle in the Greek, but this is a minor aspect of his activity. Of all the 'grands classiques', apart from Racine whose claims we shall examine, only Fénelon seems to me to deserve the title of hellenist.

We have always known, or thought we knew, that Racine was a better Greek scholar than his contemporaries, and so indeed he was. He went to school at Port-Royal, where the language was better taught than anywhere in France. More than that, he has left quantities of writings directly connected with his studies and attesting their thoroughness – notes in the margins of his texts, extracts, 'remarques', or translations. Do these warrant us in saying that he really gained a deeper understanding of the spirit of Greek literature than his contemporaries? Enough to stand against the tastes and tendencies of his age? And can we say that his familiarity with the classics explains, even in part, why his work so much surpasses other playwrights' of the time?

There is a well-known passage in his first preface to *Britannicus*:

> Que faudrait-il faire pour contenter des juges si difficiles? La chose serait aisée, pour peu qu'on voulût trahir le bon sens. ... Mais que dirait cependant le petit nombre de gens sages auxquels je m'efforce de plaire? De quel front oserais-je me montrer, pour ainsi dire, aux yeux de ces grands hommes de l'antiquité que j'ai choisis pour modèles? Car, pour me servir de la pensée d'un ancien, voilà les véritables spectateurs que nous devons nous proposer; et nous devons sans cesse nous demander: 'Que diraient Homère et Virgile, s'ils lisaient ces vers? que dirait Sophocle, s'il voyait représenter cette scène?'

The 'ancient' he quotes is Longinus. But does this mean that Racine had been 'formé' by Sophocles (or Sophocles and Euripides)? We have here really two interconnected problems: the standard of his Greek scholarship, and the relation between it and his work as a poet. By way of preliminary, I propose, in the following pages, to examine these points: at what period of his life did Racine read the two Attic playwrights? in what spirit did he read them? and what traces of their influence can we detect in his earliest essays in drama?

We possess seven copies of Greek tragedians annotated in Racine's hand, one of Aeschylus, four of Sophocles and two of Euripides. Though these annotations bear no date, I cannot agree with those who attribute them to the youth of the poet. The Aeschylus has the publication date of 1663; in one Sophocles, Racine has translated and commented on the note of a scholiast which reappears, with the reference, in the second preface to *Andromaque* (of 1676); but besides this there is the fact that all these annotations are quite unlike those that can be dated with certainty from the years of his boyhood studies – by reason of their handwriting in the first place, but also in their subject matter and the intellectual maturity they show.

For the studious years at Port-Royal, there is one irrefragable piece of evidence – the two volumes of Plutarch annotated and dated in the pupil's hand (1655 and 1656 respectively). These notes, abundant and quite uncritical, are for the most part simply what Mesnard called them, 'une table des matières très développée'. Some apply the expressions of Plutarch to Christian, or specifically Jansenist teaching; but the biographers who claim to read in these the schoolboy's personal reflections have assuredly not remembered what was the spirit in which his teachers worked, and what methods they used –

> Le régent doit avoir soin de faire marquer à la marge ... les sentences et les belles pensées. ...
> On engagera les écoliers à recueillir les sentences qu'on trouve en chemin, et à les apprendre par cœur. (Arnauld)

> On leur faisait voir que tout est plein de pièges et de dangers dans le monde. ... Les maîtres prenaient le plus souvent occasion de ce qu'ils trouvaient dans Cicéron et dans Horace, pour leur faire adroitement ces sortes de réflexions, contre lesquelles ils n'étaient point en garde. (Wallon de Beaupuis)

> Il ne faut pas craindre les digressions en ces sortes de rencontres, parce qu'elles vont à quelque chose bien plus utile que ce qu'on s'était d'abord proposé. ... Un des Conciles de Milan exhorte fort les maîtres à tourner toujours, du côté de la piété et des bonnes mœurs, tout ce qu'ils trouveront dans les auteurs profanes qui pourra y avoir du rapport. (Coustel)

These notes on Plutarch by Racine are school exercises, inspired, if not actually dictated, by a master who was never far from his side.

Beside these Plutarchs, the Greek studies that can be attributed to Racine's youth are: his extracts from St Basil, his translations of Josephus, Philo Judaeus and Eusebius, and notes in the margins of Plato and the *Nicomachaean Ethics*. All bear the sign-manual, or so to speak the *imprimatur*, of Port-Royal; nothing has any bearing on any work of imagination, nor on poetry (though Racine certainly had to study at least the Latin poets).

Did he read nothing else in Greek, nothing more attractive and at the same time more useful to the future poet? We know the legend of the two copies of Heliodorus confiscated and burnt by Lancelot, and the other story of hours spent reading Sophocles and Euripides 'in the woods round the pool of Port-Royal': neither, of course, can be refuted, but the few positive data at our disposal do not tend to support them. Or rather, paradoxical as it may seem, they tend to confirm the story of the long Greek novel 'learnt by heart', rather than that of the readings in the woods. When, in 1662 (another certain date, since we have it in his own hand), Racine wrote his *Remarques* on the first ten books of the *Odyssey*, he referred several times to Heliodorus, quoting also seven other Greek writers, but not even mentioning Sophocles or Euripides. Their bare names occur in his writings for the first time in 1666 (*Lettre à l'auteur des Imaginaires*).

If now we open the copies of the two tragedians in which his notes appear (as for Aeschylus, at that time little understood or appreciated, Racine's notes on him contain nothing very significant), we shall notice first how often he picked out felicities of expression, appreciative as always of 'sentences' or 'beaux sentiments':

> Arrêter les ailes de ses soupirs.

> Metaph: *pascitur in suis campis.*

> Les espérances ont une Vénus ...

At the same time he looks closely at the portrayal of characters and passions, studying the devices by which the dramatist displays them. Thus,

> Au milieu de la douleur d'Electra et des regrets qu'elle fait sur la mort d'Oreste, Chrysothémis vient lui dire qu'il est venu. Cela fait un fort bel

effet. Car les regrets d'Electra sont interrompus, et sa douleur n'en devient
que plus violente. Ainsi la pitié va toujours en s'augmentant . . .
Dispute des deux sœurs.
Leur caractère paraît bien ici. L'une est intrépide et fière, l'autre timide,
mais honnête, et sans perdre le respect . . .
Oreste vient lui-même, apportant le vase où il dit que sa cendre est
enfermée. Il s'adresse à Electra. C'est le dernier période de sa [her] douleur, et où le poète s'est épuisé pour faire pitié. Il n'y a rien de plus beau
sur le théâtre que de voir Electra pleurer son frère mort en sa présence, qui
en étant lui-même attendri, est obligé de se découvrir . . .
Reconnaissance d'Oreste. Cette reconnaissance est merveilleusement
pathétique et bien amenée de parole en parole, en se répondant tous deux
fort naturellement et tendrement . . .
Il représente dans Electra une joie aussi immodérée que sa douleur était
excessive . . .

Here – as also in Homer – he finds picturesque dramatic effects which
he appreciates and notes, although they are never employed in his own
plays:

Sophocle a un soin merveilleux d'établir d'abord le lieu de la scène. Il se
sert pour cela d'un artifice très agréable, en introduisant un vieillard qui
montre les environs du palais d'Argos à Oreste, qui en avait été enlevé tout
jeune. Le *Philoctète* commence à peu près de même: c'est Ulysse qui
montre à Pyrrhus tout jeune l'île de Lemnos . . . L'*Œdipe Colonéen* s'ouvre
par Œdipe aveugle qui se fait décrire par Antigone le lieu où il est. Ces
trois ouvertures, quoique un peu semblables, ne laissent pas d'avoir une
très agréable diversité et des couleurs merveilleuses.

(On Sophocles' *Electra*.)

In the same way he notes the actions and speeches of the chorus, and
even a description (which he found in a commentary) of its movements
in the orchestra during the *stasima* – that chorus which a (no doubt
unexpected) stroke of fortune was to enable him to use one day
himself on an amateur stage. In spite of this, he reads the Greeks –
and we can see it more clearly here than in the *Remarques sur l'Odyssée*,
for here he is studying predecessors in his own genre – with the eyes
of a man of his own day: he divides the text into 'acts' and 'scenes',
he studies the way incidents are 'prepared', the invention of 'couleurs'
to motivate the entries and every action of the characters:

Acte 1er, scène 1re. Le pédagogue explique le lieu de la scène, le temps et
le sujet même.

La scène est devant la porte du palais d'Agamemnon.
Pylade est présent.
Lever du soleil . . .
Oreste explique tout le sujet qui le fait venir . . .
Oreste rapporte le commandement de l'oracle pour préparer le spectateur
à n'avoir pas tant d'horreur de tout ce qu'il vient faire.
Nœud de la fable.
Scène 2. Electra vient seule, et ils s'en vont pour n'être point vus . . .
Elle rend raison pourquoi elle vient pleurer hors du logis . . .
Scène 3ᵉ. Chœur de filles qui viennent pour la consoler.
Le Chœur est de filles d'Argos . . .
Scène 4ᵉᵐᵉ. Chrysothémis vient . . .
Elle sort pour aller porter des offrandes au tombeau d'Agamemnon . . .
Songe de Clytemnestre.
Ce songe de Clytemnestre vient bien au sujet, pour envoyer Chrysothémis
au tombeau d'Agamemnon, où elle trouve des cheveux d'Oreste, qui y a
été aussi: ce qui fait un fort bel incident . . .
Chœur tout seul.
Il semble pourtant qu'il adresse sa parole à Electra, qui ne rentre point dans
la maison durant toute la prière; et il y a apparence qu'elle se promène
devant la porte, sans s'en éloigner, comme on peut voir par le premier vers
de Clytemnestre . . . (Ibid.)

In the first preface he published, Racine claimed that 'tous mes
acteurs ne viennent point sur le théâtre que l'on ne sache la raison qui
les y fait venir'. Here he finds this rule being observed by Sophocles –
though it was never formulated as a rule, to my knowledge, before
d'Aubignac and Corneille.

The same attitude of mind makes him pick out in Sophocles,
wherever he meets it, that respect for verisimilitude which Aristotle
had advocated in plot-construction, but which seventeenth-century
theorists insisted on unrelentingly 'dans les moindres actions re-
présentées au théâtre'. This search for realism Racine expects to find in
Sophocles too – and he finds it, even where Greek convention required
the introduction of song and dancing. The third choric song in *Ajax*
refers to 'dances learnt without a teacher': this, Racine notes, is 'pour
excuser la danse d'"un chœur de soldats, qui ne doit point avoir appris
à danser' !

Annotating Sophocles, Racine keeps up the tone of respectful admiration. Euripides, on the other hand, he criticizes without a qualm. His
long series of notes on *Medea* picks up every point that seems to him

weak or awkward, every incongruity in the tone, every violation of
tragic dignity on the one hand, or simplicity on the other:

La nourrice de Médée fait le prologue ...
Scène 1. Le gouverneur des enfants de Médée les amène sur la scène.
Ainsi tout le sujet est expliqué par une nourrice qui s'entretient avec un
pédagogue. Ils s'en acquittent bien et par de beaux vers; mais je doute que
Sophocle eût voulu commencer une tragédie par de tels personnages ...
Cette moralité est agréable, mais peu tragique ...
Pourquoi cette moralité, au lieu de dire simplement: Je sors, puisque vous
avez souhaité de me voir ... ?
Malheurs des femmes [This is Medea's great speech.]
Nous achetons un maître bien cher.
Tout cela est plus comique que tragique, quoique beau et bien exprimé ...
Médée rentre dans le sujet ...

In the poet's *Phoenician Maidens*, he pauses at the places where the
unity of action seems to him endangered:

[The scene with Antigone on the ramparts] n'est point de l'action; mais
le poète a voulu imiter une chose qui est belle dans Homère, l'entretien
d'Hélène et de Priam sur les murs de Troie ...
Ces interrogations [by Jocasta] ne sont point nécessaires au sujet; mais
elles sont tendres et du caractère d'une mère. ...
Ceci est un peu plus du sujet. ...
Cette scène [between Creon and Eteocles] est languissante, et n'est point
nécessaire au sujet. ...
Cette scène de Tirésias n'est point assez nécessaire pour intéresser. ...
Ceci rentre dans le sujet. ...
Cette petite scène est du sujet, et elle est tendre. ...
Ce chœur est plus du sujet que les autres. ...
Le reste de la pièce [after the account of the two brothers' deaths] est
inutile et même languissant. ...

For Racine – whether he really thinks so, or simply echoes at times
the ideas of Aristotle and his French disciples – drama cannot indis-
criminately admit every kind of pathetic or poetic beauty. To quote
from a preface, 'On ne peut prendre trop de précaution pour ne
rien mettre sur le théâtre qui ne soit très nécessaire. Et les plus belles
scènes sont en danger d'ennuyer, du moment qu'on les peut séparer
de l'action, et qu'elles l'interrompent au lieu de la conduire vers sa
fin.'
Are we not forced to admit that, for all his sureness and delicacy of

taste, Racine to some extent reads Sophocles, and even more Euripides, in the light of Aristotelian rules they never knew? and sometimes even – dare one hint it? – in the light of the rules of d'Aubignac? Even over his Greek books he remains in thought and feeling (as how should he not?) a Frenchman of the seventeenth century. It now remains to be seen how far he could shake off these contemporary influences when he composed his first tragedies.

It has been shown that Racine's serious and productive reading of Greek plays seems to have taken place later than his visit to Uzès in 1661 to 1662 or 63 – later also, therefore, than the beginnings of his career as a dramatist. It should be recalled at the same time that, in his dramatic work, the tangible and incontrovertible traces of strong Greek influence are all grouped at the end of that career – in *Iphigénie* and *Phèdre*, with their Euripidean plots, in *Esther* and *Athalie*, with the introduction of a chorus. What are we to say in this respect of his early works?

While he lived with Canon Sconin at Uzès, preparing for the tonsure and spending some of his leisure copying out extracts of Virgil, Horace, Pliny the Elder and Cicero, and later making commentaries on Pindar and the *Odyssey*, his correspondence is composed of lively epistles in the Voiture vein, studded with light verse; they are written to be handed round, and he knows that they 'courent les rues'. They are full of quotations of Ariosto (in 1661), Virgil (particularly in 1662), and several other poets, Latin and French. But it would have been out of place to talk of scholarship; except to give a half-joking account of the austerity of his life in Uzès, Racine does not write a word about his studies. Of the five tongues with which Le Vasseur credits him, Greek is the only one never employed in this correspondence. 'Il y a assez de pédants au monde sans que j'en augmente le nombre.'

The young wits he addresses in this style are the same who counsel him in his earliest literary ventures. Le Vasseur it was who had 'prescrit des règles' for the (lost) sonnet to Mazarin, Le Vasseur and Racine's 'cousin' Vitart who sponsored *Amasie* at the Marais, and Vitart who took *La Nymphe de la Seine* to show to Chapelain and Perrault. La Fontaine, to whom, bashfully, Racine sent *Les Bains de Vénus* for comment, was not as yet even the author of the *Contes*.

And his poetic ventures up to this time had been exactly suited to the company he kept. He writes two sonnets, three occasional odes in the manner of the day, the melodious and empty *Stances à Parthénice, Les*

Bains de Vénus, of which the title, and a few allusions that have been preserved, tell us all we need to know. . . .

These verses make plentiful use of mythology, but it is the mythology of courtly gallantry:

Plaisirs, Jeux, Grâces, Ris, Amours, (*Ode sur la convalescence*, 2)

with Mars, 'la Vertu', 'la Victoire', Venus and her 'court', the Nymph of the Seine attended by naiads (and Tritons too, till Chapelain had them taken out because they are not fresh-water creatures). It is the same style in the letters: 'Je jure par toutes les divinités qui président aux prisons (je crois qu'il n'y en a point d'autres que la Justice, ou Thémis en termes de poètes).' In short, a conventional mythology in which M. Chapelain could give points to Jean Racine.

Clearly at this time Racine was leading a double life: on the one hand still trying to please his grandmother and aunt the nuns, his uncle the Canon, and his old masters the *Solitaires*, while on the other 'il se fait loup avec les loups'.

His classical interests still seem to belong exclusively to the Port-Royal half – he owed them to Port-Royal, and of all his private tastes it was very likely the only one he dared indulge without alarming his mentors. Probably he translated Josephus, Philo and Eusebius to please them (unless it was the ex-Jansenist Duc de Luynes). Nor need he feel any hesitation in letting the good Canon look over his *Remarques sur l'Odyssée*.

But the theatre, with practically the whole of present-day poetry, belonged inevitably to the other side, the worldly and forbidden side, of life. When he talked plays, went to plays, or planned plays, it was with Le Vasseur, La Fontaine and Vitart. But Port-Royal had willed it so. It did not take the famous letter of Mère Agnès to tell him that actors were 'des gens dont le nom est abominable à toutes les personnes qui ont tant soit peu de piété', nor the *Visionnaires* to prove that Nicole looked on playwrights as 'public poisoners'.

The Racine of these years is then a budding Greek scholar – budding, since it is not certain that he has so far advanced his studies at all in the one direction in which they are destined to bear fruit. And he is a budding dramatist. But no bridge has been established between the two virtualities which divide his intellectual life. We cannot call him, at the outset, a dramatist under Greek influence.

Or, if there is a Greek influence discernible in these years, it is not that of Euripides, but Heliodorus. We have only to look at the titles of

the still-born dramatic projects of 1661–3. The correspondence refers
to two; Grimarest and Louis Racine add the third. They are: *Amasie*,
from a source in Ovid, or perhaps Heliodorus; *Les Amours d'Ovide*;
and *Théagène et Chariclée* (the hero and heroine of Heliodorus' novel).
I have studied elsewhere the very suggestive coincidence in date
which seems to connect two of these uncompleted projects with two
plays, performed in Paris, by Gabriel Gilbert:

> June 1661: Racine is preparing to write *Les Amours d'Ovide* for the
> Hôtel de Bourgogne.
> July 1662: the Palais Royal puts on Gilbert's *Théagène* (a lost play,
> presumably a pastoral).
> June 1663: the Hôtel de Bourgogne puts on *Les Amours d'Ovide*, a
> *pastorale héroïque* by Gilbert.
> 1663: Racine considers writing – or writes – a *Théagène et Chariclée*.

It seems possible that Racine's *Théagène* was conceived as a reprisal
against this *précieux* poet who had succeeded in getting his own *Ovide*
accepted (a complete travesty of the subject in the taste of the day), in
the place of the laboriously documented work that Racine was never
able to finish; and I suggested that this disappointment inflicted,
perhaps unwittingly, by Gilbert, had the effect of strengthening in
our poet, *par esprit de contradiction*, his attachment to historical truth or
literary sources. This attachment is visible already in his letter describing his preliminary work on Ovid, and none of his prefaces written
later fails to mention it. The same sort of thing happened a few years
later, I believe, when his quarrel with Corneille served to confirm him
in the principles most directly opposed to his opponent's practice.

Can it be, then, that Gilbert's good offices were responsible for the
first step towards a *rapprochement* between the scholar and the playwright in Racine?

The second step may have been due to Jean Rotrou.

To understand *La Thébaïde*, we must not place too much reliance
on the preface, written twelve years later. Racine was by then the
author of *Iphigénie*, and we can see him endeavouring to place his
earliest play under the aegis of the Greek tragedian to whom he had
owed his recent triumph. 'Je dressai à peu près mon plan sur les
Phéniciennes d'Euripide. Car pour la *Thébaïde* qui est dans Sénèque' –
it does not deserve, he says, the name of tragedy.

We need not go to the other extreme, and give credence to the tales of Grimarest, La Grange-Chancel and Brossette, according to which Molière had 'donné le plan' of the tragedy to the young poet, advising him to 'rajuster' the *Antigone* of Rotrou. But the proof that Racine was 'asked' to write *La Thébaïde*, and submitted all its scenes to the scrutiny of 'friends' whose names are unknown, lies in the preface and Racine's letters of 1663. And on the question of its sources, the indulgent Mesnard delivered a judgement, a full century ago, which only the blindest prejudice could call in question:

> Ce que l'on remarque sans peine dans sa *Thébaïde*, c'est l'imitation directe de Rotrou pour la conception et la composition de plusieurs scènes, comme pour les détails du dialogue; beaucoup de traits heureux, et vraiment tragiques, fournis par Sénèque; enfin l'influence de Corneille. . . .
>
> Le plan d'Euripide ne ressemble nullement à celui de Racine. L'entrevue de Jocaste et de Polynice, et la scène de la conférence des deux frères, en présence de leur mère, voilà tout ce que l'on trouve de commun entre la pièce grecque et la nôtre.

There is then, after all, one scene at least (the last in Act IV) derived directly from Euripides. Racine seems to have believed what he states in his preface, that Rotrou had used this scene before him: in fact, he had not. There is irony in the thought that the older writer led his imitator to look into the Greek source that he himself had been too hurried or too incurious to consult – and thus, for all we know to the contrary, to open Euripides for the first time.

La Thébaïde is certainly a first attempt at collaboration between Racine the Greek scholar and Racine the poet, but no more than that. It owes more to Seneca than to Euripides, and more to Rotrou than to Seneca. The handling of the plot and the psychology of the characters – with Hémon hazarding and losing his life for the love of his princess, and Créon moved by ambition to inflame the hatred between the two brothers – owe nothing to antiquity. The sombre atmosphere, the theme of destiny and that of the injustice of the gods, these are to be found in every Senecan tragedy of the seventeenth century, including the still recent *Œdipe* of Corneille.

The second tragedy, *Alexandre*, has nothing Greek in it beyond the name of its hero and, if we like, its relative simplicity of action:

> Enfin la plus importante objection que l'on me fasse, c'est que mon sujet est trop simple et trop stérile. Je ne représente point à ces critiques le goût de l'antiquité. Je vois bien qu'ils le connaissent médiocrement. (First preface)

But, in the absence of any more precise reference and any trace of actual influence, it is more natural to see in these phrases an echo of the attacks which d'Aubignac had recently been making on the *Sertorius* and *Sophonisbe* of Corneille and their 'polymythie', in his *Dissertations* of 1663.

Racine treats his historical sources (it is true that they include Greek writers as well as Quintus Curtius, the only name cited in the preface) with a mixture of respect and casualness – the authentic utterances of Porus and Alexander have been retained, the battle which ends the play did in fact take place; but of the two princesses who inspire the action, one, Axiane, never existed, and the other, Cléophile, never met either Taxile or Porus. The two great rivals, both equally 'tendres' and 'généreux', are heroes out of novels or tragi-comedies. All picturesque touches, all concrete details, connected with the invasion of India have been sacrificed, just as all the atmosphere of Greek legend is missing in *La Thébaïde*.

Assuredly, in later works, the contribution of the Greek scholar becomes more pronounced.[2] But in his earliest plays he was scarcely more 'Greek' than Corneille – only a little different from Rotrou or Gilbert. We cannot say that the first two plays show his art or his taste to have been 'formés' by familiarity with Sophocles and Euripides.

SOURCE: Revised and translated by the author from 'Sophocle et Euripide ont-ils "formé" Racine?' in *French Studies*, v (1951).

NOTES

1. Of the sixteenth-century translators, only Amyot was still popular. The first Homer appeared in French in 1681, the first two tragedies of Sophocles in 1692. Aeschylus and Euripides were not available in French. But all Greek writers had been translated into Latin – usually literally and without elegance.

2. Not very much in *Andromaque*, and very little in the plays from *Britannicus* to *Mithridate*. Why a change occurred then, is another question, still obscure (see my *Racine et la Grèce*, ch. XXVI). The bigger question, what Greek literature contributed to Racine's conceptions of tragedy, to his poetic powers, or simply to his pre-eminence in his field, has never been satisfactorily answered, and perhaps never will be. It is too hard, for one thing, to be sure quite what he saw in it.

JULES BRODY

Racine's *Thébaïde*: an analysis (1959)

THE indifference with which Racine's first play is usually treated cannot be accounted for merely by the number of its defects. One wonders what would have been the fortunes of *La Thébaïde* had it not been fated to languish in the shadow of *Andromaque* and *Phèdre* – had it been allowed to follow the laws of natural selection among its peers. Would we not, perhaps, view *La Thébaïde* more kindly if it had crowned the career of a Rotrou, or even a tottering Corneille? People seem not so much dissatisfied with the play itself as with Racine for having written it.

La Thébaïde has been disparaged in a unique way. It is not scorned as Babbitt scorned Rousseau, or Brunetière the Naturalists. It is disdained discreetly, benevolently, with the deference that no one would wish to refuse the poet of *Phèdre*. Critics seem to have been more bent on showing why *La Thébaïde* is un-Racinian than on studying it and understanding it as drama.

It was once possible to say that Racine did not really have his heart in this first venture, that the subject and even the structure of the play had been suggested by Molière. Although this view has been discredited by Mesnard, it is still not uncommon to hear that *La Thébaïde* was conceived under the influence of the declining Corneille. One critic (Carrington Lancaster) has even been prepared to say that Racine chose a Greek subject because his elder had dramatized the Oedipus and Golden Fleece legends a few years earlier. But with his thorough classical culture might not Racine have gone to Greek antiquity almost instinctively? Would he have needed the example of Corneille? Those who see the theme of *La Thébaïde* as primarily political are able to make a somewhat better case for Cornelian influence. But they assume exactly what requires to be proved. For no

one has ever shown that the theme of Racine's play is primarily
political, or that the spirit, inspiration and tragic focus of *La Thébaïde*
are at all in Corneille's heroic vein.

Racine's first play surely owes something to Corneille. That this
should be so was perhaps inevitable. But this fact is hardly as important
as it has been made out to be. While the assertion of Corneille's influence, serving as a convenient peg on which to hang *La Thébaïde*,
does much to satisfy the historian's love of order, it does little to
illuminate the problems raised by a close and honest reading of the play
itself. It will never tell us, for example, what Racine could have meant
when he described *La Thébaïde*, a good many years after its composition, as 'le sujet le plus tragique de l'antiquité' (Preface). And yet
this question is basic. It leads one to ask whether this youthful work
does not contain the elements of the poet's mature tragic vision. It
leads one to ask also whether *Andromaque* is really Racine's first 'Racinian' tragedy.[1]

Those who have studied the relation of *La Thébaïde* to earlier versions
have been more interested in alleging 'influences' than in laying bare
differences. The researches of Mesnard and Lancaster furnish between
them a substantial catalogue of lines imitated, similarities in plot and
characterization, and parallels in style and structure. But these facts,
however valuable, are of necessity disconnected, and tell us little in the
end about what could be called Racine's *interpretation* of the Theban
story. One still wants to know in what way, if at all, Racine departed
from his originals. The question is whether we can view *La Thébaïde* –
as we do, say, Gide's *Œdipe* or Giraudoux's *Électre* – as a reinterpreta-
tion of an ancient legend, having a different emphasis, a fresh view of
human motives, and a reorientation of tragic interest.

The sources usually given for *La Thébaïde* are Euripides' *Phoenician
Maidens*, a fragment by Seneca bearing the same title, and Rotrou's
Antigone. There are also two sixteenth-century versions, which Racine
probably did not use: Garnier's *Antigone, ou La Piété* (1580) and Jean
Robelin's *La Thébaïde* (1584). It is doubtful too whether he owes anything to Statius' *Thebais*. Modern authorities still agree with Mesnard
that Racine drew more than he admits from Seneca and Rotrou, and
less from Euripides than is implied in his preface.

The lines from Seneca which Mesnard reproduces in his notes may
well have inspired certain lines in *La Thébaïde*. But the *Phoenissae* as a
play can contribute little, if anything, to our knowledge of Racine's

intimate conception of his subject. Although the recurrence of words like *cruor, sanguis, scelus, odium*, etc., suggests that Seneca's version had stressed themes which prove to be central in Racine, the fragmentary, formless state in which it has come down precludes our viewing it as a total interpretation of the Thebaid legend.

Euripides' *Phoenician Maidens* stresses a theme that is barely discernible in *La Thébaïde*: the fortunes of Oedipus. Eteocles and Polyneices 'have confined their father closely, that his misfortune . . . might be forgotten'. Enraged at their impiety, Oedipus heaped 'most unholy curses on his sons, praying that they may have to draw the sword before they share [his] house between them'. The struggle between these *frères ennemis* is conceived of as a further episode in the life of Oedipus the King.

In Aeschylus' *Seven against Thebes* the city itself had been the principal character. *The Phoenician Maidens* reflects this tradition. By contrasting the patriotism of Menoeceus with the selfishness of Creon and his nephews, Euripides keeps the civic theme well in the foreground. The young hero's suicide was, so to speak, a political act: he died that an ancient city might live. In the minds of the other characters his death marks a signal phase in the historical cycle that began with Cadmus, the city's founder (see especially lines 930–41 and the penultimate choral ode, lines 1019 ff). The sacrifice of Menoeceus, moreover, was ordered by Teiresias who, Euripides was careful to specify, had just come from restoring peace to Athens. His role in *The Phoenician Maidens* is that of the professional saver-of-cities.

The emphasis in *The Phoenician Maidens* falls on Oedipus and Thebes. The absence of these two motives in *La Thébaïde* indicates that Racine intended a radical shift of dramatic interest. By the time the play begins Oedipus is dead. He is mentioned by name only three times (lines 83, 406, 430). If the father of the *frères ennemis* has any importance in Racine's play, it is as a symbol rather than as a person.

The references to Thebes are also perfunctory. Eteocles evokes the city and *le peuple* in arguing that his régime has popular support. But this is as far as it goes. There is no mention of the Cadmus legend; the war between the Thebans and the Argives, which had epic importance in Euripides, is reduced to a minor incident. Racine depicts the colourful Thebes of mythology in its most indistinct outlines. In his treatment of Menoeceus' suicide there is no trace of the civic theme which had loomed so large in Euripides.

The Phoenician Maidens has an unusual length of 1766 lines. But only
192 of these are devoted to Eteocles and Polyneices, who came face to
face at line 446 and part company at line 637. Their resolve to meet in
single combat is reported some 600 lines later and their fatal duel is
narrated by a messenger in a speech ending at line 1479. (In his copy of
Euripides Racine noted at this point: 'Le reste de la pièce est inutile et
même languissant'. It is impossible to determine whether these notes
were made before or after the writing of *La Thébaïde*.) The last part
of the play centres on Creon, Antigone and Oedipus. The theme of
the warring brothers barely constitutes one-third of the action. In
Euripides there is no hint of the capital scene where Racine will make
Eteocles express his fratricidal hatred of Polyneices. Jocasta's illumination which Racine was to prepare at such great length does not occur
at all in *The Phoenician Maidens*. Her death is merely reported by a
messenger.

A glance at Rotrou's *Antigone* dispels all doubts of Racine's complete
independence of his predecessors with respect, at least, to interpretation,
tone, and dramatic purpose. Though *Antigone* and *La Thébaïde* have
the same point of departure, they are oriented in different directions.
In fact, the point of departure is all they have in common.

The respective titles of the two plays indicate where the divergence
occurs. Rotrou wanted to write a play about Antigone. His first
concern was to dispose of the enemy brothers early in order to reach
his real subject. (The outcome of their single combat is related in III
ii.) Rotrou needed survivors to act out the conflict over Polyneices'
burial. Racine, on the other hand, wanted to build a complete drama
around the Eteocles–Polyneices feud, and was interested in delaying
their fatal meeting as long as he could. In each play the brothers are
brought together at a different time and for a different purpose. In *La
Thébaïde* their meeting marks the culmination of a tragedy; in *Antigone*
it serves to introduce one. Although all the bare events of Racine's
play are found in Rotrou, their dramatic functions differ basically.

If the essential conception of *La Thébaïde* is largely independent of
Euripides and Rotrou, what can be said of the oft-repeated claim of
Cornelian influence? This claim is based on the assumption that political
ambition is the play's central theme. The following comment is typical:

> There was nothing in *La Thébaïde* to suggest to its first audience that its
> author was a man who would some day revolutionize the content of
> French tragedy. It bears the outer marks of being written by a disciple of

Corneille. Its subject is the typical Cornelian one of great ambitions
competing for a great, political object, the winning of a throne. The
characters are 'great souls' pursuing their ends with fierce and unyielding
determination (A. F. B. Clark).

Gonzague Truc comes nearer the truth with the observation that in
La Thébaïde politics is strictly 'hors-d'œuvre': 'les deux frères n'en
usent que pour masquer leur haine et tenter de se justifier'. Neither of
the brothers insists on his 'gloire', the by-word of a power-hungry
Cornelian hero (the word occurs only eight times). Here, as will be
seen, the key terms are *sang* and *haine*. Close analysis will show that the
mainspring of their fratricidal struggle is a relentless, ferocious passion,
that their conflicting political ambitions are but the surface manifestation of a far more basic division.[2]

La Thébaïde centres on a tragic family rather than a single tragic
figure. With the exception of the confidants, all the characters are
related in some way to Œdipe and Jocaste. This drama unfolds among
people who are bound together by a common blood. But particularly
striking here is the uninterrupted violence done to purportedly sacred
ties of the blood. Three of the four children whom Jocaste bore
Œdipe – in an archetypally illicit mixture of bloods – figure in *La
Thébaïde*. Étéocle and Polynice, divided over the succession to their
father's throne, finally shed each other's blood as they had threatened
to do from the very beginning of the play. Their maternal uncle,
Créon, who encouraged their blood-feud, conceives a doubly illegiti-
mate love for their sister, Antigone. His passion not only borders on
incest, but puts him in an equivocal position *vis-à-vis* his son, Hémon,
who loves and is loved by Antigone. These two, in turn, are ready to
mix once again a blood whose sorry history forebodes nothing good
for the future. It is in this atmosphere of actual and imminent pollution
that the tragedy unfolds.

The first edition (1664) bore the title: *La Thébaïde, ou Les Frères
ennemis*, but in the printings of 1676, 1687 and 1697 only the subtitle
was retained. Most contemporary references to the play use *Les Frères
ennemis*, a designation which points directly to the kernel of the
tragedy. The final issue, the fate of all concerned, depends on the
course of action adopted by each of the warring brothers. The pivotal
question is: can the catastrophe be averted, or, in Racine's own terms,
can the 'bad blood' dividing the brothers somehow be made 'good'?

Will natural feelings, ties of the blood, suffice to bridge a gap created, ostensibly, by conflicting political interests?

The central role of the blood-bond in *Les Frères ennemis* can be seen in Racine's very choice of language. The word *sang* is used sixty-nine times in all. Repetition of this kind is, of course, a constant in Racinian poetry; but in no other play, according to available statistics, is a single word used so frequently. In the present case these numerous occurrences of the word *sang* are not by any means accidental. For it turns out that the fate of all concerned in fact depends on their respective attitudes towards the blood which flows in their veins.

The characters fall into two distinct categories. Some regard the blood of Œdipe as inherently good, a symbol of virtue and justice. Others realize that their blood cannot but be a source of crime and corruption. For Jocaste and Antigone, who share the first view, blood represents peace, harmony, and family solidarity. They want to believe the blood-bond strong enough to reunite the divided brothers. Polynice's attitude differs from theirs only slightly. His claim to the Theban throne is grounded on an hereditary privilege, a blood-right. For him *sang* signifies justice and legitimacy. To Étéocle, however, the 'sang incestueux' (921) from which he and his brother are sprung is a well of hatred which, he hopes, will eventually destroy Polynice and leave his own sway uncontested. Créon holds essentially the same position but tries to use the 'bad blood' between his nephews to put them both out of the way and retain the empire for himself.

On a linguistic level the knot of the tragedy is the puzzle of the word *sang*. On the strictly dramatic level, however, the problem is to interpret this ambiguous oracle pronounced early in the play:

'Thébains, pour n'avoir plus de guerres,
Il faut, par un ordre fatal,
Que *le dernier du sang* royal
Par son trépas *ensanglante* vos terres.' (II ii 393-6)

Antigone, who, with Hémon, is the first to hear this pronouncement, well aware of her family's criminal history and of the local deities' vindictiveness, interprets 'dernier' instinctively to mean 'the last drop, inclusive':

O Dieux, que vous a fait ce sang infortuné,
Et pourquoi *tout entier* l'avez-vous condamné?
N'êtes-vous pas contents de la mort de mon père?
Tout notre sang doit-il sentir votre colère? (II ii 397-400)[3]

Later in the play, however, inspired by the heroism of Ménécée, Créon's youngest son, who, as the 'last' (i.e. youngest) in Œdipe's line, thought to propitiate the gods with the gift of his life, Antigone takes heart and is willing to believe that her cousin has not died in vain, that her earlier interpretation of the oracle had been premature (III iii 617 ff., 671–4, 691). But Jocaste, who has lived and suffered more, remains sceptical (III iii 692–9). Yet, at one point, even she shares Antigone's new optimism (III iv 771–8), only to return to her former doubts when events fail to meet her expectations. Because the meaning of the oracle is not made clear until the final scene of the play (v vi 1498 ff.), the characters must waver throughout between hope and despair.

Now, the ambiguity of *sang* and the obscurity of the oracle are but two different statements of the same problem. For, if the blood is not infected it is capable of being redeemed by the suicide of Ménécée. But if it is irretrievably bad, then the extinction of the line is inevitable. And so, when the oracle is pronounced the actors in the tragedy are given an assignment by the indifferent, if not maleficent, deity. In the remaining portion of the play they are to decipher the oracle as best they can, uncover the true nature of the family blood, and determine their relation to one another and Destiny.

From the outset both Créon and Étéocle evaluated the situation correctly. They knew that their blood was irretrievably corrupt and that the sentiments and values that governed other families could not prevail against the instincts of Œdipe's progeny. Though Créon simulated grief over the death of Ménécée, falsely raising Antigone's and Jocaste's hopes with a gesture of repentance and a plea for the reconciliation of his nephews, he never for a moment believed such a reconciliation possible. He was thoroughly aware that the blood-bond between Étéocle and Polynice would unite them in hatred rather than in love – that it would precipitate the catastrophe rather than avert it:

> ... quand de la nature on a brisé les chaînes,
> Cher Attale, il n'est rien qui puisse réunir
> Ceux que des nœuds si forts n'ont pas su retenir.
> L'on hait avec excès lorsque l'on hait un frère. (III vi 880–3)

Créon does not indicate the cause of their hatred explicitly as a corruption of the blood, but the implication is clear. His speech foreshadows this one by Étéocle:

> Nous étions ennemis dès la plus tendre enfance;
> Que dis-je? Nous l'étions avant notre naissance.
> Triste et fatal effet d'un *sang* incestueux!...
> On dirait que le ciel, par un arrêt funeste,
> Voulut de nos parents punir ainsi l'inceste;
> Et que dans notre *sang* il voulut mettre au jour
> Tout ce qu'ont de plus noir et la haine et l'amour. (IV i 919-30)

Before any actual attempt at reconciliation has been made we know, along with Étéocle and Créon, that reconciliation is impossible. We know that the 'bad blood' is incorrigibly bad. We know what the other characters have yet to learn. It is on this process of learning – the reluctant repudiation of a precious illusion – that Racine centres his tragedy.

Polynice, though never a fully tragic figure, is a case in point. Racine was not content to follow the traditional differentiation between him and Étéocle. He took special care to distinguish him from his brother, to give him the *beau rôle*. All the disinterested characters in the play are on his side; they testify frequently and at length to his moral superiority. His aristocratic political orthodoxy is contrasted with Étéocle's rabble-rousing. Antigone clearly prefers Polynice, who, unlike Étéocle, is capable of fraternal and filial feeling and is not easily excited to violent language and behaviour.

Most of what we learn about Polynice is through direct testimony from himself and the other characters. But Racine uses more subtle devices to prejudice the reader in his favour. Polynice is surprisingly fair in his verbal treatment of his brother. In a play where *haïr* and its derivative noun occur some forty-odd times, it is significant that Polynice is not made to use either even once with reference to his brother. In the two places where he does admit to hatred a nice detour is employed. Racine does not raise Polynice's emotions to this pitch of violence until rather late in the play. The first instance occurs towards the end of the fourth act:

> *Jocaste.* Mon fils, son règne plaît.
> *Polynice.*   Mais *il m'est odieux*. (IV iii 1165)

and the other shortly afterwards:

> Et moi je ne veux plus, tant *tu m'es odieux*,
> Partager avec toi la lumière des cieux. (IV iii 1177-8)

In both these cases Polynice is saved from using the transitive forms, *je le hais* and *je te hais*. Even in these cold affirmations the agency of hatred is left, by grammatical indirection, with Étéocle. One might go so far as to translate the last example as: 'You make yourself hateful to me.' The words *haine* and *haïr* are strictly confined to the vocabulary of Étéocle.

On the surface, Polynice's personal and moral advantage automatically lends weight to his claims, making it appear as if Justice were on his side. But his very superiority only serves to accentuate the irony of his role. In this respect he approaches tragic stature. For Polynice justifies his conduct and supports his claim to the throne by appealing to the very blood that has sealed his guilt:

> Le *sang* nous met au trône, et non pas son caprice:
> [i.e. du peuple]

> Ce que le *sang* lui donne, il le doit accepter ... (II iii 480-1)

> Dois-je chercher ailleurs ce que le *sang* me donne? (IV iii 1112)

> Que le *sang* me couronne; ou, s'il ne suffit pas,
> Je veux à son secours n'appeler que mon bras. (IV iii 1133-4)

In three other places he makes an identical appeal, but without using the metaphorical *sang* to express hereditary right:

> Je veux devoir le sceptre *à qui je dois le jour*. (IV iii 1118)

> Vous voulez que mon cœur, flatté de ces chimères,
> Laisse un usurpateur *au trône de mes pères*? (IV iii 1151-2)

> *Jocaste.* Il a pour lui le peuple.
> *Polynice.*   Et j'ai pour moi les Dieux. (IV iii 1166)

Unaware that the very principles he invokes in support of his claim work against him towards the punishment and extinction of the blood of Œdipe, Polynice never assumes full tragic proportions. He dies firmly convinced that his cause is legitimate.

Jocaste wavers between poignant perception and self-delusion. This ambivalent tendency allows her role alone in *La Thébaïde* to take on tragic dimensions. Her hopes are grounded in the illusion that the blood is fundamentally good, capable of transcending what appears to

be a political difference dividing her sons. This conviction, however, is
shot through with flashes of insight into the real implications of their
consanguinity. In the beginning of the play she apostrophizes the Sun:

> Tu ne t'étonnes pas si mes fils sont perfides,
> S'ils sont tous deux méchants, et s'ils sont parricides:
> Tu sais qu'ils sont sortis *d'un sang incestueux*,
> Et tu t'étonnerais s'ils étaient vertueux. (i i 31–4)

Also, in later moments, she suspects that an inherent criminality rather
than a political difference is responsible for their estrangement (i iii
111–14). Not until the third act does Jocaste use the word *haine* with
reference to her sons. (Thereafter she uses *haine* and *haïr* quite freely,
723 ff, 780, 1027.) She doubts that Ménécée's death really portends
peace:

> La haine de mes fils est un trop grand obstacle. (iii iii 692)

This admission is costly, and had she not been so completely given to
self-deception, she might at this point have lost her faith in the blood-
bond. But this insight had to be reinforced before she could have her
final illumination. Jocaste cannot be made entirely to abandon hope
even by such an avowal as this:

> Hélas!
> Ils détournent la tête, et ne m'écoutent pas!
> Tous deux, pour s'attendrir, ils ont l'âme trop dure:
> Ils ne connaissent plus la voix de la nature. (iv iii 1029–32)

This sense of futility, however, is secondary and contrapuntal to the
main motive in Jocaste's behaviour. Like Polynice she insists on the
sacred prerogatives of consanguinity without realizing the peculiar
destiny of her own family:

> Ah! mon fils,
> Quelles traces de *sang* vois-je sur vos habits?
> Est-ce du *sang* d'un frère? ou n'est-ce point du vôtre?
> (i iii 45–7)

> Vous pourriez d'un tel *sang*, ô ciel! souiller vos armes?
> (i iii 71)

> Et doit-il être enfin plus facile en un autre [Ménécée]
> De répandre son *sang* qu'en vous d'aimer le vôtre?
> (iii iv 727–8)

> Surtout que le *sang* parle et fasse son office. (IV iii 983)

> *Polynice.* Il suffit aujourd'hui de son *sang* ou du mien.
> *Jocaste.* Du *sang* de votre frère?
> *Polynice.*   Oui, Madame, du sien. (IV iii 1061–2)

> Mille sceptres nouveaux s'offrent à votre épée,
> Sans que d'un *sang* si cher nous la voyions trempée.
>   (IV iii 1147–8)

Jocaste's illusion takes on tragic proportions as she tries to translate it into action. In her mind *sang* stands for solidarity, cohesion, proximity, and her aim on the level of action is to make Étéocle and Polynice come together, to make them do physically, effectively, what they refuse or are unable to do affectively. Jocaste fails to consider that 'meeting' can signify collision as well as union. Her interpretation of *sang* is ironically tragic in that it leads her to hasten and precipitate the clash she wants most to avert.

Jocaste, however, is not merely bent on her sons' meeting; it is basic to her strategy that they come together in the palace halls where they were born and spent their youth. She is not content with Étéocle's suggestion that they go see Polynice in his quarters (III v 809–10). When, finally, she has brought them together she tries to soften their hearts by evoking the atmosphere of the *foyer*:

> Vous revoyez un frère, après deux ans d'absence,
> Dans ce même palais *où vous prîtes naissance.* (IV iii 975–6)

> Considérez ces lieux *où vous prîtes naissance*:
> Leur aspect sur vos cœurs n'a-t-il point de puissance?
> C'est ici que tous deux vous *reçûtes le jour*;
> Tout ne vous parle ici que de paix et d'amour:
> Ces princes, votre sœur, tout condamne vos haines …
>   (IV iii 1023–7)

These lines recall an earlier passage where Étéocle, using identical language, grounds his hatred for Polynice on the very facts which in his mother's mind are a basis for love:

> Nous étions ennemis dès la plus tendre enfance;
> Que dis-je? nous l'étions *avant notre naissance.* (IV i 919–20)

Jocaste's words and gestures are replete with irony; they act as boomerangs:

> Me voici donc tantôt au comble de mes vœux,
> Puisque déjà le ciel vous rassemble tous deux. . . .
> Tous deux dans votre frère envisagez vos traits;
> Mais pour en mieux juger, voyez-les de plus près.
> *Surtout que le sang parle et fasse son office.*
> Approchez, Étéocle; avancez Polynice . . . (IV iii 973 ff)

Her earnest and innocent remarks are terribly ambiguous. 'Le ciel' – not Jocaste's providential gods, but an angry deity bent on punishing the house of Œdipe – has indeed brought the brothers together. Étéocle has already explained with what accents the blood speaks and what is its true 'office'. When Jocaste says 'approchez' and 'avancez' (984), she is, in effect, saying 'frappez' and 'tuez'. By inviting her sons to observe each other 'de plus près' (982) she is inviting them to act out the hatred she seeks to allay.

Racine has been careful to prepare a background against which to produce in relief the irony of Jocaste's error. Earlier Créon had been made to say:

> L'on hait avec excès lorsque l'on hait un frère.
> Mais leur *éloignement* ralentit leur colère:
> Quelque haine qu'on ait contre un fier ennemi,
> Quand il est *loin* de nous on la perd à demi. . . .
> Je veux qu'en se voyant leurs fureurs se déploient,
> Que rappelant leur haine, au lieu de la chasser,
> Ils s'étouffent, Attale, en voulant s'embrasser. (III vi 883–90)

When the moment arrives Étéocle reacts accordingly:

> Et maintenant, Créon, que j'attends sa venue,
> Ne crois pas que pour lui ma haine diminue:
> Plus il *approche*, et plus il me semble odieux;
> Et sans doute il faudra qu'elle éclate à ses yeux. (IV i 931–4)

>   Sont-ils *bien près d'ici?*
> Vont-ils venir, Attale? (IV ii 965–6)

> Qu'ils entrent. Cette *approche* excite mon courroux.
> Qu'on hait un ennemi quand il est *près de nous*! (IV ii 969–70)

In the next scene Jocaste enters with Polynice. Very little has been said before she has this pathetic insight:

> O Dieux! que je me vois cruellement déçue!
> N'avais-je tant pressé cette fatale vue
> Que pour les désunir encor plus que jamais?
> Ah! mes fils, est-ce là comme on parle de paix?
> Vous n'êtes pas ici dans un champ inhumain.
> Est-ce moi qui vous mets les armes à la main? (IV iii 1015 ff)

After a series of fruitless supplications and arguments Jocaste's negotiations come to naught and she is forced to answer this last question for herself. When Étéocle and Polynice have professed undying hatred for each other, she has no choice but to repudiate her misguided faith in the blood-bond:

> Puisque tous mes efforts ne sauraient vous changer,
> Que tardez-vous? allez vous perdre et me venger. . . .
> Le plus grand des forfaits vous a donné le jour;
> Il faut qu'un crime égal vous l'arrache à son tour.
> Je ne condamne plus la fureur qui vous presse;
> *Je n'ai plus pour mon sang ni pitié ni tendresse.* (IV iii 1181 ff)

For the first time Jocaste sees things as they are. Sensitive now to the ambiguities of her simplistic maxims she understands that *sang*, far from being an agent of solidarity, actually sets Étéocle and Polynice apart, that the *haine*, which ostensibly divided them, is alone capable of bringing them together. The highest irony of Jocaste's role is that she brought on the inevitable by trying to prevent it. Créon's report to Antigone on the outcome of the single combat may be taken as an epilogue to Jocaste's tragic error:

> La soif de se baigner dans le sang de leur frère
> Faisait ce que jamais le sang n'avait su faire:
> Par l'excès de leur haine ils semblaient réunis;
> Et prêts à s'égorger, ils paraissaient amis. (V iii 1313–16)

No one would want to reclaim Racine's first play as a hitherto neglected masterpiece. Its defects are glaring. For all practical purposes everything of importance has been said and done by the end of Act IV, and the final act is, at best, a superfluous and unstable appendage. Créon's tragic illumination is trumped up and inadequately prepared. The Créon-Antigone-Hémon love triangle is badly out of tune with the terrible tenor of the rest of the drama.

When studied closely, however, *La Thébaïde* reveals certain emphases and artistic procedures usually considered characteristic of Racine's mature art. It has an inner unity of tone and tragic interest that are significant and original. Reference to Racine's sources shows that in *La Thébaïde* his overarching concern was for that same spareness of action that was to characterize his later plays. Centring his attention on a carefully isolated incident, he fastened on a single passion which was to propel and resolve the action of his play. The most striking factor in the unity of *La Thébaïde* is the theme-word *sang* – a kind of axis which the thoughts and motives of every character must inevitably cross. The corrupt and corrupting hatred which animates and destroys the *frères ennemis* already anticipates the violent impulse that was to motivate Hermione. Their passion, like hers, does not subside until there is nothing left for it to consume. As Giraudoux has said: 'La catastrophe ne se résout jamais par une solution mais par extinction, *Phèdre* prend fin parce que Phèdre et Hippolyte, *Andromaque* parce que Hermione et Pyrrhus, *Bajazet*, parce que Bajazet et Roxane sont morts, la *Thébaïde* parce que tous sont tués et qu'il ne subsiste sur la scène que des figurants.'

In Jocaste we have the lineaments, if not the complexities, of Phèdre and Bérénice. She is the first of those Racinian women whose moral vision grows slowly and too late out of the painfully acquired awareness of their own moral blindness. In Racine's first play the terms of tragedy are the same as in his last: the most profound truths about life are the most obvious and the most dreadful to believe. Is not Jocaste the exemplar of those Racinian heroines who must first deny in order, ultimately, to admit that the inevitable cannot but be?

SOURCE: *French Studies*, XIII (1959).

NOTES

1. For some partial answers to this question and some shrewd insights into the meaning of *La Thébaïde* see J. C. Lapp, *Aspects of Racinian Tragedy*; Thierry Maulnier, 'Apparition de Racine', in his *Langages* (Lausanne, 1946) pp. 79 ff; G. Truc, *Jean Racine* (Paris, 1926) pp. 23 ff.

2. Although the basic inspiration of *La Thébaïde* cannot be Cornelian, it is possible that Racine borrowed from his predecessor certain external devices. The oracle in Act II is typical of Corneille, and the false report on the single combat (v iii), which is later belied, is almost certainly modelled on *Horace* (III, vi, IV ii).

3. Mesnard, following Père Brumoy, refused to see any possible obscurity in this oracle; he held that, on genealogical grounds, Antigone and Hémon had no business making the oracle refer to anyone but Ménécée who was, in fact, 'le *dernier* [né] du sang royal'. But, as has been recently pointed out, Racine was obviously not using the same genealogies as his sources. Louis Racine had answered Brumoy with a common-sense observation that ought to have forestalled Mesnard's objection: 'Un oracle est toujours ambigu; et ce mot, *le dernier*, peut s'entendre: *tout, jusqu'au dernier*. C'est ainsi qu'Antigone l'a entendu.' It would indeed seem that since Racine had Antigone interpret the oracle in one way and Ménécée in another, he meant the oracle to be ambiguous. His means of suggesting this ambiguity may have been clumsy, but this is beside the point. It is more important to see, as Professor Lapp pointed out, that the oracle, interpreted as Racine intended, 'serves to increase the tragic irony, and to highlight the futility of the characters' struggle' (*Modern Language Notes*, 1951, pp. 462–4).

JEAN POMMIER

Literary Tradition and Living Models in Racine's *Andromaque* (1962)

BOOKISH tradition and living models, these two factors in literary creation combine in varying measure, depending on the period, the author's individuality, and the genre. In Racine's drama, imitation – in the sense understood by the seventeenth century – seems to me to have been of preponderant importance. It is possible to disagree, and to argue that the writer in his tragedies transposed not only his own life and ideas, but the annals of his times. I cannot adopt this view, nor show things otherwise than as I see them. So, without polemics, I embark on the first part of my disquisition, which deals with the Graeco-Latin heritage.

The poet's Andromache, and ours, is *Hectoris Andromache*, the Andromache of Hector, the touching figure from that third book of the *Aeneid* which Racine must have read in his youth. You know the kind of semi-private education that was given to boys at Port-Royal: no-one is more fitted to understand it than an Englishman. Pierre Nicole was less a schoolmaster than a guide to the 'jeunes Messieurs'. He pointed out the finest passages, he was there, in the words of a manuscript consulted by Sainte-Beuve, 'pour leur en inspirer le goût'. And Nicole was a devotee of Virgil. He made them learn whole books of the *Aeneid* by heart – even the fourth (the love-episode with Dido) 'apart from a few passages'. And he could match the example to the precept; not long before his death he was capable of reciting thousands of lines from his favourite author without turning a hair. The stories told of Racine's schooldays seem less surprising when set among these feats of memory.

The tradition followed by Virgil takes us far from Racine's plot. Andromache mourns not only her illustrious consort, but her son Astyanax; Pyrrhus, whose concubine she has become, has left her for Hermione. Hector's widow has fallen into the hands of a third man, this time of her own race, her own family – her brother-in-law. Hence the surprise of Aeneas when, landing in Epirus, he finds a Greek kingdom under Trojan rule. This change of fortunes occurs at the end of our tragedy, but is brought about quite differently. Orestes' Greek attendants are forced to flee:

> Aux ordres d'Andromaque ici tout est soumis.
> Ils la traitent en reine ... (v v 1587–8)

This reversal of the situation was also in keeping, at the time of writing, with a recent restoration. But I will not anticipate.

The author of *Andromaque* refers to the *Aeneid* again, but to another book, when he remarks in his preface on the character of Pyrrhus, which had been criticised by his public. My only liberty was 'd'adoucir un peu la férocité de Pyrrhus,' he says, 'que ... Virgile, dans le second de l'*Énéide*, a poussé beaucoup plus loin que je n'ai cru devoir le faire.'

I must be forgiven for commenting that Racine has pulled rather a fast one here. Racine's Pyrrhus is a conqueror returned from the wars, demobilised if I may so put it, reigning over a peace-time Epirus. Virgil's is engaged in a most violent act of war, the capture of Troy. We see him there, with one hand dragging the aged Priam up to the altar by the hair, while the other plunges his sword into his body to the hilt. Racine did not repeat this phrase in his second preface, and one can see why.

Here I will quote another passage from Aeneas' narrative, if I may be forgiven the digression. Making his way through the darkness, the hero dimly sees the figure of a woman in hiding; in the gleam of the fires he recognises Helen. At the thought of all the ills she has caused, he seeks to kill her. But his divine mother, Venus, appears and persuades him not to. Helen? It was not her hateful beauty that laid Troy low, but the gods; yes, the gods. And Venus, opening her son's eyes to a sight hidden from mortal men, shows him the gods, *dirae facies*, working havoc on the doomed city.

Virgil was not alone in acquitting Helen. In a tragedy to which we shall turn shortly, Euripides puts the idea into the mouth of the most unexpected of judges, the deceived husband himself. True, says

Menelaus, 'she has had misfortunes' – 'through no will of her own, but by the will of the gods', οὐχ ἑκοῦσ', ἀλλ' ἐκ θεῶν. What description could be more apt for Phèdre? It is strange how we forget this pagan philosophy in which the young humanist was steeped, when we lay so much to the account of what we like to call his Jansenist upbringing.

I will go further. Not every man is the son of Atreus or Oedipus, nor every woman daughter of Helen or Pasiphaë. It is not hard to see why Melpomene favours those families, so eminently tragic: 'races funestes', in Clytemnestre's words, dynasties laid under a curse. But if, as a good poet should, Racine picks his subjects from among these destinies *out of the common run*, does this entitle us to infer that he, personally, held so pessimistic a view of our common condition? Do not *Bérénice* and even *Mithridate* tell of a different humanity?

We must close this digression. Among the witnesses of the murder of Priam, Virgil does not mention Andromache. She was there, however, so we learn from the words Racine gives to his Andromaque:

> Dois-je oublier son père [Priam] à mes pieds renversé,
> Ensanglantant l'autel qu'il tenait embrassé?
> Songe, songe, Céphise, à cette nuit cruelle ... (III viii 995-7)

A memory of horror, which has not faded with time. If we ask how much time has passed between the fall of Troy and the day of the action shown in the tragedy, a long space or a short, Pyrrhus is there to tell us:

> Ah! si du fils d'Hector la perte était jurée,
> Pourquoi d'*un an entier* l'avons-nous differée? (I ii 205-6)

And elsewhere, 'Mon cœur, désespéré d'*un an* d'ingratitude ...' The events before our eyes are a kind of epilogue to the Trojan war. Hence the violence of the sentiments of Hector's widow, particularly of her hatred for Pyrrhus.

I used the word hatred. And if anyone imputes to her other feelings he is mistaken. Not coquetry, but an instinctive diplomacy inspires her in that sixth scene of Act III in which dire necessity forces her to fall at her master's feet. All through the play, whether in her speeches or in those of Pylade interpreting her acts, what we see, displayed with overpowering force towards Pyrrhus, can be called by no other name than hate. What wonder? Not only had Pyrrhus the killer of Hector for his father, not only is he Priam's murderer, but how does he behave

to his prisoner? 'Il lui cache son fils, *il menace sa tête*' (I i 113 var.).
His head has been claimed by Oreste, but the blackmail had begun long
before the ambassador's arrival. It passes from the chronic to the
acute state to provide the 'crisis' of the tragedy. Andromaque as yet
knows nothing of the new phase when she makes her first entrance
with the famous words:

> Je passais jusqu'aux lieux où l'on garde mon fils.
> Puisqu'une fois le jour vous souffrez que je voie . . . (I iv 260–1)

How much resentment lies hidden under that veil of irony, how much
mute hostility and bitterness!

How comes it then that on this point the character of Andromaque
has been so misinterpreted? One scene has had not a little to do with it
– we shall seek it in vain in our tragedy, but it was there originally, and
remained for a considerable time. In our texts Andromaque does not
appear again after her exit at the beginning of the fourth act: but in
the original version, after the death of Pyrrhus, she came back with
her new captor, Oreste, to face Hermione; just as, in the original
version of *Britannicus*, Junie made a last entrance in Néron's presence
after the poisoning of the young prince. (Ought we to correct some
of the ideas prevalent about Racine's tact?) And, in this last appearance,
what did Andromaque say? This, in substance: 'I mourn for Pyrrhus,
as if he had taken the place of my Hector.' What should we conclude
from that? Apart from the fact that Racine did not retain the passage,
is it not obvious how completely the situation has changed by this
time? Pyrrhus has sacrificed Greece to Andromaque, and his own life
to Astyanax. Orestes' Greek retinue could not have cut him down,
had he not sent off his personal guard to protect the child. How could
the mother fail to be touched and overcome? But Racine's tragedy does
not begin at the King's death. Let us beware of judging the widow of
Hector by the widow of Pyrrhus.

During the play Andromaque encounters Hermione only once, for
a brief moment. On the stage as in the novel, there are scenes which
everyone expects but which the author has avoided, because of their
difficulties or drawbacks. Hermione – she too comes from the Greeks.
While he was in the little Languedoc town of Uzès, the youthful
Racine had studied and admired Homer's *Odyssey*. We recall Book IV,
when Telemachus and his companion arrive at the palace of Menelaus.
'The sun was setting as they came to Lacedaemon.' (How like the

opening of a chapter in a modern historical novel!) Menelaus and his kinsmen are celebrating a double wedding, and one of the brides is Hermione, who is about to leave: her father is sending her in marriage to the son of Achilles. Ἑρμιόνην, says Homer, ἥ εἶδος ἔχε χρυσέης Ἀφροδίτης, Hermione with the beauty of golden Aphrodite.

That is all. But what a vision! Did Racine foresee that he would give being to another Hermione? And what must he have thought, five years later, when he set eyes on the actress who was to create the part – Mademoiselle des Œillets, a good actress but forty-six years old, short, thin and plain? Divine vision of the Grecian singer, Hermione with golden Aphrodite's beauty, where are you now?

The tradition that makes Hermione the wife of Pyrrhus reappears in a tragedy by Euripides, *Andromache*, mentioned by Racine in both his prefaces for the character it attributes to Hermione – jealousy and 'emportements'. True, but against whom? Here again the French poet has done his best to put us on the wrong scent. The action of Euripides takes place in Achilles' country, Thessaly. Pyrrhus is on his travels, leaving at home his wife and his concubine. Some have said that Euripides intended his play to show the objections to a 'ménage à trois'. Certainly Hermione cannot stand Andromache. 'Die,' she tells her, 'or, if any should wish to save you, you must forget the pride of your old prosperity and cower in humility and fall at my knees; you must sweep my floors and sprinkle them with water, so that you may remember where you are.' Just like some Athenian citizen's wife, taking pleasure in humiliating a detested servant. One might have imagined an equally vindictive disposition in Racine's personage; but in fact, no sooner does she think she has won Pyrrhus back than her only thought is, not to turn on her rival, but to bask in her visions of happiness undisturbed. The approach of Andromaque is an intrusion:

> Dieux! ne puis-je à ma joie abandonner mon âme?
> Sortons: que lui dirais-je? (III iii 857–8)

Andromaque holds her by the knees and implores her. Hermione's refusal is given in six lines, and her scorn lies more in the tone than the words, which are unwise rather than anything else.

Such is the style of courtly tragedy; an incessant transposing of far-off models, forcing the poet not merely to modify, but to forget. How many memories he must have consigned to the darkness! We think of them only rarely, and yet ... What had caused the enmity of the

Greek Hermione? The son that Andromache had borne her husband, while she remained childless. She blamed the magic philtres of the Trojan, who rejoined: 'The real reason is that you are unpleasant to live with. Not so did I act in Hector's palace; I made myself agreeable in every way.' And how did Hector's Andromache make herself agreeable, do you suppose? Here are her words: 'O dearest Hector, for your sake I even made myself an accomplice in your loves, if at times Cypris led you astray; and many a time have I offered the breast to your bastards, to show that I bore you no bitterness. And thus I drew my husband to me by my virtue.' This time we ourselves feel the revelation is an offence to be put out of our minds. What a light on Hector's private life!

The lesson does not melt Hermione. In Pyrrhus' absence, she has sent for her father Menelaus, and means to make an end of mother and son together. But Andromache clings to the statue of a goddess, and her son has been concealed. Not very effectively, for Menelaus discovers him and drags him on to the stage. He tells Andromache: 'Either you leave the protection of the statue and let yourself be killed, or the child will perish in your place'. Racine's Pyrrhus will say: 'Your hand or your son': Menelaus says: 'Your son or your life.'

Another form of blackmail is shown in a tragedy by Seneca, also quoted in Racine's first preface – the *Troad*, or *The Trojan Women*. Here Andromache has to choose whether to surrender her son, or her husband's ashes. The unhappy woman's deliberation-speech is an over-elaborate but characteristic example of those internal conflicts that our classical playwrights have so often employed, a typical example being the *stances* of *Le Cid*.

In Euripides' play, the mother sacrifices herself for her son: 'O son, she who bore you goes down to Hades to save you from death. If you escape, remember your mother and her unhappy end; and to your father [Pyrrhus], with kisses and tears and embraces, relate what I have done. True it is that for all men, children are life.' So she gives herself up, but the scoundrelly Menelaus, once he has the mother at his mercy, is determined to sacrifice the son as well. (The Peloponnesian War was on, and the Lacedaemonian had to be shown in an evil light to the Athenian public.) But both the victims escape thanks to Pyrrhus' grandfather, Peleus, who arrives in the nick of time.

Need I emphasise the brutal nature of such scenes? Racine, of necessity, has toned it down greatly. But if he makes his Andromaque suffer, there is no need to suppose that it was because of some sadism in his make-up. Blackmail is a highly tragic thing. And it has been used by modern authors, to whom we shall now turn.

Ab Jove principium ... The great Corneille gave up writing for the stage for a time owing to the failure of his play, *Pertharite* (1651), One would have expected playwrights to shun a subject of ill omen. But no: first his younger brother, and later his youthful rival were inspired by the unsuccessful tragedy. And they succeeded – Thomas Corneille with his *Camma* (1661), Racine with *Andromaque*, which derives at once from *Pertharite* and *Camma*.

Pertharite, roi des Lombards – the play takes us into the Middle Ages (the seventh century), among characters named Grimoald, Unulphe, Edüige; barbarous names – they may have been in Boileau's mind when he gibed at the ignorant poet, who, from so many heroes, 'va choisir Childebrand'. Pierre Corneille was no ignorant poet, but a provincial who was not put off by massive tomes. If ever he saw a few dramatic possibilities in a story he let himself go, trusting to his genius and his craftsmanship to carve out a five act play from material which was not always of first class quality. He has suffered in consequence; if a whole section of his work does not earn from us the attention that it may perhaps deserve, it is because he was not as careful as was Racine to choose subjects awaking a response in his public; he was not afraid of working a little outside the great humanist tradition. When Montesquieu was in London in 1730 he replied to a question from the Queen: 'In France, Corneille is considered the greater mind, and Racine the greater writer.'

Often, since Voltaire, the resemblances have been noted between *Pertharite* and *Andromaque*. In Corneille's play too, there is a king who jilts a princess betrothed to him, for a captive queen with whom he falls in love; and a prince (the Duke of Turin) who aspires to the jilted woman's hand. Only, here, the captive queen is wrong to think herself widowed; her husband, who left her a son, has not died in exile as rumour reported. He returns, like Thésée in *Phèdre*; husband recovers wife, her suitor goes back to his betrothed, and the loser is the Duke of Turin. It is as if Oreste were to die, and Hector rise from the dead to fall into his wife's arms, while Pyrrhus fell into Hermione's. More images that Racine had to brush aside.

Let us do the same, and look only at the situations that are parallel.

King Grimoald, the Pyrrhus of Corneille, failing to obtain anything from
his captive Rodelinde by submission and entreaty, turns to threats:

> Je me ferai justice en domptant qui me brave ...
> Allez, sans irriter plus longtemps mon courroux,
> Attendre ce qu'un maître ordonnera de vous. (II v 735 ff)

To which the queen replies: 'Qui ne craint pas la mort craint peu quoi
qu'il ordonne.' The King: 'Vous la craindrez peut-être en quelque
autre personne.' Rodelinde understands: her son is threatened. A
little later, an emissary of the King intimates the terms of the bargain:

> Et la juste colère
> Où jettent cet amant les mépris de la mère
> Veut punir sur le sang de ce fils innocent
> La dureté d'un cœur si peu reconnaissant. (III i 755–8)

While he was still employing milder methods, the King had – vainly –
made his captive a generous proposal; marry me, and I undertake to
restore the throne to your son when he becomes of age. Will Rodelinde not reconsider her refusal?

> C'est à vous d'y penser: tout le choix qu'on vous donne
> C'est d'accepter pour lui [your son] la mort ou la couronne.
> Son sort est en vos mains: aimer ou dédaigner
> Le va faire périr ou le faire régner. (758–61)

The queen's reply might have come from the lips of Andromaque:

> Et le choix qu'on m'ordonne est pour moi si fatal
> Qu'à mes yeux des deux parts le supplice est égal. (773–4)

This comes very close to Racine. But a moment ago I passed too
quickly over the threat that Rodelinde should 'attendre ce qu'un
maître ordonnera de vous'. The captured woman, in antiquity, was
thrust forcibly into the master's bed. Andromaque has nothing of the
sort to fear from Pyrrhus, who is reduced to tears by her refusal. The
transition takes place in *Pertharite*, where one of the characters says to
Rodelinde:

> On vous aura fait peur ou de la mort d'un fils,
> Ou de ce qu'un tyran se croit être permis. (III ii 833–4)

The second alternative is only envisaged for a fleeting moment; in
Racine it disappears entirely. The delicacy of a polite court admits
that a captured woman may be carried off by her captor (as is Ériphile
in *Iphigénie*), but nothing more.

Corneille has invented things in *Pertharite* that are appalling, as if powerful creative faculties could not go together with taste. And side by side with these, an analysis of the passion of love so accurate and delicate that, in this field which is his own, Racine could pass for the pupil.

I am thinking of the dialogue between the ex-betrothed of the King and the Duke who wants to marry her. Like Hermione, Edüige calls on her lover to serve her hatred and punish the fickle. The Duke refuses, and explains as follows:

> Mettre à ce prix vos feux et votre diadème,
> C'est ne connaître pas votre haine et vous-même;
> Et qui, sous cet espoir, voudrait vous obéir,
> Chercherait le moyen de se faire haïr.
> Grimoald inconstant n'a plus pour vous de charmes,
> Mais Grimoald puni vous coûterait des larmes.
> A cet objet sanglant, l'effort de la pitié
> Reprendrait tous les droits d'une vieille amitié
> Et son crime en son sang éteint avec sa vie
> Passerait en celui qui vous aurait servie.
>   Quels que soient ses mépris, peignez-vous bien sa mort,
> Madame, et votre cœur n'en sera pas d'accord.
> Quoi qu'un amant volage excite de colère,
> Son change est odieux, mais sa personne est chère ...
> Ainsi n'espérez pas que jamais on s'assure
> Sur les bouillants transports qu'arrache son parjure ...
> Votre haine tremblante est un mauvais appui
> A quiconque pour vous entreprendrait sur lui;
> Et quelque doux espoir qu'offre cette colère,
> Une plus forte haine en serait le salaire. (II i 399ff)

We may feel that such a warning might have saved Oreste. In fact it was his undoing, since it provided Racine with the programme for his catastrophe – this theory of the vicissitudes of the heart, what a magnificent dramatic effect!

> Et son crime en son [Pyrrhus'] sang éteint avec sa vie
> Passerait en celui [Oreste] qui vous aurait servie.

Where the clear-sighted foresee and draw back, the blind rush in. Racine had only to fill in Corneille's dotted line. I can imagine him feeling in his heart that slight thud of which Musset speaks, warning the writer of a gift from fortune.

I thought it preferable to deal at some length with *Pertharite*, rather than disperse our attention over other models. Everyone knows that they exist in great numbers, and not only in the tragic genre. It is a comedy of Corneille that provides one of the best-known details in the role of Oreste. In *Mélite ou les fausses lettres* (published in 1633) a certain Éraste (the name is not so far from Oreste) has a kind of mental breakdown, with hallucinations. He thinks he is in the underworld, struggles with the Eumenides, and calls to his aid the spirits of the abyss:

> Sus, de pieds et de mains
> Essayons d'écarter ces monstres inhumains . . .
> Écrasons leurs *serpents*; chargeons-les de vos chaînes . . .
> Pour ces *filles d'Enfer* nous sommes trop puissants. (IV viii 1365 ff)

An onlooker appears, and expresses the opinion on hearing this speech that Éraste has 'perdu le *sens*'. We have all recognised the madness of Oreste:

> Hé bien, *filles d'Enfer*, vos mains sont-elles prêtes?
> Pour qui sont ces *serpents* . . . ? (*Andromaque*, V v 1637–8)

Even the very rhyme *puissants–sens* recurs right at the end of *Andromaque*, in Pylade's last words. The imitation is signed and sealed. The frantic gesticulations of madness, which provoke laughter in *Mélite*, produce horror in Racine. He acclimatises all these borrowings with the same miraculous art.

So too with what he takes from the novelists of his own time. Not that he held the genre in high esteem. 'Je croyais', he wrote in 1666, 'que ces sortes d'ouvrages n'étaient bons que pour désennuyer l'esprit, pour l'accoutumer à la lecture, et pour le faire passer ensuite à des choses plus solides.' (I wonder what 'choses plus solides' our novel reading prepares us for today?) If the phrase was meant seriously, perhaps Racine was adapting to his purposes certain admonitions of his Port-Royal masters, who are reported to have confiscated his copy of the Greek novel *Theagenes and Chariclea*. Once his own master, he probably made up for lost time with more modern writers; and the experience was profitable, as we can see, among other *rapprochements*, from the two I shall quote.

In the *Cassandre* of La Calprenède (1642–3), Alexander loves his captive Statira but is not loved in return. Tempering her refusal with

words of praise, she informs him plainly that there is too much bloodshed between them: 'Quelque vertu qui éclate visiblement en vous,
je ne puis vous considérer autrement que comme le meurtrier de nos
sujets et le meurtrier de mon père.' And she begs him: 'Souffrez que
ce qui est de Darius passe le reste de sa vie en tranquillité, dans quelque
petit coin des terres qui furent autrefois à lui.' Was it with this passage
in mind that Racine puts a similar wish into the mouth of Andromaque
– to be allowed to live hidden with her son 'en quelque île déserte'
where 'd'être veuve et mère elle ait la liberté'? I note, too, that Statira's
confidante is called Cléone – like the confidante of Hermione.

Now let us open *Bérénice*; not Racine's play, but the novel of Segrais
(1640). Titus has ravaged Judaea. 'O terre jadis si delicieuse,' he exclaims, 'que les rigueurs de Bérénice vous vengent bien de celles que
j'ai exercées sur vous! Votre cruel vainqueur languit dans un esclavage
plus tyrannique que celui où il a réduit vos peuples.' Pyrrhus refines
still further on this theme of *précieux* gallantry:

> J'ait fait des malheureux, sans doute; et la Phrygie
> Cent fois de votre sang a vu ma main rougie.
> Mais que vos yeux sur moi se sont bien exercés! . . .
> Vaincu, chargé de fers, de regrets consumé,
> Brûlé . . . (I iv 313 ff)

I am not denying, in a general way, that certain expressions or figures
of speech may arise as it were spontaneously from a given situation.
Shall we conclude that this was the case here? It would be somewhat
imprudent, considering how extraordinary was Racine's memory,
and how widespread was imitation in literature at the time.

Imitation! Even the writers most jealous of their own originality
have studied this practice, for which they have sometimes evolved
expressive descriptions. Valéry, for instance, has said: 'Le lion est fait
de moutons assimilés.' Racine is composed of all these *minores*, Gilbert,
Quinault or Thomas Corneille, whom he has digested so perfectly.
But – and Valéry might have realised this – the lion does not assimilate
only sheep. He may adopt a more invigorating diet, and feed on
another lion. Racine has done this with those illustrious ancients,
Euripides, Virgil, etc., whom he cites in the first preface to *Britannicus*;
he has done it with Pierre Corneille himself.

And since I am in the vein of animal similes, I will hazard another.
I was reading recently a letter of Racine's dating from his last years.

It belongs, I think, to 1697, is addressed to the poet's sister, and deals with an edict making it compulsory to declare armorial bearings (we can guess why – to bring money into the treasury by taxation). I know, he writes, that the arms 'de notre famille sont un rat et un cygne' (forming the rebus *Ra-cine*). And he recalls the lawsuit which their grandfather brought against a painter for portraying on the windows of the house a wild boar instead of a rat. The grandson would not have shown the same scruples, far from it. How gladly would he have dispensed with the rat to which his senior was so attached! What could be more unsuitable? The swan, yes; it could be retained alone; otherwise – let us quote his own words – 'Je voudrais bien que ce fût en effet un sanglier ou la hure d'un sanglier, qui fût à la place de ce vilain rat.' So much nobler and more aristocratic! The artist in falsification was quite right.

So be it. But we who care little for Messire Jean Racine, *conseiller secrétaire du Roi et gentilhomme ordinaire de sa chambre*, what emblem shall we choose for our poet? What but the 'buveuse de rosée' that visits 'le lys du coteau'? No less than his friend La Fontaine did Racine go his rounds 'de fleur à fleur'. So then, neither rat nor boar; but, beside the swan, a honey-bee.

This poetic bee we have watched rifling the store of ancients and moderns alike. But one of the latter has been omitted – none other than Racine himself, whose earlier work has left some marks on *Andromaque*. I ask the reader's indulgence for a very ungainly word, but one denoting an important phenomenon; self-imitation. The writer repeats himself through a sort of facility which is not to be confused with the obsessions of psycho-analysis. This is the worst way in which the work can form the workman, as Valéry puts it. Racine had only had two tragedies acted and published, and already at times he was walking in his own footsteps. Had this increasing weight of the past something to do with his final renunciation? Some have said so.

What seems certain in any case is, that he did not write Oreste's mad-scene without remembering that of Créon, at the end of his own *Thébaïde*. It was a case of self-imitation in a theme which 'faisait fureur' at the time. The same theme can be seen long after, I believe, in however attenuated a form, in the fourth act of *Phèdre*, when the unhappy queen, driven out of the universe by forbears who judge her crimes, seeks to take refuge 'dans la nuit infernale'. With this difference, that she remains sane enough to know that she is the victim of an illusion, when she says to Minos 'Je *crois* voir de ta main tomber l'urne terrible.' Observations of this kind could send one back to Brunetière's evolutionary theories: on the stage, just as in nature, we see the perpetuation of forms, their type still recognisable in their degenerate state.

La Thébaïde had been performed in June, 1664. In December of the next year Racine scored his first success with *Alexandre le Grand*. In this play, Axiane the queen has her Oreste in the person of the weakling Taxile. Listen to this dialogue:

> *Axiane.* On dit que tes désirs n'aspirent qu'à me plaire . . .
> Sais-tu par quels secrets on peut toucher mon âme?
> Es-tu prêt . . . ?
> *Taxile.*   Ah! Madame, éprouvez seulement
> Ce que peut sur mon cœur un espoir si charmant.

—This last hemistich occurs in the mouth of Pyrrhus—

> Que faut-il faire?
> *Axiane.*   Il faut, s'il est vrai que l'on m'aime . . . (IV iii 1162 ff)

But this Hermione is a Cornelian character. She bids Taxile go and fight, not commit a murder.

And what actress 'created' this role of Axiane? This is the kind of question that literary critics will do well to ask themselves. The Axiane in *Alexandre* was that Mademoiselle des Œillets whom we have already named as taking the part of Hermione in 1667. As he composed this or that scene of his new tragedy, how could Racine fail to see and hear the style of the woman who was to interpret the part?

With the space at our disposal, the third section must be brief; and some will consider very niggardly the space I have thus left, *in fine*, for the living models – the first of whom, in their view, is Racine himself. To those who incline towards confessional tragedy, I have no need to name the long work in which they will find these beliefs elaborated: they know it. In reality, nobody has ever imagined that Racine, at the moment of creating his plays, dismissed his personal experience from his mind, and so to speak dehumanised himself. Only, in what manner did he use this experience? There lies the whole question. I cannot convince myself that it was by putting himself into

the play with his associates, under names drawn from legend or
history. The most I can do is to perceive here and there in *Andromaque*
some momentary emergence, some slight trace of personal sensibility,
such as the one I shall quote. We remember the account given by
Cléone to her mistress after she has watched the nuptial procession
pass by. She paints without attenuations the triumphant air of Pyrrhus:

> Je l'ai vu vers le temple ...
> Mener en conquérant sa nouvelle conquête;
> Et d'un œil qui déjà dévorait son espoir

– I borrow from the early editions this audacious and telling expression,
which has been replaced –

> S'enivrer en marchant du plaisir de la voir. (v ii 1433 ff)

And who, in 1667, was playing this Andromaque who aroused such
fierce desire? Marquise du Parc, whose superb figure and bearing struck
all her contemporaries with admiration: *incessu patuit dea*. This pleasure
of the senses, this gratified pride, Racine must have felt on many an
occasion, contemplating his mistress. That we find some reflection of
them here, I would willingly accept. But let us admit conjectures
of this sort only with caution: too much readiness would tell against
us.

If, on the other hand, we pass from Racine's biography to the history
of his times, we shall find events which influenced, beyond a doubt, the
composition of *Andromaque*. Here I have no illusion that I am bringing
up anything new, for everything, practically, has already been said in a
well-known article, many years old already (1924), that by Jacques-
Émile Morel on 'La vivante Andromaque'.

This name the writer gives to Queen Henrietta Maria, or 'Henriette
de France', the wife of Charles I – a woman who was made to suffer
in her love for her sons even before she was a widow. Parliament
restricted her contacts with them, for fear that, as an ardent Catholic,
she would turn them into Papists. We have a note in which she answers
an accusation by saying: 'Le prince de Galles n'est venu que pour
fêter le jour de naissance de sa sœur.' The phrase shows under what
kind of surveillance she lived. And the nobleman to whom that
invidious role fell had once, it seems, been a rejected lover of hers. So
the parallel goes quite a long way.

The Queen had had to cross over into France in 1644, but the death of Charles I led to new persecutions against his family, at least after the treaty of alliance between Cromwell and Mazarin in 1653. Henriette's eldest son, the future Charles II, was obliged to leave France with his two brothers. What do we find in *Andromaque?* The accusation that Pyrrhus 'élève en sa cour l'ennemi de la Grèce'; and later on, this:

> Leur haine pour Hector n'est pas encore éteinte.
> Ils redoutent son fils. (I iv 269–70)

Cromwell, too, had 'poursuivi' the offspring of Charles I and a Catholic queen.

Pascal's speck of gravel having had the effect we know, Charles II was restored to his throne and made his entry into London in 1660. What a revenge, not for Catholicism of course, since he was a Protestant, but for the legitimist principle! What a cluster of associations linked with the Stuart restoration must have stirred in the audience's minds, when in the temple Pyrrhus crowned the widow of Hector and recognised Astyanax 'pour le roi des Troyens'!

When Racine staged his tragedy, Henriette de France still lived, in the seclusion of Chaillot and Colombes. She did not die till two years later. But in 1662 her daughter (born in Exeter), Henriette 'd'Angleterre', had married Louis XIV's brother. It is to this young princess that *Andromaque* was dedicated. The poet in his *Épître* attributes all his success to the patronage of Madame. 'On savait', he writes, 'que Votre Altesse Royale avait daigné prendre soin de la conduite de ma tragédie. On savait que vous m'aviez prêté quelques-unes de vos lumières pour y ajouter de nouveaux ornements.' There was nothing abnormal in those of noble or princely rank showing interest in works of literature. Richelieu used to work together with the authors he commissioned; and even Louis XIV, though in his case . . . ! It is enough to turn to the dedication of *Les Fâcheux*: I owe the success of this comedy, writes Molière, 'non seulement à cette glorieuse approbation dont Votre Majesté honora d'abord la pièce, . . . mais encore à l'ordre qu'elle me donna d'y ajouter un caractère de Fâcheux dont elle eut la bonté de m'ouvrir les idées elle-même, et qui a été trouvé partout le plus beau morceau de l'ouvrage.' (The hunting-scene, so it is believed.) Sometimes the author did not give way: Molière held out once, against Madame in fact, when she tried to make him strike out the reference in the last act of *Le Misanthrope* to 'notre grand flandrin de vicomte' who spent his time spitting into a well to make ripples. If the master of comedy had yielded, Madame's refinement would have lost us this touch of realism.

No such disagreement was likely to arise between her and Racine. The resemblance between the situations was too striking not to affect her. Her father had written her mother letters of great feeling. Even supposing they had not been 'connues de toute la terre', as Bossuet says, can we imagine that the daughter of Charles I and Henriette de France would not have mentioned them – not have shown them – to her poet? Racine's old editor, Paul Mesnard, has commented that in the eighth scene of Act III in *Andromaque*, when the Trojan queen recalls Hector's farewell, his words are not those he speaks in the *Iliad*. It would be vain to look in Homer for the equivalent line: 'Je te laisse mon fils pour gage de ma foi.' But the King of England had written to his wife in his last letter (the text we have is in French): 'Je suis satisfait puisque mes enfants sont près de vous. . . . Je ne puis vous laisser de gages plus chers et plus précieux de mon amour.' A modern thread, surely, which Racine wove, without the slightest disharmony, into the ancient tapestry.

Our excerpt from the dedication was not complete. 'On savait enfin,' Racine went on, 'que vous l'aviez honorée [ma tragédie] de quelques larmes dès la première lecture que je vous en fis.' Tears which fell, perhaps, on the relics the princess was holding. 'Elle avait les yeux noirs,' says one account, 'vifs et pleins de ce feu contagieux que les hommes ne sauraient regarder sans en ressentir l'effet: *ses yeux paraissaient eux-mêmes atteints du désir de ceux qui les regardaient.*' Imagine the poet, not yet thirty, in the presence of the princess who was less than twenty-five; the one reading lines from *Andromaque* as Racine knew how to read, and both exchanging glances of the kind that reveal so much on the stage. But the tears dimming the fire of those dark eyes were perhaps contagious too. Should we add a stanza or two to Sainte-Beuve's piece *Les Larmes de Racine*? Should we conclude that these scenes, which were no part of it, lent the tragedy some of its most moving graces?

Assuredly nothing could be less like the play of 1667 than the one that closed Racine's career, a quarter of a century later. Yet the creation of *Athalie* also was not to be without its links with English history: it is impossible to understand some of its intentions unless we remember the luckless endeavours of the dispossessed James II. But I will not trespass outside *Andromaque*. Suffice it if we can conclude that this, the second major event in our seventeenth-century dramatic history (the first being *Le Cid*), would not have been altogether what it was but for that spectacle so fraught with weighty lessons – a royal family and its destiny.

SOURCE: Translated by R. C. Knight. Presidential address to the Modern Humanities Research Association (1962).

P. F. BUTLER

The Tragedy of *Bérénice* (1949)

Sur toute joie, pour l'étrangler, j'ai fait le bond sourd de la bête féroce.
(A. Rimbaud, *Une Saison en Enfer*)

Bérénice is, of all Racine's plays, the one which has called forth most criticisms, even among his most fervent admirers. The subject is unsuitable for tragedy; so say not only Saint-Évremond or 'son ennemi Boileau', but Louis Racine, who is moved to laughter by it, Voltaire and La Harpe, who treat it with a condescension bordering on contempt. Renan was almost the only man in the nineteenth century who deeply enjoyed Racine's favourite tragedy; Sainte-Beuve, in a formula which criticism took up in a universal chorus, could see in it nothing but a 'ravissante élégie,' which ranked for him among the poet's minor works. Even after the *Bérénice* of Michaut, the first study to give the play the attention it deserves, it remains the most controversial of his tragedies, the one which has given rise to the most contradictory verdicts. The 'mélodieuse faiblesse', the 'comédie de cœur' of Sainte-Beuve is for Jules Lemaître a drama of heroic will-power, another *Polyeucte*, and for M. Dubech an essentially political play, in which Rome plays the leading role. But this Roman tragedy, which to Renan appeared profoundly Greek, is for M. Bechtum Le Ducq 'la Tragédie Française type'; and far from feeling in it the inspiration of *Polyeucte*, several critics make reservations concerning the 'héroïsme affiché' of its characters. To crown all, this Cornelian tragedy *manqué* is often held up as the Racinian tragedy *par excellence*. In the eyes of Michaut 'le chef-d'œuvre profane de Racine', to M. Brisson it is a 'prouesse de salon', a 'tragédie insincère', an 'œuvre factice'.

Bérénice, as Paul Mesnard wittily put it, seems unlucky for critics. Indeed, nowhere is the deceptive simplicity of Racine's art more dangerous, and he who advances beyond the noble classical façade with its serene ranks of columns is soon lost in disquieting labyrinths, haunted by strange Minotaurs. In these few pages I wish to study the

characters rather than the structure of the play, and taking as established
M. Michaut's demonstration of the dramatic character of *Bérénice*,
draw attention to its tragic quality. Why does Titus send Bérénice
away *invitus invitam*? Why does Bérénice accept the separation? A
strange dénouement for a tragedy, and a tragedy by Racine! What has
Titus in common with Pyrrhus? Is Bérénice really a sister of Hermione
and Roxane, who seek to bring all misfortune, if they cannot bring all
happiness, to the object of their love? Or have we here simply a
youthful affair, giving way to more serious concerns? But the intimate,
passionate tie which has held Titus and Bérénice together for five
years is as far removed from the frenzies of *Bajazet* as from the youthful
ardours of Achille and Iphigénie. Achille – and I do not deny that he
is everything a fiancé should be – burns above all to conquer Troy; but
the love of Bérénice has transformed the heart and the life of him
who made it

un plaisir nécessaire
De la voir chaque jour, de l'aimer, de lui plaire, (II ii 423-4)

and Bérénice

passe ses jours, Paulin, sans rien prétendre
Que quelque heure à me voir, et le reste à m'attendre.

(Ibid. 535-6)

If not the weakness of their love, is it then the strength of their
wills that explains the separation of these two lovers? This is the
Cornelian explanation of the play – that Titus and Bérénice, like
Rodrigue and Chimène, like Sévère and Pauline, sacrifice their love
to their duty, 'et sur *leurs* passions *leur* raison souveraine' makes them
submit to the obligations of the supreme seat of authority in the
Empire. I do not say that interpretation is absurd. Racine has been too
often shown as exclusively the painter of weak souls. Roxane is not
weak; Phèdre would die rather than betray her marriage vow;
Monime summons up the force to send away Xipharès. But the
Cornelian explanation does not really account for the drama of Racine.
The situation in *Bérénice* is Cornelian, but the characters are not; and
even when they seem to be acting in conformity with the Cornelian
code, the motives inspiring them are of quite another order. *Bérénice*
is in fact an act of defiance to Cornelianism – in the structure of the
play, as Racine himself emphasises, in its psychology, which adopts

positions opposite to that of Corneille, and in its repudiation, implicit
but radical, of every Cornelian value.

Fervent and tender, Bérénice has neither the barbaric splendour of
Roxane, nor the quasi-supernatural halo that irradiates Phèdre, but
she too stands in the forefront of the drama: the hopes and anxieties,
the angers and the rebellions which lead her by degrees from the happy
confidence of the first act to the stark desolation of the fifth, regulate the
progress of the tragedy. No rare metaphors adorn her passionate
entreaty, no sparkle relieves this deliberately effaced style; there is
only the masterly rhythm of a verse with musical inflections like a
phrase of Mozart, only the singing of the human voice:

> Ah cruel! est-i ltemps de me le déclarer?
> Qu' avez-vous fait? Hélas! je me suis crue aimée.
> Au plaisir de vous voir mon âme accoutumée
> Ne vit plus que pour vous. . . . (IV v 1062–5)

> Dans un mois, dans un an, comment souffrirons-nous,
> Seigneur, que tant de mers me séparent de vous?
> Que le jour recommence, et que le jour finisse,
> Sans que jamais Titus puisse voir Bérénice? (Ibid. 1113–16)

Need we wonder that among the Romantics some sensibilities felt
the spell of Racine's incomparable violin music so strongly as to forget
all the rest and see in *Bérénice* nothing but an elegy? But Bérénice is
very far from being a character of pure pathos, after the manner of
Les Juives or *L'Écossaise*, or a Romantic 'qui ne sait que son cœur'. Not
with Antiochus alone do we see how cold and hard this elegiac soul
can be ('Hé quoi, Seigneur! vous n'êtes point parti?'). With Titus
himself, what bursts of haughty anger, what explosions of outraged
pride! She deludes herself in the beginning, and who would not
share her error? But what lightning intuition, what clear-sighted
energy in the breathless struggle with Titus, entreating, threatening,
arguing, passionate and humble in turns, prepared to sacrifice anything
to save the essential, defending their common happiness inch by inch,
defending Titus himself against Titus.

> Ah, Seigneur, s'il est vrai, pourquoi nous séparer?
> Je ne vous parle plus d'un heureux hyménée:
> Rome à ne plus vous voir m'a-t-elle condamnée? . . .

> Hé bien, Seigneur, hé bien! qu'en peut-il arriver?
> Voyez-vous les Romains prêts à se soulever? . . .
>
> Quoi! pour d'injustes lois que vous pouvez changer,
> En d'éternels chagrins vous-même vous plonger?
>
> (IV v 1126-8, 1137-8, 1149-50)

Elegiac and dramatic, the character of Bérénice is also tragic by the nature of the conflict in which she is engaged. 'Un amant et une maîtresse qui se quittent,' said Voltaire, 'ne sont pas un sujet de tragédie.' But the tragic essence is surely 'the spectacle and the emotion (fear or pity) of human misery . . . created by the essential conditions of life, by the mysterious violence of destiny, by the often ironical play of an incomprehensible divine force which confounds and crushes man' (G. Lanson). Bérénice, like Psyche of old, sees her happiness vanish at the moment when she thought it was complete, all her joy changes to bitterness, and from the tenderest, most genuine love issues the savage 'duel' of Baudelaire's lovers. In the decisive battle she fights against Titus, Bérénice has to bear the weight of circumstances she can in no way change: neither the destiny of her birth which made her a queen, nor the foreign blood in her veins, can be abolished. And lastly, Bérénice stands alone exposed to the hostility of an entire people, of this inexorable spectre that Titus conjures up between her and himself: 'Rome . . . l'Empire . . .'

But this tragedy of circumstance, a tragedy external, and not unlike that of Corneille, combines in Racine with another, more subtle and more inward. The whole play in fact tends to replace the pressure of circumstance by the more delicate, but equally cruel and no less inevitable, play of the hidden motive forces in the heart. It is not only her royal dignity and her alien origin that cause the ruin of Bérénice, it is everything in her that is noble, and even Roman. Devotion to the public good, the sense of honour and duty, it was Bérénice who gradually nurtured these in the dissolute young prince from Nero's court. 'Je lui dois tout, Paulin,' Titus confesses,

> Récompense cruelle!
> Tout ce que je lui dois va retomber sur elle. (II ii 519-20)

Above all we must see that we do not interpret as mere rhetoric that explicit threat of Titus – that if Bérénice dies, he will die. This genuine psychological *coup de théâtre* has the effect of transferring to her the

whole burden of the decision. Here again it would be wrong to think
that the dilemma is unreal. An ironic fate restores her liberty to
Bérénice: the choice is hers; but what a choice! For she can only save
Titus by losing him. We know how Hermione would choose, how
she does choose. But Hermione was overcome by jealousy. Racine
has spared his Bérénice this canker. For her he has reserved a more
exquisite pain, with no end and no escape – Bérénice must live that
Titus may live. And if she lives on after her disaster, it is not because
this Palestinian Elvire has raised her dagger only to drop it again in
floods of tears. To preserve Titus alive Bérénice renounces what to
her is dearer than life,

> For exile hath more terror in his look,
> Much more than death . . .

The terrible mutilation she has done everything to evade, she in the end
is called upon to effect; it falls to her to lay the knife to her own flesh
and cut herself off from Titus for ever.

It is right then that Bérénice, like Andromaque, should give her name
to the play, since it depends on her whether the tragedy shall end in a
threefold suicide or a threefold renunciation. But if Bérénice gives
the conflict its solution, it is Titus who formulates it, his initiative
that sets it in motion. Titus in any case is by no means as static, nor
is the outcome so certain, as it has been claimed. And, most important,
it is from the soul of Titus that the forces emerge which create the
tragedy.

The immediate reason for the Emperor's decision is the fact that the
law of Rome forbids him to marry Bérénice. Rome hates royalty, and
Bérénice is a queen; Rome despises alien races, and Bérénice is a Jewess.
Rome is unceasingly present in the tragedy, with her power, which
makes and unmakes kingdoms, her great past, and her massy pomp
of gold and purple:

> Ces flambeaux, ce bûcher, cette nuit enflammée,
> Ces aigles, ces faisceaux, ce peuple, cette armée,
> Cette foule de rois, ces consuls, ce sénat . . . (I v 303–5)

But Racine's Rome is not that of Corneille. The eloquent and patriotic
Romans of *Horace, Cinna, Nicomède,* are as far removed from the
dangerous wild beasts of *Britannicus,* as Livy is from Tacitus and

Suetonius. And it is in the light of *Britannicus* that *Bérénice* should be read, as Racine himself invites us to read it (lines 351 ff). What Titus has to fear is not the timid magistrates or the cringing Senate who let Claudius marry his brother's daughter. No *potestas*, no legal authority, stands in the way of the imperial will. 'Anything is permissible to me, against anyone', said Caligula, *omnia mihi et in omnis licere* (Suetonius), and Paulin echoes him:

> Vous pouvez tout. Aimez, cessez d'être amoureux,
> La cour sera toujours du parti de vos vœux. (ii ii 349–50)

But Titus looks to 'un plus noble théâtre' (356); he wants Paulin to be spokesman for 'tous les cœurs'; he seeks to know 'ce que les Romains pensent'. It is to public opinion, then, that he would conform. But in first-century Rome – and in Racine's writing – the people has become indistinguishable from the populace. Formidable no doubt, but at the same time contemptible, this 'public opinion' is nothing but blind xenophobia, a 'reste de sa fierté' that 'survit dans tous les cœurs après la liberté' (lines 385–6), the hatred and rancour of a dethroned Sovereign People. It is impossible to mistake the implications of certain lines:

> Jules céda lui-même au torrent qui m'entraîne.
> Si le peuple demain ne voit partir la reine,
> Demain elle entendra ce peuple furieux
> Me venir demander son départ à ses yeux. (iii i 731–4)

> Qui? moi? j'aurais voulu, honteuse et méprisée,
> D'un peuple qui me hait soutenir la risée? (iv v 1179–80)

Rome in *Bérénice* is less the court and the servile Senate than that 'foule insensée' (v v 1319), cruel and mocking, with its primitive reactions, the crowd of the Circus and its games – still invested, by the great name of Rome, with a vague aura of sanctity. How far removed is this Rome, whose equivocal glory has never been better portrayed by Racine than in *Bérénice*, from that stirring image, the mother of heroes in Cornelian tragedy!

So Caesar is afraid of riots? To think that would be to misjudge his courage ... Titus only fears having to shed Roman blood. And then, although the whole world like Antiochus takes the marriage as certain, Rome murmurs but does nothing. If then we grant that *Bérénice* is a 'political' play, we must at least admit that Titus is moved by considerations of principle, rather than swayed by immediate necessity or external pressure: as guardian of the law, he will in no way compromise its sacred character, and he refuses to risk a battle, however improbable, which it would be distasteful to have to fight.

Does this suffice to explain the imperial decision? Is it not rather as if Racine was at pains to make it as gratuitous as possible and deprive it of all substance? For the fact is that Titus sacrifices Bérénice to a law which he knows to be neither just nor reasonable; one which, even accepting certain risks, it is in his power to repeal. More than this, Bérénice does not ask to reign, cares little for the rank of empress; Bérénice does not even ask that Titus should marry her; she asks only to be allowed to see him and love him. This makes nonsense of all the political reasons: yet Titus jibs. Were those critics right who cast doubts on his love? Or does Racine reject a compromise solution only in order to save his play, even at the cost of psychological probability? I do not wish to be accused of turning Titus into a hypocrite; I question neither his sincerity nor his love; I am only asking the questions Titus puts to himself:

> Car enfin Rome a-t-elle expliqué ses souhaits?
> L'entendons-nous crier autour de ce palais?
> Vois-je l'État penchant au bord d'un précipice? ...
> Tout se tait; et moi seul trop prompt à me troubler,
> J'avance des malheurs que je puis reculer. (IV iv 1001ff)

This duty, always so clear to Corneille's characters, sometimes eludes Titus' grasp; yet, even when it seems to vanish, or at least lose all inevitability, Titus repulses Bérénice, and so resolutely that at times he seems to be pursuing not glory but destruction. Bérénice sees the truth when she divines that the obstacle is not simply Rome, but Titus:

> Tout l'Empire a vingt fois conspiré contre nous.
> Il était temps encor: que ne me quittiez-vous? ...
> Je pouvais de ma mort accuser votre père,
> Le peuple, le Sénat, tout l'empire romain ...
> Je n'aurais pas, Seigneur, reçu ce coup cruel,
> Dans le temps que j'espère un bonheur immortel,
> Quand votre heureux amour peut tout ce qu'il désire,
> Lorsque Rome se tait, quand votre père expire,
> Lorsque tout l'univers fléchit à vos genoux,
> Enfin quand je n'ai plus à redouter que vous.
> *Titus.*   Et c'est moi seul aussi qui pouvais me détruire. (IV v 1073 ff)

This line illumines the whole tragedy like a flash of lightning. In this essential minute souls are laid bare and face each other in their nudity. In the sacrifice dictated to Titus by duty, what passion is it that surreptitiously finds assuagement? And this fever to trample on all he holds most dear, what is it but the vertigo of destruction, a kind of strange and terrible death-wish?

This death-theme, this *Todesmotiv*, runs in muted tones through the whole tragedy:

> Je n'examine point si j'y pourrai survivre. (II iii 552)

> Je sens bien que sans vous je ne saurais plus vivre,
> Que mon cœur de moi-même est prêt à s'éloigner;
> Mais il ne s'agit plus de vivre, il faut régner. (IV v 1100–2)

> Je n'aurai pas, Madame, à compter tant de jours ...
> Vous verrez que Titus n'a pu sans expirer ...
>
> (Ibid. 1122, 1125)

It becomes dominant in the astonishing reversal of the fifth act, when Titus, suddenly forgetting Rome and the Empire to which he meant to devote himself, considers the solution of suicide which so shocked the Cornelian faction.[1] The reversal is only apparent, the continuity complete. Rome has never been for Titus what it was for Horace – the god for whom one fights, dies, kills brother and sister, for whom one will even quit the field amid jeers. To the more august name of Death, Titus is willing to sacrifice both Rome and Bérénice. For death is no less present in this tragedy without murders than in the bloodthirsty *Bajazet*. It is death, more even than Rome, that obsesses Titus, and whose insidious whisper comes to him 'comme un ordre secret de ne plus résister' (V vi 1414). Andromaque too, choosing her own death, chose also to risk the life of her Astyanax, and the 'innocent stratagème', by which Racinian heroes seek to escape from their dilemma and find justification in their sacrifice, only betrays their deep-seated inclination and their most hidden preference.

Here perhaps appears the difference between Racine's *Bérénice* and a play of Corneille. It is in the first place that the injuries inflicted on one another by Titus and Bérénice are far deeper and more incurable – whereas in *Le Cid* a just, human, reasonable and providential king comes to release Chimène from her duty of vengeance, and stops the combat when blood is about to flow. It is also that the Cornelian sacrifice, that of Auguste for instance, bears with it its own reward; it gives the hero access to a richer life, a higher plane of liberty and joy. On the far side of martyrdom there opens for Polyeucte the mystical vision of eternal beatitude. But for Titus and Bérénice, this amputation of a passion having the vigour of youth and bound up with the noblest part of themselves, so far from being a means of self-fulfilment, leaves them as it were crippled, or, to borrow Claudel's forceful expression, 'opérés de leur raison d'être'. Bérénice, it is true, gives up Titus, but what is there here akin to the victorious jubilation of the Cornelian will? Bérénice consents to live, as men consent to die, in an impulse of abnegation which is an act of pure love. Corneille's Bérénice conquers her love and gives Titus up the moment the Senate consents to the marriage – her *gloire* is satisfied (*Tite et Bérénice*, v v). But in the final sacrifice of the Racinian heroine there seems to be a mortal lassitude:

> Je crois, depuis cinq ans jusqu'à ce dernier jour,
> Vous avoir assuré d'un véritable amour.
> Ce n'est pas tout: je veux, en ce moment funeste,
> Par un dernier effort couronner tout le reste:
> Je vivrai, je suivrai vos ordres absolus.
> Adieu, Seigneur. Régnez, je ne vous verrai plus.
>
> (v vii 1489–94)

And Titus leaves the contest broken, bloodless, in the horror and detestation of himself:[2] 'Moi-même je me hais' (iv vi 1213). Where are those Cornelian shouts of triumph?

> Je le ferais encor, si j'avais à le faire …
> Je suis maître de moi comme de l'univers …
> Où le conduisez-vous? – A la mort. – A la gloire …

But the contrast goes still deeper. For it is quite true that on the Cornelian plane, in Cornelian language, Titus has conquered his passions, and duty claims him. But what turbid passions are mingled with that duty! And if it is irresistible, is it not because of the dark forces that sustain it and throng behind it? Passion and duty – this antithesis, so clear and reassuring in the drama of Corneille, is dissolved and clouded in the destructive alchemy of *Bérénice*. The whole proud fortress of Cornelian ethics staggers, its most unassailable positions turned and occupied without a blow.

Antiochus too has suffered from the vicissitudes of *Bérénice*. For

Faguet he was the most important character in the play; his wailings, according to Daniel Mornet, are simply a nuisance. Antiochus deserves 'ni cet excès d'honneur, ni cette indignité'. His role contains some of the best-known lines in Racine, and his dramatic utility is no longer disputed. But this is the point: is he anything else but a 'utility'? Here again, the figure only takes on its full importance when considered from the tragic angle, when we remember that Racine is above all a tragedian. If Antiochus is unable to influence the development of the drama directly, if he is of all its characters the most 'agi', it is not for want of force and character in the companion-at-arms of Titus and the conqueror of Jerusalem; it is because he is caught up in a mesh of circumstances and feelings which makes it impossible for him to take any action. Antiochus drags along with him a passion which is un-requited and rendered hopeless by the mutual love of the other two, and the fatal coincidence of being made the messenger of Titus draws down on him the hatred of Bérénice. He too has outbursts of bitter passion –

> Je fuis des yeux distraits
> Qui me voyant toujours ne me voyaient jamais
>
> (I iv 277–8)

– or revolt –

> Dieux cruels! de mes pleurs vous ne vous rirez plus   (v iv 1302)

– like Oreste, to whom he has been compared, and whose melancholy and fatalism he shares. But Titus' friendship, and the watchful com-passion which makes him unable to bear the suffering of Bérénice, complete the process of tying his hands. He it is who comes to beg Titus to go back to Bérénice. His fury and exasperation in the fifth act are turned, not against either of them, but against himself. And if, in lines worthy of Sévère, he wishes Bérénice 'mille prospérités l'une à l'autre enchaînées' (v vii 1464), he adds:

> Je conjure les dieux d'épuiser tous les coups
> Qui pourraient menacer une si belle vie
> Sur ces jours malheureux que je vous sacrifie. (1466–8)

Antiochus is another ἑαυτὸν τιμωρούμενος, who takes up and accom-panies in a minor key the theme of fatality that dominates Titus and Bérénice.

This urge to self-destruction, so eminently tragic, occupies a considerable place in the complex network of motives actuating the personages in *Bérénice*; but it would be a mistake to think that it is found only there. Of how many characters could it be said, as it is of Oreste, 'Le coup qui l'a perdu n'est parti que de lui'! It is Monime who betrays Xipharès, Atalide seals Bajazet's doom. And who makes the marriage of Mithridate impossible, but Mithridate? It is he who brings to life that other love buried in Monime's heart, and by his deceits drives into hostility a girl at first resigned, but now defiant:

> Vous seul, Seigneur, vous seul, vous m'avez arrachée
> A cette obéissance où j'étais attachée;
> Et ce fatal amour dont j'avais triomphé ...
> Vos détours l'ont surpris, et m'en ont convaincue.
>
> (*Mithridate*, IV iv 1339 ff)

'Ye gods,' prayed the old King of Pontus,

> Épargnez mes malheurs, et daignez empêcher
> Que je ne trouve encor ceux que je vais chercher!
>
> (Ibid. II iii 525-6)

But he was jealous, he desired not Monime's hand alone, but her heart, he wished to know, to be sure. Titus loves, he is loved, he is a ruler; he has all that a malevolent Fate has refused Phèdre, Bajazet, and Oreste. ... But Fate needs no other instrument than ourselves to achieve our misfortune.

If then *Bérénice* is what it has been called, a *gageure*, we can I think concede that Racine has won it. *Bérénice* is a play that is entirely psychological, and yet it is in a real sense a drama, a tragedy – not a 'comedy of the heart'; a play without external events, but not a play in a sealed chamber, for the characters live out their private fates under the formidable pressure of a hostile world. We do not seek to turn an unjustly neglected drama into Racine's supreme masterpiece, nor even the typical Racinian tragedy, still less the typical French tragedy. That *Bérénice* is less dramatic than *Andromaque* or *Bajazet*, less rich in poetry than *Phèdre* or even *Iphigénie*, is possible; but less tragic, no. To see in it only an idyll, an elegy, even though ravishing, indicates a surprising misconception of what constitutes the essence of tragedy. This Racinian Fate, lurking in the depths of men's and women's hearts, inextricably mingled with their being yet dragging them where they would not go, is no less manifest in Titus than in Oreste or Phèdre.

This great darkness, that rises from the depths of souls and submerges them, is no less redoubtable than 'Vénus toute entière à sa proie attachée', no less irresistible than the 'impitoyable Dieu' who 'seul *a* tout conduit'. *Bérénice*, so implacable and so tender, so touching and so tragic, is not unworthy of the writer of *Andromaque*, *Phèdre* and *Athalie*.

SOURCE: Translated by R. C. Knight. From *French Studies*, III (1949). (A recast version appears in *Baroque et classicisme dans l'œuvre de Racine* (1959) pp. 232 ff.)

NOTES

1. Cf Abbé de Villars, *Critique de Bérénice* (1671): 'J'avas pourtant eu quelque espérance que le caractère de Titus serait héroïque ... mais quand je vis que tout cela n'aboutissait qu'à se tuer par maxime d'amour, je connus bien que ce n'était pas un héros romain, que le poète nous voulait représenter. ...'

2. Otway's *Titus and Berenice*, a much abridged adaptation of Racine's *Bérénice*, ends with the following lines:

> *Titus.* She's gone and all I valu'd lost.
> Now Friend, let *Rome* of her great Emp'ror boast.
> Since they themselves first taught me cruelty,
> I'll try how much a Tyrant I can be.
> Henceforth all thoughts of pitty I'll disown,
> And with my arms the Universe o'er-run,
> Rob'd of my Love through ruins purchase fame,
> And make the world's wretched as I am.

This Titus conceiving designs of vengeance is not Racine's, but a possible extension of the same figure. 'Praeter saevitiam suspecta in eo luxuria erat', says Suetonius, in his composite portrait of the man he elsewhere calls 'amor et deliciae generis humani'.

JEAN DUBU

Artistic Reasons for Racine's Silence after *Phèdre* (1953)

(In memoriam Gaston Broche)

OUR values are those of Racine's days no longer, yet, even after Jean Pommier's and Raymond Picard's careful and convincing analyses, can it be assumed that merely human or social reasons weighed with the poet and brought about his decision to withdraw from the stage after *Phèdre*, which proved a lasting success despite the intrigues (and alarms perhaps) of the first few nights? The appointment as historiographer royal was indeed a remarkable worldly achievement for a poet 'born at La Ferté-Milon', as the lampoonists of the day seldom lost an opportunity to recall – just as an unromantic marriage brought regular habits and drew a veil of respectability over the errors of the past; and Racine had succeeded in establishing a delicate balance, between elements as distinct as the King's favour (including that of his favourites), his own ambition (an orphan's lifelong desire for revenge over fate adverse) and his personal convenience.

What about the artist's claims? ... Some critics would probably object from the start that it is taking too modern, too romantic a view, to consider that Racine, the well-known careerist, might have given more than a few brief careless moments to such subsidiary matters. Yet there is ample evidence that, thereafter, he did not neglect his past tragedies; by careful and repeated corrections he showed that they were still alive for him; he even added to his lyrical and dramatic works. Saint-Simon's penetrating remark: 'None of the poet in him, an utter man of the world and, towards the end, a thorough gentleman', provides a clue: the same sense of proportion was at work all the time, the tact it inspired was already well known. The poet was there all right, yet socially poets can be unbearable; Racine's subsequent life would show that one poet, despite the accepted disrepute of the body as a whole, could behave properly and even becomingly. And yet remain a poet. Was not the man who later composed *Esther* and *Athalie* the same man, for all his change of attitude towards his previous works, as the author of *Phèdre* and even *Iphigénie*? Had not the artist willingly accepted (and perhaps secretly welcomed) this silence for reasons of his own, marks of which can be found precisely in his works?

If *Phèdre* marks a turning-point in the dramatic technique of Racine, so much so that Giraudoux could write of it as 'the first of a series of plays of terror' (a series never written), it was with *Iphigénie* that the new theme appeared of which the last four completed tragedies of our author were to bear the mark, and with them the two projects known to us only by rumour – I mean the direct intervention of the supernatural, joined with a new way of looking at Death and using it for dramatic effect.

In the tragedies before *Iphigénie*, the supernatural involves no more than the existence of gods who are invoked at a moment of stress: their moral reality in the heroes' eyes amounts to no more than a poetic form of words. Frequently the gods are merely a collective plural, and the grammatical distinction differentiating them from God in the singular – the concept to which the author had been accustomed by a monotheistic religion – becomes imperceptible. In the first performances of *Bérénice*, and even in the first edition, the heroine refers to 'les Dieux' (see particularly lines 145, 312, 591); the abbé de Villars pointed out the inconsistency of this polytheism in the mouth of a queen of Jewish extraction, and Racine repaired the mistake, even substituting 'au Ciel' for 'aux Dieux' in a line of Titus:

Plût au Ciel que mon Père, hélas! vécût encore! (II iv 600)

Such expressions are rather an automatic reflex – one dare not say a *cheville* – than a dramatic and psychological reality. The gods, though inevitable dramatic properties, find their scope severely limited. Right at the end of *Andromaque* we do see Oreste fall a prey to the Erinyes, it is true; but, striking as that scene is, and great as is the pathos it confers on Racine's dénouement, the Erinyes do come in at the end. We had neither seen them nor guessed at their existence until that moment, and even their victim did not realize that he had to fear them. In fact, these men and women are actuated by passions and sentiments still very close to instinct, as has often been pointed out, both by their violence – which Racine sought to portray above all else – and by their spontaneity. They have no questionings about the origins of what they undergo, they are too busy suffering and defining the results. And death, in the prevailing social atmosphere where nothing exceeds the importance of psychological observation, is simply a means of ending it all – the poet may sometimes neglect to use it, if he is satisfied that his drama is full of 'la violence des passions', 'la beauté des sentiments', and 'l'élégance de l'expression', to quote the preface to *Bérénice*.

With *Iphigénie*, the climate changes. We return to subjects from Greek literature, such as the apparent (but only apparent) source of *La Thébaïde*, and that which undeniably contributed to Racine's success with *Andromaque*. *Iphigénie* was the first of his tragedies to be inspired for the greater part by Euripides, and it shows a change of ground which was to become more marked, and has only been generally noticed, in *Phèdre*. The starting-point of the drama is not now, primarily, a conflict of passions, but an order from the gods; or, if we prefer to look at it another way, the conflict of Agamemnon's ambition with Achille's *gloire*, and Clytemnestre's mother-love, combated by the submission of Iphigénie, all starts with the oracle of Calchas and Diana's will. The theomachy, the Battle of the Gods, which in Homer and the Greek dramatists accompanies and explains the human drama, thus finds its way on to the French stage, and with it the beginnings of a justification on the metaphysical plane; Calchas, the precursor of Mardochée and Joad, the mediator, priest and prophet, never appears, but everything depends on his oracles which no one thinks of contradicting. Thus the Cartesianism of an entirely secular psychology is tinged with the irrational greatness and poetry of an arbitrary divine will, and, at the same time, death acquires a new meaning.

Andromaque's acceptance of suicide had been there to show that Racine, very early on, had learnt to use death as a dramatic device; but Pyrrhus, the character principally concerned, never learns of the decision she reached at Hector's tomb: so that, from one point of view, that decision only becomes the subject of one dramatic scene, between herself and Céphise. *Bérénice* goes further and shows suicide threats used as a form of blackmail, unblushingly, by the three characters: but we have moved from early Greek history to imperial Rome, and moreover, if any of them know that their suicide will bring about the suicide of a crowned head, they feel morally obliged to renounce it, on pain of being unworthy of the crown they wear themselves. A *bienséance*, dictated by the seventeenth-century abhorrence of regicide, restrains these members of the most exclusive club conceivable – three sovereigns in their own right. (We may recall the awe with which Saint-Simon relates the unprecedented occasion in 1700 which brought together at Versailles *three kings*, and all the details of protocol invented for it.) In these projects of suicide we have, then, only a means of justifying the dénouement. Whereas, in *Iphigénie*, death acquires two new characteristics: it becomes imminent, and *inescapable*. It is not simply the just wages of wickedness and guilt, or the elegant way out chosen by a contemporary of Petronius – the victim longs to live. The evolution of the poet's thought in this respect is striking. He stresses it in the preface to *Iphigénie* when, taking up the cudgels for Euripides, he quotes the tragedy of *Alcestis* and offers us a fragment of his own translation of the play – of which, we remember, he destroyed the draft unpublished. Alcestis on the point of death, 'a l'image de la mort devant les yeux', in Racine's own words. He has, then, given much thought to the scenic and dramatic value of a dying figure and its farewells to life. We realize now what steps have led him to show us a Phèdre already dying as the play opens, and returns of that delirium which was only one episode rather suddenly introduced towards the end of *La Thébaïde* and *Andromaque*.

But Racine's meditation had not borne all its fruits when he brought out *Iphigénie*. The tyranny of *vraisemblance* made him timid, and he preferred an inconsistency, justified in the preface by superficial *a posteriori* arguments, to the perfect logic according to which a heroine, once condemned by the goddess, must die. After accepting the beliefs of Greek religion to the extent of admitting that Calchas is an infallible seer, we are bound to consider Ériphile's death, and the error over the identity of the victim, rather disappointingly facile solutions, however well they may square with the laws of the genre. Racine feels clearly that he had to submit to a compromise, and his explanations show that he was not happy about it; he takes refuge behind the *bienséances*, which forced him to save Iphigénie's life at any cost, and the desire to spare the audience 'un miracle qu'il n'aurait pu souffrir parce qu'il ne le saurait jamais croire'.

In *Phèdre*, the imminence of death is made much more palpable and convincing than in *Iphigénie*. Never out of our sight, it is justified in many different ways. On the plane of the psychology of passion, the poet works in, side by side with his habitual touches, details drawn

from physiology and coenaesthesia, which bring home to the audience
the desperate struggle taking place in the heroine's body; highly
particularised details which would have been most out of place had no
explanation been given us on a transcendental plane at the same time:

C'est Vénus toute entière à sa proie attachée. (I iii 306)

The success of this creation is certainly due to its psychological consistency – awareness of imminent death intensifies Phèdre's tendency
to introspective withdrawal, itself logically the source of her passion
on the moral plane, and reawakens the mystical tendency, which is
only another aspect of the tendency to introspection.

The new value attached to the supernatural, and to death, leads finally
to interiorization of the drama, a progress from the point of view of the
unities – for the scene of action is no longer physical but psychological,
now that the debate takes place, not on the stage, but within an individual's consciousness; but the immediate effect of this noteworthy
progress is to destroy the equilibrium of the drama as Racine had
hitherto conceived it. Thésée, Aricie, Œnone and even Hippolyte
are not of the same metal as Phèdre and still belong to the world of
romanesque values. Phèdre alone undergoes an ordeal that commands
our whole attention, and does so to the detriment of the attention we
should normally pay to her companions on the stage. Hence a shift
of plane and emphasis which had one important result – that of endow-
ing Phèdre alone with that variation which is truly life. Fénelon has
put this point very acutely in his *Lettre à l'Académie.* 'Il fallait laisser
Phèdre toute seule dans sa fureur. L'action aurait été unique, courte, vive
et rapide.' Paul Valéry too, whose *Jeune Parque* owes so much to a perceptive study of *Phèdre*, reduced his poem to a soliloquy, having
grasped that internal torment is self-sufficing, that the consciousness
can have no worthy interlocutor but itself, and any witness other than
reader or audience will always be an unwelcome intruder. But in the
interval had come *Hamlet*, brought from London to France one day
by Voltaire; whereas Racine was writing in the third quarter of the
seventeenth century, for a court and a public who expected their five
acts, and for companies which refused to sacrifice any of their time-
hallowed major roles. So he cast his study of a woman dying of sinful
passion in the form of a tragedy of the accepted type; but his new
themes, in spite of himself, displaced its centre of gravity.

So far, one might have seen Racine divided, broadly speaking, between two, or maybe three, patterns of distribution for his characters: one woman between two or three men (*Bérénice, Mithridate*), two women in conflict and opposed to two men (*Alexandre, Andromaque, Bajazet* – the celebrated quartet), two women, of different generations, opposed to several men (*La Thébaïde, Britannicus, Iphigénie*). In more than one way *Phèdre* belongs to the third category, and here Jean Pommier's subtle remark concerning Phèdre's age should be borne in mind, where he quotes:

> Va trouver de ma part ce *jeune* ambitieux. (III i 799)

Indeed, there is a delicate shift, so that half a generation divides Phèdre from Hippolyte (and Aricie), and probably the same from Thésée and Œnone. Part of the Queen's trouble comes from the fact, which Racine may have *felt* rather than clearly realized, that she becomes aware gradually (in Act IV, particularly) of being no longer a *jeune femme*, but a *femme jeune*. In the new production of the play at the Théâtre Français (1960), the emphasis was laid, by means of the colour schemes of the costumes, on the existence of three couples, what one might call three *natural* couples: Phèdre and Thésée, Hippolyte and Aricie, Théramène and Œnone: this sophisticated device made Phèdre's passion appear all the more monstrous (particularly in Act II, scene v, when the three characters each belonged to one of the three different pairs).

But the distinctive thing about the play seems to us that all those features which, until this point, Racine used to distribute skilfully between touching and unpleasant characters alike, making us feel compassion for Hermione *and* Andromaque, different though the degree and, perhaps, the quality of that compassion might be, here are piled on the one figure of Pasiphaë's doomed daughter. Convinced that she is incestuous in her love, the almost mystic victim of fate, feeling Death near her, alone and bereaved in the midst of a primeval nature where emotions little different from instinct are the rule, such is the Cretan queen; to these Racine adds dishonour, jealousy, poison at last – as the means to what a suicide!

> Par un chemin plus lent descendre chez les morts . . . (v vii 1636)

Recently, H. T. Barnwell has clearly and most aptly shown how this was necessary to produce the final phase of tragedy: the recognition of errors through enlightenment reconciling the hero with his fate,

and wounded nature with itself. Yet all admirers of the play have
noticed the exceptional wealth of psychological traits and dramatic
features lavished on *one* character, and the utter unbalance brought
about by such profligacy. Despite the author's acknowledged craftsmanship, the other characters look thin; even, at times, sound hollow.
Indeed, the younger couple, which comes straight from the *romanesque*
intrigue dear to the seventeenth-century playgoer, is steeped in a
'climate of politeness' (Stegmann) which may seen insipid.

A queer fate, that of Hippolytus, raised in Euripides' play to the
rank of a demi-god (whence, no doubt, the strange haze of holiness
and religious feeling that still lingers around him), this strange oblate,
this votary of Diana with his downright, uncouth chastity, doomed
by our classical stage and its requirements to a veritable transfiguration.
The deep generosity which, here, is the foundation of his personality
stands in utter opposition to Phèdre's endless, tormented variation.
With La Fontaine's Adonis, his near-contemporary, he shares a
courteous kindness, raised to heroism in respect of Thésée and the
queen herself. Yet, proper rather than passionate, he develops little.
Does he ever really demonstrate that love which he confesses to
Théramène and that Aricie more or less compels him to admit?
Death, which strikes him first, seems not to touch him. Unless Théramène's memory fails him, there was no room in Hippolyte's last
words for any regret of life – or Aricie. Businesslike, he is satisfied with
trying to restore her to his father's favour.

So with Aricie. Not that she is not finely delineated, but Racine,
in search of a character apt to create a sharp contrast, innocent, pure,
graceful so as to enhance Phèdre's monstrosity, fails, exactly as with
Hippolyte, to endow her with real tragic strength.

Like *La Thébaïde* and *Iphigénie*, *Phèdre* uses the character of a father
and the background of a patriarchal society. Now the three fathers
have one common feature which brings us back to our subject: each
is somehow responsible for his child's death – Créon, the most detest-
able, through personal ambition; Agamemnon through ambition, and
political forces too: his daughter's death is by no means his direct
responsibility, but the oracle's. Hence a conflict, and the deep humanity
of this man 'who never appears on a level with the situation and for
whom the freedom of choice was a fatal present' (F. K. Dawson).
Quite different is Thésée: in one sense, his position is the reverse of
that of Mithridate. The latter is in love, and not yet Monime's husband.

His jealousy makes him tragic – his son's rival, with his age against him. He is pathetic in so far as he has been entertaining illusions over his power to command her love, and this fails him at the very moment all the rest fails him as well: victory, crowns, allies. But Thésée does not feel jealousy for a single moment: the only task he sets himself is to avenge the Queen's honour; so that he does not appear as a deceived husband, but as a credulous man. The contrast is sharp between him and the characters in other Racinian tragedies, so laden with history, so conscious of the past, their own and that of the group they belong to. Thésée simply forgets who Phèdre is, where she comes from; he does not take the hint when Hippolyte ventures:

> Phèdre est d'un sang, Seigneur ... (IV ii 1151)

Father and son are equally single-minded. Thésée's credulousness does not work only as a blind acceptance of Phèdre's and Œnone's assertions, but in relation to Neptune. In *Iphigénie*, the real believers were the two girls on one side, and the mob of soldiers on the other. Euripides' hardly disguised rationalism in the handling of the plot has passed into Racine's play. One may even detect a slight political tension between the King of Kings and the High Priest.

Thésée is quite different: his relationship with Neptune is personal, and his critical powers nil. Œnone herself – the only character beside him to feel parental love towards another on the stage, and in this respect she ranks not far from Clytemnestre – did not expect that he would summon such extraordinary aid:

> Un père en punissant, Madame, est toujours père.
> Un supplice léger suffit à sa colère. (III iii 902–3)

Such simple and intense notions are highly poetical and dramatic; they help greatly to create a suitable atmosphere to contrast with Phèdre's subtler touches of introspection. To those who might deem Iphigénie too much of a seventeenth-century princess, Clytemnestre too much a Bourbon queen and Alexandre another Enghien or Lauzun, Thésée could but come as a reminder of much earlier days: several centuries of civilization truly separate the two sets of characters. Whether this comes from the Greek original matters less here than the price paid for such vivid evocation of a legendary, instead of a historic, past: characters of a coarser intellectual grain, and the adoption of a strange compromise in the handling of religious matters.

Racine is evidently careful to avoid the trap into which he fell when writing *Bérénice*. Paradoxically he does almost the reverse. Mentions of gods, whether by name or collectively (as 'les Dieux', 'le Ciel', etc.) are barely fewer in *Phèdre* than in *Iphigénie* (at a rough count, 76 to 105), bearing in mind that there are fewer speaking characters and fewer occasions for exclamation. But at the same time polytheistic references (to gods conceived of as plural) are 38 to 65, and references with a definitely monotheistic ring become relatively more numerous. And the result should not be underrated: when in either play any character, instead of referring to 'les Dieux', mentions 'le Ciel' - e.g. when Agamemnon exclaims:

> Non, je ne croirai point, ô Ciel, que ta justice
> Approuve la fureur de ce noir sacrifice
>
> *(Iphigénie,* I i 121-2)

or when Phèdre exclaims:

> Détestables flatteurs, présent le plus funeste
> Que puisse faire aux rois la colère céleste, (IV vi 1325-6)

- Racine is adroitly drawing on his audience's religious habits and experience to create the necessary sympathy with his heroes. When, some fourteen years later, Joad says:

> ... Ce roi que le Ciel vous redonne aujourd'hui *(Athalie,* IV iii 1371)

does he speak differently? Thésée's Neptune is a *Dieu vengeur*, just like Joad's Iahweh, and each is a *dieu cruel*.

Arnauld, long before J. Lemaître, had grasped this aspect of *Phèdre*, and applauded it; he even tried to reassure the author. Here was a man with a faith seasoned enough to withstand the controversies we remember, who had come to see in the world, as his like tends to do, nothing but illustrations of his faith. But Racine was no austere, sublime theologian, no convert rooted in unshakable certainties; rather, even in his beliefs, and similar in this to the ancient Greeks he had so long frequented, for whom every truth offered a double face, Racine hesitated between the psychological truth dear to those who had been his masters and models in the art of moving a select, sophisticated public, and the truth of a revealed metaphysics, implanted in him from youth by Port-Royal with the same pedagogical zeal to which he owed the discovery of the glorious polytheism of Olympus. (It was the same strangely split mentality with which Montaigne in his day had had to come to terms; it seems, to a point, characteristic of our French civilization, split between the secular and the sacred.) Could he then, at a time when he felt within him once again

Les repentirs, les doutes, les contraintes,

accept a form of symbiosis, a compromise, whereby the force and authority of an inward, almost mystical experience acquired within the Christian religion were by him bestowed on the fabled history and heroes of paganism?

We see then that, to the other considerations, personal or social, which may have weighed with him, his artist's conscience may have added reasons of a technical and moral kind – he felt the need, without ceasing to give pleasure or respect the strict laws of his genre, of restoring the inward equilibrium of his work and removing a contradiction, which had become flagrant, between his own metaphysical beliefs and those that his heroes illustrated on the stage. In the absence of texts to confirm this hypothesis beyond doubt, we would willingly leave it as a mere conjecture; but it seemed that a short discussion of *Esther* and *Athalie*, those flowers that came to bloom on the further shore of our poet's mysterious silence, would be relevant and might confirm our contentions.

The last two plays abandon Greece, for a people of believers having close and obvious links with Christianity. Some of its members have a religious fervour which makes it possible to show a human character as the mouthpiece of God – like Calchas, behind the scenes in *Iphigénie* – Mardochée, then Joad. Introspection, psychological explanation, diminish, but the audience's legitimate demand to see the causes of the action is fully satisfied on the metaphysical plane. Assuérus yields less to Esther's sensual charm, or to violent passion like that of Phèdre in her delirium, than to the grace of Iahweh whose instrument the Jewish girl is. Athalie, 'la superbe Athalie', terror-stricken by a dream, brings up before our eyes, accustomed to a more scientifically rational universe, all the baleful fascination of the unconscious. Despite her age, she is closer to a Phèdre at war with ancestors and goddesses, than to Agrippine defying Néron to his face. Like Phèdre she tries appeasement, incense, sacrifice: can we see the widow of Claudius offering her son even the incense of flattery? Emperor-worship, here, is beside the point. We have two worlds radically different; but in the second,

and especially in the last two plays, the dramatic unity which we saw
endangered by a disproportionate development of introspection has
been restored. *Phèdre* had meant the end of the unity created by shared
struggles and mutually inflicted pain. With *Esther* and *Athalie* appear
pain and emotions endured in common under the hand of a single God,
whose existence established the unity of the world and the drama.
No longer have we as in Phèdre a victim sacred in the true sense of
'set apart', and facing death in the presence of minor characters aghast
or uncomprehending. All, good and evil alike, are in the hand of
God.

At this point it is impossible not to recall that *Œdipe* which Fénelon
and Longepierre tell us Racine dreamed for a moment of writing. J.
Vanuxem reminds us, appropriately, that a line from the *Œdipus Rex*
of Sophocles is to be found in *Esther*, and two more in *Athalie*, and we
know for a fact that Racine annotated it in two editions of the Greek
text; but R. C. Knight has found no indication enabling us to date the
annotations, and thereby the poet's interest in the subject (cf above,
p. 164). If the three quotations justify us in assuming that the play was
in his mind in the years 1668–90, must we not suppose that he gave up
the project because at this moment, only the Judaeo-Christian order,
by the profound truth of the responses it awoke in him, seemed to him
worthy of the dream, and of man's attention? No other subject seems
to him acceptable save that scruple of predestination which the
Christian order has reconciled with individual liberty – and which in
his day was so often reasserted, so topical. Through it, with no less of
verisimilitude, all characters equally recover a liberty to which it
forms the metaphysical counterpoise: the drama recovers its equilibrium on well defined philosophical bases.

As symbols of the less individual, more collective, more subordinate
role of destiny as Racine now conceives it, stand the choruses. They
restore to drama the lyrical side for which the author had such gifts,
which now he could no longer use to paint the passions of lovers.
If the Bible provides the themes, the ancient Greeks inspire the structures (the play without love interest – exactly as *Œdipus*). Thus the
strictly intellectual approach tends to give way to one based rather on
the senses. On to the Bible story are grafted words drawn from the New
Testament, appealing directly to the sensibility of the public – and of
the players; and the poet knows he can rely on the simplicity, the
naïvety even, of these young girls to form a welcome novelty for the

jaded palates of a theatre-going society, as well as on the music, the singing, the crown jewels, the tapestries from the royal stores, and the truly liturgical atmosphere of great court occasions. What a theatre this was, this improvised stage rigged up in the convent school of Saint-Cyr with princely sumptuousness, this palace playhouse such as Versailles itself did not possess, its curtain rising on the timeless vistas of a story drawn from Holy Writ! A site of ideal import, where the ambiguity proper to poetry might triumph, purified as if by miracle of all profaner admixture. How we can sympathise with the author, after the encouragement of *Esther*, when he failed to obtain any worthy performances for *Athalie*!

And yet is the literary expression given here to religion so fundamentally different from what any Parisian, for almost fifteen years, could have heard declaimed by the two Champmeslés for the price of a few *sols*? The playwright takes his stories from a new source, the poet cannot detach himself from his language. This is the same thing, surely, that had happened to Le Brun and Poussin a few years before, when (as J. Vanuxem has shown) they deliberately translated their biblical themes by forms and details from the repertory of pagan Greece and Rome. Was Racine consciously trying to rival his former self, or was he not rather the slave of his own craftsmanship? Giraudoux has accused him of copying himself at this moment: might one not suggest that, from the time of *Iphigénie* or at least of *Phèdre*, his work had been anticipating the place and the dramatic value he was eventually to give to the religious element?

Looked at in this way, his retirement in 1677 appears not simply as the act of a courtier and historiographer anxious to please a royal patron; nor is it the sudden impulse of a soul assailed by scruples, seeking to accord its life with a rule till then neglected or uncomprehended in some of its demands (compromise was inevitable in that world of actors – and actresses; the source of his earnings was considered scandalous); this retirement also appears as the result of the artist's disquiet at the incompatibility of two metaphysical worlds, realizing that to certain people they may appear to be equated, and recoiling before the ambiguity he has thus expressed. Given his chance by the pious foundress of an educational institution, he prefers to break with the fables of pagan antiquity because they ring false to his religious experience; but, in the universe he chooses now, the inspiration – like an underground river emerging to create the cool of an oasis in the desert sands – the inspiration remains the same, and the craftsmanship is still nourished by the same classical models of unchanging quality. The crisis of middle life, less sudden perhaps than some have said and some still say, beginning as it seems as early as *Iphigénie* (because of *Iphigénie*, for all we know), cut short after *Phèdre* the unwitting disciple of the ancients: their rival, as *Esther* and *Athalie* attest, it did not harm.

SOURCE: Translated by Jean Dubu and R. C. Knight. Revised from 'Quelques raisons esthétiques pour le silence de Racine après *Phèdre*', in *XVIIᵉ Siècle*, xx (1953).

Select Bibliography

COLLECTED WORKS

Œuvres, ed. P. Mesnard, 8 vols and 2 albums (Hachette, 1865–73, etc.) ('Les Grands Écrivains de la France').

Théâtre complet, ed. G. Truc, 4 vols (Société des Belles-lettres, 1929–30) ('Les Textes français'). Original spelling and punctuation.

Œuvres complètes, ed. R. Picard, 2 vols (Gallimard, 1950), ('Bibliothèque de la Pléiade'). The latest complete and scholarly edition.

Théâtre complet, ed. M. Rat (Garnier, 1960).

Œuvres complètes, ed. P. Clarac (Seuil and Macmillan Co. of New York, 1962) ('L'Integrale'). No variants given.

SINGLE PLAYS

(*a*) English editions; introduction and commentary in English except where stated.

Britannicus, ed. P. Butler (Cambridge U.P., 1967). Extensive bibliography.

—— ed. W. H. Barber (Macmillan and St Martin's P., 1967).

Bérénice, ed. W. S. Maguinness (Manchester U.P., 1929, 1956).

—— ed. C. L. Walton (Oxford U.P., 1965).

Bajazet, ed. C. Girdlestone (Blackwell, 1955). Entirely in French.

Mithridate, ed. G. Rudler (Blackwell, 1943). Entirely in French.

Phèdre, ed. R. C. Knight (Manchester U.P., 1943, 1955).

Athalie, ed. P. France (Oxford U.P., 1966).

(*b*) Collection 'Mises en Scène' (Éditions du Seuil). Line-by-line commentaries by producers of noteworthy Paris productions, illustrated (but without scholarly authority).

Bajazet, mise en scène et commentaires de X. de Courville (1947).

Phèdre, mise en scène et commentaires de J.-L. Barrault (1946, 1959).

Athalie, mise en scène et commentaires de G. le Roy (1952).

ENGLISH TRANSLATIONS

In blank verse unless otherwise stated. (Racine's poetic style being what it is, no translation must be expected to convey the full flavour.)

The Dramatic Works of J. Racine. A metrical English version by R. B. Boswell ('Bohn's Standard Library') (H. G. Bohn *et al.*, 1846, etc.).

Bérénice and *Esther*, trans. John Masefield and published separately (Heinemann, 1922).

The Best Plays of Racine, translated in English rhyming verse by Lacy Lockert (Princeton U.P., 1936).

Racine's Mid-career Tragedies, translated in English rhyming verse by Lacy Lockert (Princeton U.P., 1952).

Jean Racine, *Five Plays*, trans. Kenneth Muir (MacGibbon & Kee and Hill & Wang, a Mermaid Dramabook, 1960). *Andromache, Britannicus, Berenice, Phaedra, Athaliah.*

Phaedra, trans. John Cairncross (Droz, Geneva, 1958).

Phaedra and other Plays [*Iphigenia, Athaliah*], trans. John Cairncross (Penguin Books, 1963, 1966).

Andromache and other Plays [*Britannicus, Berenice*], trans. John Cairncross (Penguin Books, 1967).

Phaedra and Figaro. Racine's *Phaedra* trans. Robert Lowell (Farrar, Straus & Cudahy, 1961).

Racine, *Phaedra*, trans. Robert Lowell (Faber, 1963). By general consent, a free paraphrase in a very different poetic idiom.

BIOGRAPHY AND CRITICISM

A. Adam, *Histoire de la littérature française au XVIIe siècle*, 5 vols (Domat, 1948–56) IV 277 ff, V 39 ff.

R. Bray, *La Formation de la doctrine classique en France* (Hachette, 1927; Nizet, 1951).

H. Bremond, *Racine et Valéry. Notes sur l'initiation poétique* (Grasset, 1930).

G. Brereton, *Jean Racine, a critical biography* (Cassell, 1951).

—— *An Introduction to the French Poets. Villon to the present day* (Methuen 1956; University Paperbacks UP5, 1960). Ch. VI.

P. Butler, *Classicisme et baroque dans l'œuvre de Racine* (Nizet, 1959).

J.-G. Cahen, 'Le Vocabulaire de Racine', in *Revue de linguistique romane*, XVI, nos. 59–64 (Droz, 1956).

A. F. B. Clark, *Jean Racine* (Harvard U.P. and Oxford U.P., 1939).

P. Claudel, *Conversation sur Jean Racine* (Gallimard, 1956).

Corneille and Racine: Parallels and Contrasts, ed. R. J. Nelson (Prentice-Hall, 1966). All texts but two in French.

A. A. Eustis, *Racine devant la critique française, 1838–1939* (U. of California P., 1949).

P. France, *Racine's Rhetoric* (Oxford U.P., 1965).

P. H. Frye, *Romance and Tragedy* (Jones, Boston, 1922; U. of Nebraska P., 1961). 'Racine', pp. 205 ff.

M. Fubini, *Jean Racine e la critica delle sue tragedie* (Sansoni, Società tipografico editrice nazionale, Turin, 1925).

J. Giraudoux, *Jean Racine* (Grasset, 1930); and in the same author's *Littérature* (Grasset, 1941) pp. 27–55, and other collections. Trans. P. M. Jones (Fraser, Cambridge, 1938).

L. Goldmann, *Le Dieu caché. Étude sur la vision tragique dans les 'Pensées' de Pascal et dans le théâtre de Racine* (Gallimard, 1955). Trans. P. Thody, *The Hidden God* (Routledge & Kegan Paul and Humanities P., 1964).

—— *Racine* (L'Arche, 1956).

J. D. Hubert, *Essai d'exégèse racinienne: les secrets témoins* (Nizet, 1956).

R. Jasinski, *Vers le vrai Racine*, 2 vols (A. Colin, 1958).

R. C. Knight, *Racine et la Grèce* (Didier-Boivin, [1951]).

H. C. Lancaster, *A History of French Dramatic Literature in the Seventeenth Century*, 5 parts in 9 vols (Johns Hopkins P. and Presses Universitaires Françaises, 1929–42; Gordian Press, 1966). Parts IV and V.

G. Lanson, *Esquisse d'une histoire de la tragédie française* (Columbia U.P., 1920; 2nd ed. Champion, 1927).

J. C. Lapp, *Aspects of Racinian Tragedy* (Toronto U.P. and Oxford U.P., 1955, 1964; Canadian University Paperbacks, no. 28).

V. Lugli, *Racine* (Formiggini, 1926).

T. Maulnier, *Racine* (Librairie de la Revue Française, 1935; Gallimard, 1936, 1947, 1954).

—— *Lecture de* Phèdre (Gallimard, 1942).

F. Mauriac, *La Vie de Jean Racine* (Plon, 1928).

G. May, *Tragédie cornélienne, tragédie racinienne* (U. of Illinois P., 1948).

W. G. Moore, *Racine: Britannicus* (Arnold, 1960; Studies in French Literature, no. 1).

P. Moreau, *Racine, l'homme et l'œuvre* (Boivin, 1943; Hatier, 1952).

D. Mornet, *Jean Racine* (Aux Armes de France, 1944).

O. de Mourgues, *Racine, or The Triumph of Relevance* (Cambridge U.P., 1967).

—— *Autonomie de Racine* (Corti, 1967). Revised and translated version of the preceding.

R. Picard, *La Carrière de Jean Racine* (Gallimard, 1956, 1961).

—— *Corpus racinianum: Recueil-inventaire des textes et documents du XVIIᵉ siècle concernant Jean Racine* (Les Belles Lettres, 1956).

—— *Supplément au 'Corpus racinianum'* (Les Belles Lettres, 1961).

—— *Nouveau supplément, Troisième supplément*, in *Jeunesse de Racine* (La Ferté-Milon, 1963) p. 5 ff (1966) pp. 3 ff. See also J. Dubu, *Raymundi Picard 'Corpori raciniano' addenda*, ibid. (1960) pp. 30 ff.

J. Pommier, *Aspects de Racine. Suivi de l'histoire littéraire d'un couple tragique* [Phèdre and Hippolyte] (Nizet, 1954).

J. Scherer, *La Dramaturgie classique en France* (Nizet, [1950, 1954]).

L. Spitzer, *Linguistics and literary History* (Princeton U.P. and Oxford U.P., 1948). 'The "récit de Théramène" ', pp. 87 ff.

G. Lytton Strachey, 'Racine' (dated 1908), in *Books and Characters* (Chatto and Harcourt, Brace, 1922) pp. 3 ff, and *Literary Essays*, in the *Collected Works* (Chatto, 1948) pp. 58 ff.

G. Truc, *Jean Racine: l'œuvre, l'artiste, l'homme et le temps* (Garnier, 1926).

M. Turnell, 'Jean Racine', in *The Classical Moment* (Hamilton, 1947, 1964) pp. 131 ff. Embodies articles of 1939.

E. Vinaver, *Racine et la poésie tragique* (Nizet, 1951, 1963). Trans. P. M. Jones, *Racine and poetic Tragedy* (Manchester U.P., 1955).

K. Vossler, *Jean Racine* (Hueber, 1926; Roland, 1948).

B. Weinberg, *The Art of Jean Racine* (Chicago U.P., 1963).

Katherine E. Wheatley, *Racine and English Classicism* (U. of Texas P., 1956).

E. E. Williams, *Racine depuis 1885, essai de bibliographie raisonnée* (Johns Hopkins P., 1940).

Notes on Contributors

SIR C. M. BOWRA, F.B.A., M.A., D.Litt., Warden of Wadham College, Oxford; author of *The Heritage of Symbolism*, *Sophoclean Tragedy*, and many other studies of classical and modern literature.

JULES BRODY, Ph.D., Professor of Romance Languages and Associate Dean of Faculty at Queen's College (University of New York); author of *Boileau and Longinus*, editor of *French Classicism: a critical miscellany*.

PHILIP F. BUTLER, Ph.D., D.ès-L., Lauréat of the University of Lausanne, Professor of French in the University College of South Wales and Monmouthshire, Cardiff (University of Wales); author of *Baroque et classicisme dans l'œuvre de Racine*, and of a critical edition of *Britannicus*.

JEAN DUBU, Professeur Agrégé at the Lycée Saint-Louis (Paris), tutor at the Institut d'Anglais (Sorbonne, Annexe Censier); Secrétaire Perpétuel of the Académie Racinienne (La Ferté-Milon and Uzès), organiser of the annual Sessions Raciniennes at Uzès and of the 1er Congrès International Racinien (Uzès, 1961); editor of the periodical *Jeunesse de Racine* and of a critical edition of *Racine, Lettres d'Uzès*.

LUCIEN GOLDMANN, D.ès-L., Professeur at the École Pratique des Hautes Études (VIth Section, University of Paris) and Directeur of the Centre de Sociologie de la Littérature at the Institute of Sociology (University of Brussels); author of *Le Dieu caché: étude sur la vision tragique dans les* Pensées *de Pascal et dans le théâtre de* Racine.

R. C. KNIGHT, M.A., D.ès-L., Professor of French in the University College of Swansea (University of Wales); author of *Racine et la Grèce*, and of critical editions of *Phèdre* and Corneille's *Nicomède*.

JOHN C. LAPP, Ph.D., William H. Bonsall Professor of French at Stanford University; author of *Aspects of Racinian Tragedy*.

JEAN POMMIER, D.ès-L., Member of the Académie des Sciences Morales et Politiques (Paris), Professeur Honoraire at the Sorbonne and the Collège de France; author of *Aspects de Racine, Créations en littérature*, and many works on nineteenth-century and modern French literature; general editor of the *Revue d'Histoire littéraire de la France*.

GEORGES POULET, Docteur en Philosophie et Lettres, et en Droit (Liège), Professor of the History of French Literature in the University of Zürich, sometime Reader at the University of Edinburgh and Professor at Johns Hopkins University; author of *Études sur le temps humain, La Distance intérieure, Les métamorphoses du cercle, Le Point de départ, Mesure de l'instant*.

R. A. SAYCE, M.A., D.Phil., Reader in French Literature in the University of Oxford and Fellow of Worcester College, Oxford; author of *The French Biblical Epic in the Seventeenth Century, Style in French Prose*, and a critical edition of Corneille's *Polyeucte*.

LEO SPITZER (d. 1960) was Professor of Romance Languages at Johns Hopkins University and previously held posts at the universities of Vienna, Bonn, Marburg, Cologne; author of *Romanische Stil- und Literarstudien* and *Linguistics and Literary History*, and of many articles of stylistic criticism.

THEOPHIL SPOERRI, Dr Phil., Honorary Professor in the University of Zürich, previously Professor of French and Italian Literature; author of works on Pascal and Dante; was an editor of the periodical *Trivium*.

JEAN STAROBINSKI, D.ès-L., Dr Med., Professor of the History of Ideas and of French Literature in the University of Geneva, sometime Assistant Professor at Johns Hopkins University; President of the Société Jean-Jacques Rousseau and of the Rencontres Internationales de Genève; author of *Jean-Jacques Rousseau: la transparence et l'obstacle*, of *L'Œil vivant* and *L'Invention de la liberté*.

EUGÈNE VINAVER, M.A., D.Litt., D.ès-L., Professor of French Literature in the University of Wisconsin, Emeritus Professor of the University of Manchester; editor of Racine, *Principes de la tragédie, en marge de la* Poétique *d'Aristote*; author of *Racine et la poésie tragique* and of works on medieval literature, French and English.

H. M. WAIDSON, M.A., Dr Phil., Professor of German in the University College of Swansea (University of Wales); author of *Jeremias Gotthelf* and *The Modern German Novel: a mid-twentieth-century survey*; translator, *inter alia*, of Gotthelf's *The Black Spider* and Goethe's *Kindred by Choice*.

Index